THE HERITAGE OF
EARLY AMERICAN HOUSES

THE HERITAGE OF EARLY AMERICAN HOUSES

Introduction by
Vincent Price

Text by
John Drury

COWARD-McCANN, INC.
NEW YORK

Produced in association with Country Beautiful

COUNTRY BEAUTIFUL: *Publisher and Editorial Director:* Michael P. Dineen; *Executive Editor:* Robert L. Polley; *Senior Editors:* Kenneth L. Schmitz, James H. Robb; *Associate Art Directors:* Wilbur Howe, Mitchel L. Heinrichs; *Photography:* Douglas C. Green; *Editorial Assistants:* Lawrence D. Kenney, Carolyn Muchhala; *Marketing Director:* Thomas R. Given; *Sales Manager:* James P. Green; *Executive Assistant:* Judy Hammond; *Circulation Manager:* Trudy Schnittka; *Production:* Michael Swan; *Editorial Secretary:* Donna Vincent; *Fulfillment:* Judy Conklin, Nola J. Cronick.
Special Consultant: John W. Luedtke, Acting Curator of Decorative Art, Milwaukee Public Museum. All photographs not otherwise credited are by Douglas C. Green.

Frontispiece: George de Wolf House, Bristol, Rhode Island.

CONTENTS

NEW ENGLAND

MIDDLE ATLANTIC

INTRODUCTION

One of the most rewarding and enjoyable ways to learn about America's past is to visit the dwellings which were built during the more than 350 years of our history. The distinguished homes in this volume, built before 1850 are extraordinarily well preserved and authentically furnished and therefore provide excellent examples of the splendid architecture and art, adroit craftsmanship and great variety of decorative styles from our colonial period and the decades of the early republic. It has long been my belief that our lives can be immensely enriched by contact with and appreciation of the finest things produced by cultures, past and present. There is much in this book for those who enjoy fine things—portraits by Sully, handsomely carved furniture by Chippendale, Hepplewhite and Belter, delicate plaster work in the elegant Adam style, exquisite Oriental carpets, superb silver and china, expertly wrought woodwork, and magnificent gardens—all made more appealing by the patina brought to them by age.

But equally important is learning about the people who lived in these houses, who built and designed them, who furnished them, raised families in them and loved them. By studying these dwellings we find the answers to some fascinating questions about these people: Were their tastes ostentatious or conservative, were they wealthy plantation owners or statesmen or men of learning, were they of strong religious persuasion, what misfortunes did they suffer, what pleasures did they enjoy? Some are famous, such as William H. Seward, George Rogers Clark and John C. Calhoun, but some of the most interesting are relatively unknown, such as Ocean Born Mary, who was named by a pirate captain.

We owe a debt of gratitude to the individuals and groups who have struggled to preserve these historic houses against the ravages of time and uncomprehending man. Except for their persistent efforts on our behalf, the tangible evidence of the culture and history of early America would be considerably diminished and our nation would be much the poorer for it. It is because of their dedication that we have the treasures described and displayed in these pages.

Vincent Price

WADSWORTH-LONGFELLOW HOUSE

Portland, Maine

WHERE A FAMED POET WAS NURTURED

Often I think of the beautiful town
    That is seated by the sea . . . .
    And my youth comes back to me.

And Deering's Woods are fresh and fair,
    And with joy that is almost pain
My heart goes back to wander there,
And among the dreams of the days that were,
    I find my lost youth again.

These few lines from Henry Wadsworth Longfellow's poem, "My Lost Youth," are enough to convey the essential happiness of his boyhood and youth in Portland, Maine. In this now quiet seaport town, there still stands the venerable house where America's most beloved poet lived during his infancy, boyhood and young manhood, where he wrote his first poems, where he decided on a literary career, and where he often visited until his death in 1882 at the age of seventy-five years. That dwelling is the Wadsworth-Longfellow House, built 183 years ago by the poet's maternal grandfather, General Peleg Wadsworth, an adjutant general of the Massachusetts militia during the American Revolution. The house is now owned by the Maine Historical Society.

It was at a New Year's Day wedding held in the front parlor of this house in 1804 that the distinguished Wadsworth and Longfellow families were united and thus brought fame to one of Maine's oldest habitations. On that day Zilpah Wadsworth, daughter of General Wadsworth, whose family traced its descent to John and Priscilla Alden, became the wife of Stephen Longfellow, a young Portland lawyer who later was a selectman, state senator, congressman, trustee of Bowdoin College and president of the Maine Historical Society. He also, of course, was the father of a poet known to almost every school child in the United States.

When General Wadsworth first came to the seaport city of Portland in 1784 to make his home, he initially built a general store and barn on the land he bought in that thriving community. Then, in

Henry Wadsworth Longfellow spent his youth in this tree-shaded brick home in the seaport city of Portland, Maine.

Above: The portrait in the hall is of Longfellow when he was a professor at Bowdoin College. Below: On the old schoolmaster's desk in "Henry's Room" the poet wrote one of his most famous poems, "The Rainy Day."

the spring of 1785, he began work on the construction of a two-story brick house adjoining the store—the first brick house in Portland. At a later date a third story and various architectural embellishments were added to the house, giving it the appearance it has today. Among the Wadsworth children brought to this house when it was completed was Zilpah, then eight years old and afterwards to become the mother of the poet.

Although Zilpah and Stephen Longfellow lived in this house for one year after they were married in 1804, they moved out of it to the home of Captain Samuel Stephenson, whose wife was Stephen Longfellow's sister, and it was in the Stephenson house that Henry Wadsworth Longfellow was born on February 27, 1807. When the future poet was eight months old, however, his family moved back to the original Wadsworth home, and there, as stated before, he lived during his infancy, boyhood and young manhood. This return to his mother's ancestral home was made possible when General Wadsworth, after serving in Congress, built a new home for his family on a country tract of seven thousand acres presented to him by the government "for soldierly service" after he made a token payment.

One biographer of Longfellow has commented, "For a writer who was to be, on the whole, a poet of acceptance, rather than of rebellion and rejection, there was a peculiar felicity in all the circumstances of Longfellow's origin and early life; a felicity in the time, the place, the family. . . ." Portland, during the years Longfellow lived there, was thriving in its most vigorous, expansive period, as was New England generally. One visitor during this time said of Portland, "No American town . . . is more sprightly."

At the same time that it was a stimulating place in which to live and grow up, Portland was also a community with a history. It had been bombarded during the Revolution and almost destroyed; one of the houses burned was that of Longfellow's great-grandfather, Stephen. In 1813, during Longfellow's youth, residents could hear in the distance the guns of the British and American ships, the *Boxer* and the *Enterprise,* in their famous battle. Another powerful influence on Longfellow was the nearby sea itself which pervades much of his best poetry.

It was in the old Wadsworth manse, then, that Henry Wadsworth Longfellow was reared in a cultured household, read books, wrote his first poems, and from which he daily went off to classes at Portland Academy, and later, at Bowdoin College. While living in this house Longfellow wrote his first published poem at the age of thirteen. Entitled "The Battle of Lovell's Pond," it was printed in the Portland *Gazette* on November 17, 1820. However, with the exception of his sister Elizabeth, whom he let in on the secret, no one in his family knew that he was the author of the poem, which was signed "Anon."

As it happened, young Henry, following his graduation from college in 1825, was immediately offered and accepted a professorship of languages at Bowdoin. But before taking up his teaching duties, he went on a European tour. He remained at Bowdoin College until 1835 when Harvard University offered to appoint him to a chair of modern languages and belles-lettres. On accepting, the

future author of "The Song of Hiawatha" and "Evangeline" left the old Wadsworth home in Portland and moved to Cambridge, Massachusetts, where he lived until his death in 1882, in the mansion now known as the Craigie-Longfellow House.

In the meantime, the Portland house in which Longfellow grew to manhood, was owned and occupied by the poet's younger sister, Anne Longfellow Pierce. She had married George Washington Pierce, a lawyer and state legislator, in 1832. When his untimely death occurred in 1835, his widow continued to live in the old Wadsworth house, remaining there until her own death in 1901 at the age of ninety years. Here she was often visited by her famous brother. It was on one of these visits in 1855 that Longfellow was inspired to write "My Lost Youth," the previously mentioned poem in which he paid tribute to his native city of Portland. Having no children, Mrs. Pierce left a will donating her family home to the Maine Historical Society, which received it in June 1901. The society has maintained the house with its Wadsworth and Longfellow pieces and memorabilia.

Originally two stories high, in 1815 another story was added by Stephen Longfellow, who also gave it the appearance of a Federal-style dwelling, a style that came into vogue at the beginning of the nineteenth century. Here may be found a dignified entrance portico supported by two Doric columns, symmetrically arranged windows, a low-pitched hip roof, and paired chimneys at each end of the house—all familiar elements of the Federal style.

An entrance hall in the center of this fifteen-room house leads to a rear door opening into the garden. The hall features a staircase which has a pedestal and bust of the author on the landing; also in the hall is a large painting of the poet when he was a professor at Bowdoin College.

The front parlor, with wide plank floors and wainscoting, is furnished entirely with Longfellow family pieces. Among the most interesting is a handsome piano that belonged to the poet when he lived in Cambridge, and which was transferred here to replace a spinet piano, the first such in Portland. An attractive fireplace, faced with marble, dominates the room. The living or sitting room contains, in addition to many other family heirlooms, the poet's favorite chair, his mother's sewing table, and, in one corner, a doorway leading to the "Little Room," which displays a double dinner set of Staffordshire ware given to the poet's mother on her wedding day in 1804.

The old kitchen, with its spacious fireplace, contains many family cooking and baking utensils. Here, too, is the serviceable dresser featuring a display of britannia and earthenware articles. Across the hall from the kitchen is the old dining room which was originally General Wadsworth's room and later came to be known as the den and "Henry's Room." On the walls is a reproduction of the original wallpaper, but the item of principal interest in the room is the old schoolmaster's desk between the two windows looking out on the garden. On it in 1841 was written one of the poet's most famous poems, "The Rainy Day."

Remaining intact is the poet's sleeping room, with its four-poster bed, in which he slept when visiting his younger sister, Mrs. Pierce. His last of many visits here was in the summer of 1881. One of the sleeping rooms in the house has been redesigned with glass cases containing the dresses of the Wadsworth and Longfellow ladies.

It would seem to be singularly appropriate that the historic boyhood home of a poet who frequently wrote of the past and who had such happy memories of his youth—both rare enough among American authors—would be so well and authentically preserved. It is a celebration of the attitude once expressed by the Reverend Samuel Longfellow to a friend: "I hope they will leave some of the old places intact, for we need links with the past generations; there are few enough in America at best."

Above: The entrance hall leads to a rear door which opens into the colorful garden.

Opposite top: The front parlor is furnished entirely with Longfellow family pieces including the piano that belonged to the poet while he was at Cambridge. Opposite bottom: The family cradle rests near a lovely canopied four-poster bed.

Above: The pre-Revolutionary Ocean-Born-Mary House, named after an almost legendary occupant, is still faced with most of the original clapboards. Right: A rectangular fanlight and an eagle pediment, indicating the patriotic sentiments of the owner, decorate the front entrance of the Georgian-style home.

OCEAN-BORN-MARY HOUSE

Henniker, New Hampshire

A HOUSE OF LEGEND

One of the most curious and fascinating legends of much-legended New England has to do with a two-story colonial residence in the small town of Henniker, New Hampshire, a dwelling now widely and oddly known as the Ocean-Born-Mary House. It was built more than two hundred years ago, and has been restored and furnished with colonial pieces and household articles by its current owners, Mr. and Mrs. David Russell. Their historic dwelling at Henniker (just west of the state capital at Concord) is located on a hill above the Contocook River.

The story began, according to local lore, in 1720 when a young newlywed couple of Scotch-Irish descent, James and Elizabeth Wilson, left Londonderry, Ireland, for the American colonies, specifically for Londonderry, New Hampshire, a recently established settlement in which James Wilson and several other Scotch-Irish men had been granted tracts of land by the Crown.

When about one-third of the way across the Atlantic, the sailing vessel carrying the Wilsons was stopped, boarded and looted by the crew of a pirate ship. The sailors and male passengers of the Wilson vessel were bound with ropes, the women were huddled into main deck cabins, valuables were gathered into parcels, and the pirate captain was making a last-minute check below decks when he came into a cabin where lay a woman passenger in the bunk. Surprised that his pirate gang had overlooked her, he commanded the lady to get dressed and hurry up to the main deck.

The woman was young Mrs. James Wilson. Instead of obeying the pirate captain's command, however, she lifted a corner of the blanket and showed him why she could not get up. A new-born baby girl was at her side. The hard-boiled captain was startled, his face began to soften, he stood silent for a few minutes. Then he asked, "Have you named her yet?" Mrs. Wilson said no. "Well," he went on, "will you let me name her? If you do, I'll unbind all the men of your ship, return the valuables, and leave the ship unharmed."

When the young mother agreed, the captain leaned over the infant and whispered softly and tenderly the name "Mary." Then, with the suggestion of a tear in his eye, he explained that Mary was his mother's name (one version of the legend has it that Mary was

The sixteen-stair "bridal" staircase is so named because each step represents one year of the bride's age, usually sixteen.

Above: The clock on the kitchen mantel, known as a "figure eight," is flanked by whale oil lamps, pewter dishes and several tin items. Below: A sign nearby indicates the considerable age of the dwelling.

the name of his wife). The captain then left the cabin, carried out all of his promises to Mrs. Wilson, and returned a short time later with a generous portion of fine brocaded silk. "This is a gift for your little daughter," he said. "Let it be part of her wedding gown when she grows up and becomes a bride."

Thus it was that the woman who became "Ocean Born Mary" came to the New World. The Wilsons reached Boston in due time, then journeyed on to Londonderry, New Hampshire, and in that town Mary Wilson grew to womanhood. And on the day in 1738 when, at the age of eighteen, she married Thomas Wallace, her wedding gown was fashioned from the pirate captain's gift of brocaded silk.

In the years following, Thomas and Mary Wallace became the parents of a daughter and four sons, the oldest of whom was Robert Wallace. When Robert grew to manhood and entered the business world, he often admired the fine old colonial homes he saw on business trips to Portsmouth, saying to himself that one day he hoped to own such a house.

In 1767 a number of Scotch-Irish families, including the Wallaces, moved from Londonderry northwestward to Henniker on the Contocook River. By that time, Robert Wallace, who was then in his early thirties, had sufficient means to build for himself a "town house" of the kind he had admired in Portsmouth. Work on the house was begun soon after his arrival at Henniker in 1767 and thus there arose a residence now known as the Ocean-Born-Mary House. The name derives from the fact that his mother, popularly known as "Ocean Born Mary," lived with him in this house for many, many years, and that she was something of a town personality. She died in 1814 at the age of ninety-four and was laid to rest in the Center burial ground at Henniker.

As may be seen today, the Ocean-Born-Mary House is a well-proportioned example of the Georgian style of architecture. Here are the two dormers in a hip roof that marked the colonial style and which disappeared with the rise of the Federal mode of design. Here, too, is a fine colonial door with original HL hinges and a Crusader cross on the inside to keep witches out. The doorway is enhanced by a rectangular fanlight and surmounted by a decorative pediment. The house is of wood construction and its clapboarded exterior is remarkably well preserved for a dwelling as old as this. The windows have twelve-over-twelve panes.

A spacious, paneled, entrance hall in the center of the house leads to the bridal staircase of simple but dignified design. Bridal staircases have sixteen steps and were so named because brides were often sixteen years of age. These staircases also customarily have short risers and wide treads and thus were unusually comfortable for those days. To the right of the top of the staircase is the loom room, a work room that was never finished. It contains an interesting loom well over a century old, as well as a display of some old textiles, such as linsey-woolsey blankets. To the left of the staircase is a smoke house built into the chimney. The fire in the kitchen fireplace below cooked and smoked the bacon and ham which hung on hooks still to be seen inside the chimney.

On each side of the hall are large, commodious rooms with inviting fireplaces and windows with paneled shutters that slide into the walls—a feature known as Indian shutters. The front room, known as the Eagle Room, derives its name from a large painting of

an eagle symbolizing the United States which occupies most of the overmantel. This is said to be the largest overmantel in New Hampshire, measuring forty inches in height and five feet in width. Arched above the eagle's head are sixteen stars, indicating there were sixteen states in the union when the painting was completed before 1803.

Beneath the cornice in this room is a remarkable pomegranate frieze which dates from the eighteenth century. The striped rug covering the floor was made over a hundred years ago on the loom upstairs. The wallpaper is believed to be original.

The kitchen has a large fireplace, measuring eight and one-half feet, with a twelve-pie Dutch oven attached and a three-ton granite hearthstone on top.

The master bedroom is sometimes referred to as the Lafayette Room because of a local tradition that the great French general and statesman stopped overnight here on his triumphant return visit to the United States in 1824-1825. Among the furnishings of the master bedroom is a cupboard above the fireplace which held the master's hot toddy and which was known as the master's toddy chest.

Of particular interest in the house is a framed piece of the brocaded silk that the pirate captain gave to Ocean Born Mary Wallace and that formed part of her wedding dress. The bridal gown itself is now on display in the National Museum at Washington.

Beneath the cornice in the Eagle Room is a lovely frieze in a pomegranate design symbolizing abundance. The striped rug was woven over a century ago on a loom which is still preserved in the home.

19

Photos: Margaret Rother

20

GENERAL JOHN STRONG HOUSE
West Addison, Vermont
A LANDMARK OF THE LAKE CHAMPLAIN COUNTRY

In the richly historic Lake Champlain country, on the Vermont side of the lake, stands the General John Strong House, one of the most celebrated old houses in New England. It is as widely known for its architecture and restored interior appointments as for the man who built it nearly 175 years ago, the man for whom it is named. Still on its original site, it stands today in the midst of the landscaped Daughters of the American Revolution State Park and is annually visited by hundreds of sightseers who approach it from the nearby Lake Champlain Bridge.

John Strong, who served not only as a general of the Vermont militia and as a state representative, but as the first judge of Addison County, initially came to the state from Connecticut in 1765, ten years before the American Revolution. He settled in an area that is one of the most historic on Lake Champlain. The place was then known as Chimney Point. It was at this promontory of land that Samuel de Champlain, the great French explorer and "Father of New France" in America, landed on a July day in 1609 and bestowed his name on the 120-mile-long lake he had discovered, which now separates the states of Vermont and New York.

At the time Champlain arrived here with his followers and a small group of friendly Algonquin Indians as guides, he encountered on what became the New York side of the lake a band of hostile Iroquois Indians. He defeated them in a short battle—an action that resulted in enduring hatred of the French by the powerful Iroquois, especially during the French and Indian War of 1754-1763. Before the outbreak of that war, however, a number of French settlements had been established on Lake Champlain, one of them being at what later became known as Chimney Point.

Whether General John Strong knew it or not is uncertain, but the French settlement at Chimney Point was originally known as Fort de Pieux. When Lord Jeffrey Amherst, in command of the English forces aiding the Indians during the French and Indian War, planned on invading the lake's French settlements, the colonists at Fort de Pieux deserted their village in 1759 and, a year later, roving bands of Mohawk Indians burned it to the ground, leaving only the stark black forms of chimneys silhouetted against the sky. Hence arose the name of Chimney Point.

Above: Blue and white wallpaper in an antique design adds to the appeal of the entrance hall. A broad white archway divides the hall near the handsome staircase.

Opposite top: "Chimney Point" mansion, circa 1795, where General John Strong spent his last years, is a noteworthy example of the Federal style of architecture. A Palladian window and gabled entrance portico add to the charm of the house. Opposite bottom: A lovely Sheraton sideboard from the Strong family completes the dining room furnishings.

Above: Many interesting documents and memorabilia associated with General John Strong are displayed in his office. Below: A large breakfront cabinet, also located in the office, holds a collection of fine china.

Photos: Margaret Rother

With the arrival of John Strong and a few friends in 1765, the villages of Addison and West Addison were already in existence and both had hopes of becoming future lakeports. It was at West Addison, or Chimney Point, that John Strong settled with his family. His first home was a log cabin built on the foundations, or cellar hole, of an earlier French house ruined by the Indians. Then came the opening of the American Revolution in 1775. When the English began invading the Lake Champlain country, most villagers, including the Strong family, fled southward to Massachusetts and Connecticut. Later, John Strong became a leader of the valiant Green Mountain Boys during the Revolution.

It was a year after the signing of the Treaty of Paris in 1783, which formally ended the American Revolution, that John Strong rounded up his scattered family and returned to Chimney Point. He built a modest wooden house, and became active in public affairs of that part of the state. At the time he served as Addison County's first judge, that county's northern boundary was at the Canadian border. Eventually, John Strong became a man of influence and means. He soon felt the need for a newer and larger house.

Thus it was that, in 1795, he began construction on the spacious, two-story, brick residence that survives today at West Addison as one of Vermont's outstanding landmarks. Meanwhile, his second son, Samuel Strong (who also was a general of militia), had completed for himself an imposing residence still standing in the nearby town of Vergennes, Vermont. It required the elder Strong two or three years to finish work on his Chimney Point mansion, the bricks of which were made by workmen on his farm.

In this comfortable mansion General John Strong spent the remainder of his days. He died in 1816 and was buried in nearby Lakeview Cemetery. In the decades following, five generations of the Strong family lived in the house. Then in 1934, the revered old landmark was purchased by the Vermont State Society, Daughters of American Revolution, whose members restored and furnished the residence with such good taste that it is now regarded as a leading "house museum" of the New England region.

Set back on a wide lawn, the General Strong mansion presents a distinguished facade in the post-colonial or Federal style of architecture, a simpler style than the preceding Georgian mode of design. Of particular interest is that characteristic of many Federal-style houses—a dignified Palladian window on the second floor above the gabled entrance portico. A gabled pediment on the cornice adds to the mansion's architectural appeal.

Beyond the front door, which contains the original John Strong lock, is a handsome entrance hall, decorated in blue and white wallpaper of antique design and marked by an archway over the staircase leading to the second floor. The master bedroom and another large room known as the ballroom are over the main part of the house. The north or back wing contains three smaller bedrooms.

Among the furnishings in the hall are three eighteenth-century comb-back Windsor chairs with knuckle arms and a painting of a Revolutionary group by the New England artist, Julian Scott (1846-1901). A scroll-top grandfather's clock rests on the stairway landing.

In the elegant parlor, with its Federal-style furnishings, there are numerous oil paintings, among them portraits of John Strong's son, Samuel, and the latter's wife, Mercy Bloomer. Other furnishings found in the dining room include a Sheraton sideboard from the Strong family as well as a Sheffield plate tea set and Doulton china. A nearby office used by General Strong contains documents and memorabilia associated with him. Some of the doors in the mansion contain original door knobs and hinges, the latter including the corkscrew type.

Not least among the attractions of this historic landmark is the large old kitchen, with its great fireplace, baking oven, original floor boards, cooking utensils and secret "hidey-hole." As a few bands of Indians still roamed the countryside then, John Strong took the precaution of building into his spacious house a family hiding-place cleverly concealed as a part of the big brick chimney in the kitchen and originally reached through a well in a closet of one of the second-floor bedrooms. It was large enough to hold six or seven people.

A local tradition about this family "hidey-hole" is that at one time a large portrait of George Washington hung over the mantel in the kitchen and that the portrait had one transparent eye through which a member of the Strong family in the "hidey-hole" could observe any intruders in the kitchen.

The kitchen contains numerous articles from pioneer days. The main attraction, however, is the secret "hidey-hole," large enough for seven people, which is built into the chimney of the great fireplace.

23

Above: Ironmaster's House, one of the oldest dwellings in America, has steeply pitched gables, diamond-paned casement windows and a second-story overhang—all elements of the Tudor style. Right: The restored Saugus Ironworks was established over three hundred years ago.

IRONMASTER'S HOUSE "SCOTCH"-BOARDMAN HOUSE

Saugus, Massachusetts

HOME LIFE AT THE SAUGUS IRONWORKS

The authentically restored blast furnace, forge, blacksmith shop, rolling mill, water wheels, etc., of the seventeenth-century ironworks in Saugus, Massachusetts, is now widely known as the birthplace of America's iron and steel industry and as a kind of smaller New England version of Colonial Williamsburg. There are, however, two frame dwellings in Saugus that, surviving from the earliest days of the Massachusetts Bay Colony, have an even wider, more human, appeal than the ironworks, especially for women visitors and children.

One of these houses, the Ironmaster's House, believed to have been built between 1636 and 1640, is located on the grounds of the restoration. Two miles away is the oddly named "Scotch"-Boardman House, dating from about 1686. They are among the oldest houses in America and are of great historical and architectural importance. For one thing, they are eloquent reminders of the fact that the earliest settlers in America did not live in log cabins, a form of construction introduced much later by Swedish settlers in Delaware.

When, in 1647, a group of London capitalists called the "Company of Undertakers for the Iron Works in New England," set up the ironworks on the Saugus River, some ten miles north of Boston, part of the land acquired by the company had been owned by Thomas Dexter, an early settler of nearby Lynn. Some local historians believe that the Saugus dwelling now famed as the Ironmaster's House was originally built by Thomas Dexter about the year 1636. But there is no clear proof of this, and the structure has always been known simply as the Ironmaster's House, not being identified with any particular ironmaster at Saugus. When the ironworks was established here, the settlement was at first known as Hammersmith after a similarly named ironworks town in England.

This charming door knocker is an ornamental addition to the exterior of the weathered, clapboarded building.

Eventually, however, the Saugus ironworks declined and finally fell into ruin and disappeared late in the 1670's. But the Ironmaster's House managed to survive, coming into the possession of the Taylor family of Boston, a wealthy family of merchants who also operated a gristmill at the Saugus River site. Then, in 1712, the house was sold to Daniel Mansfield, and it remained in the Mansfield family during the American Revolution and up until 1840. After that, it was owned by numerous families and finally, in 1915, was bought by Wallace Nutting, the noted author and authority on New England antiques, who restored the then aging building.

But this restoration project turned out to be too costly for Nutting and the old Ironmaster's House was about to fall into ruins and disappear altogether when, in 1942, a group of graduates of the Ford Trade School purchased it for $10,000 with the intention of moving it to Greenfield Village, that group of historic buildings set up by the Ford Motor Company at Dearborn, Michigan. However, the citizens of Saugus objected to this proposal, and, with the aid of county and state authorities, the house was kept on its original site. In 1943 the house, and the site of the iron works, was taken over by the newly formed First Iron Works Association, Inc.

It was this association, in cooperation with the American Iron and Steel Institute, which preserved the ancient Ironmaster's House and restored the forge, blast furnace, blacksmith shop, rolling mill, water wheels and other buildings in its vicinity. Situated on a grassy elevation overlooking the ironworks, its clapboards weathered brown by the passing years, the house is two stories high with a steeply pitched gable roof, a large central chimney, diamond-paned casement windows and that Elizabethan element brought from England by the first colonists—a second-story overhang on the facade with ornamental drops at each end of it. Over the entrance door of the house hangs an old iron signal bell used to warn workers of approaching hostile Indians.

There are four rooms in this dwelling, two on the ground floor and two on the second floor, all furnished with period pieces. Of particular interest are the keeping room and Great Room, with its exposed ceiling timbers and its ten-foot-wide fireplace. In and about the fireplace are pot hooks, cranes and other iron articles made at the Saugus Ironworks. The oak and cherry press cupboard dates from around 1680. From the same period are the elaborately carved

Top: The double overshot water wheels still operate the Rolling and Slitting Mill.
Bottom: Late seventeenth-century pieces decorating the Great Room include an oak and cherry press cupboard, a Bible box with fancy chip carving and a gateleg table. The original floor boards are almost two feet in width.

Above: During the day, the crane top bed was conveniently folded against the wall. To the left is an early pipe rack and, in the foreground, a small paneled chest with applied moldings. Left: Among other noteworthy furnishings are a crude candelabrum and a press cupboard with split-spindle décor, the oldest in the house.

The iron bell over the door at Ironmaster's House was used to warn workers of approaching hostile Indians.

wainscot chair, dating from around 1660, and the Governor Carver chair from a little later in the seventeenth century. Also in the keeping room is a late eighteenth-century pine writing chair which is painted a greenish-gray typical of the colonial period.

It may have been that some of these articles were made by a group of Scottish prisoners-of-war captured by Oliver Cromwell's troops at the Battle of Dunbar in 1650 and sent to Massachusetts Bay Colony to labor at the Saugus Ironworks as indentured servants. It was the presence here of these Scotch workers which gave rise to the legend that the other seventeenth-century dwelling in Saugus, the William Boardman House, was originally occupied by the Scotch workmen as their rooming house. This has since been found to be untrue; the Scotch indentured servants lived in another house not far from the site of the Boardman abode and now no longer in existence. The name "Scotch"-Boardman, however, has clung to the surviving edifice and it is known by this name in the early records of the Society for the Preservation of New England Antiquities.

William Boardman, a joiner, is believed to have started construction on this house sometime after 1686 when he purchased the land on which it stands. It is known that he lived in this house with his family until his death in 1696 at the age of thirty-eight. The house remained in the hands of his descendants for the next 215 years.

In 1911, the house and its tract of land was sold to Jacob W. Wilbur, who planned for the site a new subdivision to be called City Gardens. But Wilbur seems not to have fully realized his ambition, and in 1913 he sold the Boardman house tract to another subdivider, who definitely announced demolition of the historic old landmark. It was then that the Society for the Preservation of New England Antiquities, under the leadership of William Sumner Appleton, took action, and, in the following year, became owner of the "Scotch"-Boardman House and its site.

Since then, the society has preserved as many of the architectural and decorative features of the house as possible, and is in the process of identifying them with labels. Here again is an early Massachusetts Bay Colony house still exhibiting suggestions of Elizabethan design—two stories high, steeply pitched roof, central chimney, a lean-to addition at the rear and a second-story overhang. Here, too, is the clapboard exterior of these age-old dwelling places in the Bay colony. Unfortunately, the original diamond-paned casements and ornamental drops on the overhang no longer exist.

A curious fact about the early history of the house is that at various times it stood in two counties and four towns, a situation caused by frequent local boundary changes. At one period the boundary line between Lynn and Boston ran through the middle of the Boardman house front door and, as a result, the door bore the letters "B" and "L" on its respective halves.

Above and left: The curiously named "Scotch" Boardman House has been preserved
in its entirety as a noteworthy example of the architecture prevalent
in New England during the latter part of the seventeenth century.

29

TRISTRAM COFFIN HOUSE

Newbury, Massachusetts

HISTORIC SEAT OF THE COFFIN FAMILY

The Tristram Coffin House in Newbury, Massachusetts, is an unusual example of an old New England house that grew ever larger with the passing years, with rooms, wings, lean-tos and ells having been added to it at intervals without destroying its symmetrical appearance. This venerable, clapboarded dwelling, now more than three hundred years old, has been owned continuously by eight generations of the Coffin family, one of the earliest and most prominent families of the Massachusetts Bay Colony and the beginning years of the State of Massachusetts. It is now the property of the Society for the Preservation of New England Antiquities and is furnished throughout with colonial pieces and antiques, most of them Coffin family heirlooms.

First of the family to arrive at Newbury from England was Tristram Coffin, Sr., who came in 1642 with his mother, two sisters, wife and five children. But Tristram senior was not the builder of the present house. It has not been determined where he lived with his family in Newbury. After serving as a ferryman and tavern-keeper for several years, he left Newbury and moved to Nantucket Island where he founded a celebrated branch of the Coffin family. Still standing today is that island's oldest house, built by a grandson, Jethro Coffin.

Instead of accompanying his father to Nantucket, Tristram Coffin, Jr., now a young man, chose to remain in Newbury. There, in 1653, he married Mrs. Judith Somerby, widow of Henry Somerby—an event that marks the beginning of the Tristram Coffin House story. It is generally accepted that 1654 was probably the year the house's original portion was built.

In this first section, Tristram and his wife set up housekeeping, the first of eight Coffin generations to own the house over the next 275 years. Tristram engaged in his trade of merchant tailor, assisted by one of his eleven children, an older son, Nathaniel. When Nathaniel was married in 1693, the newlyweds came to live with his parents—a move that brought about the first addition to the original Coffin

This simple clapboard home has weathered New England winters for more than three hundred years. The house was owned by eight successive generations of the Tristram Coffin family.

Above: The Coffin family coat of arms was returned by a
descendant and now hangs in the northeast parlor.
Below: Generations of Coffins set their cream to rise
in the deep earthenware pans found in the buttery.

house. After the death of Tristram Coffin, Jr., in 1704, the house
was inherited by Nathaniel.

By about 1725 Nathaniel's son Joseph had married and produced
a family which necessitated an addition which completed the portion of the house now fronting on High Road. Before Joseph's death
in 1773, one of his sons, Joshua, had married, and in 1764 this son
wrote his father a "respectfully worded letter" asking for permission
to build a further addition to the parental house "considering my
family increases so fast." This wish was granted to Joshua, the fourth
generation of Coffins to live in the Newbury landmark.

When Joshua died suddenly in 1774 at the age of forty, the family
home was inherited jointly by his two sons, Joseph and Edmund.
Edmund had the first story completely remodeled and had a second
story added to a rear corner of the house. The sixth generation to
live in the house was Joseph's son, Joshua, who added the study
or library. He was a Newbury school teacher, one of whose pupils
was John Greenleaf Whittier, later to become the celebrated New
England poet, and also a writer, scholar and historian. One of
Joshua's best known books, written while he was living in the old
ancestral house, is a *History of Newbury, Newburyport, and West
Newbury from 1635 to 1845*.

Living with Joshua before his death in 1864 was his unmarried
cousin, Lucy, daughter of Edmund Coffin, and she continued to
occupy the house until her own death in 1893. In her will, she left
the historic landmark to the children of her deceased sister, Mrs.
Elizabeth Colman, and it was two of these, Edmund Coffin Colman
and Mrs. Arthur Merriam—the eighth Coffin generation of owners—
who conveyed the revered old Tristram Coffin House to the Society
for the Preservation of New England Antiquities in 1929.

Despite the additions to the original house over the decades, the
dwelling remains essentially a low-ceilinged seventeenth- and eighteenth-century colonial abode. Two stories high and with gable roofs
and a clapboarded, weather-stained exterior, the Tristram Coffin
House has its greatest appeal in the original portion—now an ell at
the rear. The house in front of it incorporates two structures or
additions erected sometime before 1750.

Because of widespread interest in this house on the part of many
Coffin descendants, each of its low-ceilinged rooms contains numerous family furnishings and heirlooms returned to the house by
loyal descendants. In the northeast parlor, for example, may be
found the Coffin family coat of arms hanging above a fireplace
framed in Holland Delft tiles; such heirlooms as a claw-and-ball-foot
table and Chippendale chairs; and "Aunt Lucy's piano," a gift to
her because of her musical talents. In the sitting room are such
family pieces as a secretary, mirror, an Empire card table and
portraits of Edmund Coffin and "Grandmother Lucy."

An upper room in the original house contains a glass case displaying many cherished family articles, such as linen towels, pillow-
cases, delicate fans, a handsome embroidered cape and old-time
pocketbooks. The "new" kitchen features a built-in dresser of eighteenth-century design, its shelves exhibiting the family pewter.

Among the numerous family heirlooms in the northeast parlor is "Aunt Lucy" Coffin's cherished piano.

Although the original kitchen of the earliest house, where the cooking was done in a great fireplace, is furnished with a seventeenth-century oak table, this is not a Coffin family piece. A passageway in one corner of the kitchen does, however, lead to a room completely furnished with family items—one of the most interesting rooms in the old landmark. This is the dairy room or buttery. Here, on shelves of unpainted pine boards, may be seen butter- and cheese-making utensils as well as deep earthenware pans in which generations of Coffins set their cream to rise.

The continuity provided by the admirable family that has lived here until recent times has resulted in a unique dwelling that is neither museum nor period restoration, but a home which can be seen to have grown to accommodate the needs of successive generations. Mellowed and comfortable, it is a house which stands as a reminder, not only of a distinguished family but of the way of life in old New England. Because there is not the slightest trace of artificiality or contrivance it brings us closer than most historic places into direct communication with the vital past.

Above: Legendary Jethro Coffin House, built during the era of witch-craft hysteria in 1686, has an inverted horseshoe, a charm against witches, outlined in brick on the chimney. Right: This aged landmark is furnished with authentic articles of seventeenth- and eighteenth-century domestic life in America.

JETHRO COFFIN HOUSE

Nantucket Island, Massachusetts

OLDEST HOUSE ON THE ISLAND

Of all of the famous old houses on historic Nantucket Island, off the Massachusetts coast, none is better known than the Jethro Coffin House, the oldest house on the island. A plain and unpretentious early colonial dwelling, the Coffin house nonetheless has a rich background of tradition and legend. The house, furnished throughout with colonial antiques, is now owned and maintained by the Nantucket Historical Association.

Further interest in the house is added by the fact that it has a direct connection with the dwelling on the mainland at Newbury, Massachusetts, known as the Tristram Coffin House. Its builder, Tristram Coffin, Jr., was an uncle of Jethro Coffin.

The family was founded in America by Tristram Coffin, Sr., who came to the Massachusetts Bay Colony from England in 1642. After living at Newbury for several years, he moved to Nantucket Island in 1659 and became one of the ten original proprietors of the island. And it was there his grandson, Jethro, was born and grew to manhood, to become the first owner of the house now bearing his name. This dwelling is also known locally and more simply as "The Oldest House" and as the "Horse Shoe House."

When young Jethro reached the age of twenty-three, he fell in love with Mary Gardner, an island resident, who was then but sixteen, and the two were married in 1686. But contrary to popular Bay Colony custom at that time, the newlyweds instead of being invited to live in the home of either of their parents, a procedure which called for enlargement of the parental dwelling, were installed in a brand new house of their own, a joint wedding gift to them from Jethro's father, Peter Coffin, and Mary's father, John Gardner. The two men had built the house before the wedding, and the couple were married in its big West Room. Thus the dwelling became a "Honeymoon House" for the newlyweds, who immediately set up housekeeping in it.

When the fathers of the young Jethro Coffins built this typical house in 1686, they included in its design the brick outline of an inverted horse shoe on the huge brick chimney above its roof. A traditional emblem of good luck, this horse shoe may have been intended as such for the newly married couple, but one of the per-

Courtesy Nantucket Historical Association

The large spinning wheel used for making woolen or cotton thread was a necessity in every pioneer home. The yarn wheel at left is equipped with a device to indicate the number of yards that have been wound.

sistent legends about it is that it was really conceived as a charm against witches, since that was the era of witchcraft hysteria. It is from this design that Horse Shoe House takes its name.

After living in this sturdy frame abode for twenty-two years, Jethro and Mary Coffin sold it in 1708 to Nathaniel Paddock, first of several Paddock generations who were to occupy the house during the rise of Nantucket's great whaling industry. In 1840, it was conveyed to George Turner, and it remained in the Turner family until 1881 when—appropriately enough—the old landmark was acquired by Tristram Coffin, a descendant of the founder of the Coffin family in America and a well-known lawyer and leading citizen of Poughkeepsie, New York. He immediately set about restoring the house, which was falling into ruin, and opened it to the public as something of a period museum.

Before his death in 1924, Mr. Coffin offered to sell the house to the Nantucket Historical Association for a moderate price, an offer which was accepted. But it developed that further important repairs on the house were required, repairs "beyond the slender means" of the historical association. This situation soon reached the ears of Winthrop Coffin, another Coffin descendant and resident of Boston, and he agreed to finance all repairs. But he stipulated that such repairs and full restoration of the family landmark should be in the hands of experts. Thus this revered colonial house was finally restored under the supervision of Sumner Appleton, secretary of the Society for the Preservation of New England Antiquities, and Alfred E. Shurrocks, an architect who specialized in New England restorations.

Familiar items in the kitchen were the shotgun over the fireplace, the wooden ladle for stirring stews and soups, and the pierced tin lantern overhead. The crude stand (left rear) holds a limestone dripping stone used to purify water and strain out debris that might have been in the well or rain barrel.

Situated on a rise of ground known as Sunset Hill, this age-old landmark, an oblong building with a high-pitched gable roof and central chimney, is unusual in that its exterior is shingled instead of clapboarded, as was the case with most seventeenth-century homes. Like those homes, however, it faces south in order to catch the winter sunlight. Another characteristic colonial feature here is that its back slopes down to within six feet of the ground, forming a lean-to. Conspicuous, of course, is the inverted horse shoe on the chimney above the roof. Two diamond-paned casement windows are on either side of the plain central doorway.

The house contains only two original Coffin family pieces or heirlooms; however, all furnishings displayed are authentic articles of seventeenth- and eighteenth-century American domestic life. In the keeping room, with its great fireplace, may be seen a rocker; settee; rush-bottom, ladder-backed chairs; and a gateleg table that belonged to Kezia Coffin, a Tory smuggler during the Revolutionary War. At one end of the kitchen, where the usual long-barreled rifle hangs over the fireplace, is located the buttery, containing plate ware, and, at the other end, the door to a small sleeping room, often called the Borning Room. A four-poster canopy bed and a cradle which may have held a Tristram Coffin are the main attractions of a second-floor sleeping room, which also was known as the Bridal Chamber.

Of the numerous stories and legends associated with this island house, one of the most familiar has to do with the few moments of terror experienced on a summer night by Mrs. Jethro Coffin. She had returned to the house about dusk, carrying her baby son Peter, after a visit to her father's place, where she often went when her husband was away on overnight business trips to Boston. On going to bed, Mrs. Coffin found herself unusually restless and wakeful, believing that she heard strange noises in the attic, a place where the makeshift floor boards were loose.

Suddenly, there was a great crash through the attic floor and downward plunged a fierce-looking Indian. Mrs. Coffin screamed in terror. When she made a quick move to get her baby, the Indian picked himself up, pulled out a knife, and stopped her in her tracks. Then, without saying a word, he started sharpening his knife on the stone fireplace. Mrs. Coffin became desperate. In an instant, she snatched her baby, and flew through the door and out into the night. When the Indian attempted to reach for her, he fell flat on his face on the floor.

Mrs. Coffin ran to her father's house. On telling of her horrifying experience, the male Gardners lost no time in picking up their rifles and rushing to the Jethro Coffin house. There they found the Indian, still stretched full length on the floor. They found, too, that he was in a drunken stupor. He was kept in charge until he was sober. Legend has it the Gardners "taught him a lesson" that served as a warning to him and any other Indians who in future might attempt to invade houses on Nantucket Island. What the lesson was, history does not say.

Curtains were drawn around the bed at night to keep out the chilling drafts in the crudely finished bridal chamber.

Above: The Wanton-Lyman-Hazard House was nearly destroyed by a group of angry patriots during its occupancy by a leading Tory. Right: The miniature doll's cradle was probably as much in demand as its larger counterpart in the colonial American household.

WANTON-LYMAN-HAZARD HOUSE

Newport, Rhode Island

OLDEST HOUSE IN OLD NEWPORT

Among the many colonial houses in the fashionable Rhode Island resort city of Newport, a city dating back to the early seventeenth century, none has the appeal that attaches to the two-story frame dwelling at 17 Broadway in the Narragansett Bay community. If it lacks the magnificence of some of the pre-Revolutionary residences of the city, this house is nonetheless the most revered in Newport. It is historic Newport's oldest house, and, as such, stands apart from all other dwellings in the resort city. Because of the three families longest associated with it, the landmark is widely known today as the Wanton-Lyman-Hazard House and is currently maintained as a public museum by the Newport Historical Society.

About 1724, Richard Ward, who was elected governor of the Rhode Island Colony in 1740, bought the dwelling now known as the Wanton-Lyman-Hazard House from Stephen Mumford. A recently discovered record of a Town Meeting, held on July 30, 1700, shows that Stephen Mumford had complied with the town ordinances pertaining to houses on lots. From this evidence, historians believe the building was erected by Stephen Mumford around 1675.

A later owner was Martin Howard, Jr., a leading Tory of early Newport and author of the pro-English diatribe, *A Letter from a Gentleman at Halifax*. He is believed to have acquired the house sometime between 1750 and 1760, and it was in 1765, while Howard, the staunch Loyalist, was living there that an angry crowd of patriots nearly destroyed his home. When word came to Newport of the passage of the Stamp Act by England in August 1765, the townspeople were aroused. Howard and two other Tories were hanged in effigy, and a group of enraged patriots invaded Howard's house, smashing doors, windows and furnishings. But Howard and the other two Loyalists managed to flee beforehand, escaping to a British sloop of war anchored in the harbor. None of the three ever returned to Newport.

With the disappearance of Howard, his house was sold at public auction to John Wanton, a leading Newport resident. Thereafter, Wanton repaired and refurnished the damaged building and moved into it with his family. This was the first of the Wanton, Lyman and Hazard families to own and occupy the house during the eighteenth, nineteenth and twentieth centuries. And it was the family, too, of

An outstanding piece in the south parlor is the mahogany secretary made by John Goddard of Newport, who is considered one of the finest craftsmen America produced.

Preserved in the kitchen ell is one of the few examples left of a wall décor common in seventeenth-century America. The pattern of Indian red diamond cross-bars is painted on a sepia-colored background.

"Charming Polly Wanton," the vivacious and handsome daughter of the John Wantons, who made a name for herself in Newport society during the American Revolution.

When French expeditionary forces came to the aid of the Americans and established headquarters at Newport in 1780-1781, many young officers from the occupying French army were invited to social gatherings in the Wanton home. Soon Polly Wanton became the most popular girl in town. One young French officer is said to have scratched, with his diamond ring, the words "Charming Polly Wanton" on a windowpane of her house and numerous other officers praised her in their diaries.

It remained, however, for a young American Army officer to win her hand. He was Daniel Lyman, a major in General Heath's army, who married Polly in 1781. One year later, John Wanton gave his house to the newly married couple as a wedding present. Here the Lymans lived for many years afterwards. When their daughter, Harriet, married Benjamin Hazard, the old family home eventually came into the possession of the Hazards where it remained until 1927 when it was purchased by the Newport Historical Society.

40

A close study of this dwelling by architectural historians reveals that it has some interior elements of the Jacobean style of building, a style that preceded the Georgian mode. The house is of frame construction, two stories high, with a steeply pitched gable roof containing three dormers and with a central entrance door and a central chimney. Having so many different owners during its long existence, the Wanton house has seen some alterations, but on the whole, it remains as originally built about 1675.

When John Wanton repaired the house after buying it in 1765, he is believed to have encased its once-exposed interior beams and to have paneled its mantels. And after he presented the house as a wedding gift to his new son-in-law, Major Lyman, in 1782, it was the major who installed the classic portico that now enhances the front of the dwelling. Another later addition was the lean-to kitchen built at the rear of the house. The dormer windows in the roof also came later.

Evidently a part of the original house is its front cornice, formed by extending the roof a little outward to allow room for what architects call a plaster cove cornice because of its curved shape. This type of cornice is shown in Moxon's *Mechanic Exercises*, published in London in 1698, several years after the Wanton house was built. Also original with the house is its massive centrally located chimney, which at the top is in pilaster form. Interestingly, the chimney was built of brick rather than stone. Most Rhode Island chimneys at that early date were built of stone; brick did not come into common use until later.

The simple lines of the stolid oak chest are effectively enhanced by the intricately carved ornamentation.

Inside the house, a decidedly Jacobean element of design is its stairway, built against the central chimney and having three runs to the floor above. It has turned balusters, squat and widely spaced; a molded hand rail; and ball-shaped caps on the posts, with acorn-designed drops at the bottom of the posts—all characteristic details of the Jacobean style. The rooms in the Wanton-Lyman-Hazard House have been carefully furnished with period pieces and household articles of the eighteenth-century era in Rhode Island, under the supervision of the Newport Historical Society.

Among the outstanding pieces of furniture in the house are the William and Mary walnut desk and highboy made about 1690-1710 in Massachusetts and the carved oak chest, circa 1680-1700, which are in the north parlor, originally the keeping room. The south parlor contains a mahogany secretary and a mahogany ball-and-claw-foot side chair with shell-carved crest rail, both made between 1750 and 1770 by John Goddard of Newport, one of the finest furniture craftsmen America has produced. This room also has three walnut Queen Anne side chairs made about 1745 by Job Townsend, another Newport cabinetmaker.

Above: General George de Wolf began his career as one of Bristol's most lavish hosts in this palatial mansion known as Linden Place. Right: The quaint summerhouse is situated in an opulent floral setting on the landscaped grounds of the estate.

GEORGE DE WOLF HOUSE

Bristol, Rhode Island

FABULOUS LINDEN PLACE

In the days when Bristol was a leading social center of Rhode Island, one of the reigning families of that historic Narragansett Bay city was the De Wolf clan. No more eloquent proof of this may be found than in the numerous De Wolf great houses built in Bristol by various members of the family. These were imposing mansions in which they entertained graciously, welcomed famous visitors, and in general made social history during the era before Bristol was eclipsed as a millionaire's colony by more glamorous Newport.

Of the numerous De Wolf residences, however, only two remain. The most spacious, magnificent and best-known of the two is Linden Place, built in 1810 by General George De Wolf. It is also of interest as an outstanding example of the work of Russell Warren, a great Rhode Island architect who later went southward and designed some of the famous old houses in Charleston, South Carolina.

When General De Wolf commissioned Warren to design a residence for him, he stipulated that it should be "a finer mansion than The Mount," which was a palace-like dwelling built in 1808 by his uncle, James De Wolf. He also wanted it more elaborate than "Hey Bonnie Hall," a mansion also built in 1808 by another De Wolf kinsman, William. With such a *carte blanche* commission, architect Warren created what is now considered the most fabulous old house in Bristol, a city of many venerable dwellings.

Charles de Wolf, father of the builder of Linden Place, is depicted in the inimitable style of Gilbert Stuart.

After Linden Place was completed at a cost of $65,000, a large sum in those days, General De Wolf began his career in the mansion as one of Bristol's most lavish hosts. Not least among outstanding social events in the history of this Hope Street house was the day in 1817 when the general entertained President James Monroe, who then was in his first year term as the nation's chief executive. In the future, two other De Wolf kinsmen were to entertain Presidents in their palatial Bristol residences—William De Wolf, who welcomed President Andrew Jackson, and Frank E. De Wolf, who served as host to President Chester A. Arthur. In 1875, former President U. S. Grant called on Mrs. Theodora de Wolf Colt.

Now more than 150 years old, Linden Place is still playing its role as a comfortable home. It is now the residence of a great-great-

Above: Over the black marble mantel in the drawing room hangs a portrait of Andrew Jackson by Benjamin West. In the corner between windows curtained in gold silk stands a Claggett grandfather's clock. Right: A groined vault supported by four Doric columns comprises the front part of the main hall.

granddaughter of General De Wolf. She is Mrs. J. Romeo Miglietta, who also happens to be the daughter of America's most celebrated actress, Ethel Barrymore. Mrs. Miglietta is continuing the tradition of hospitality first set in motion here by General De Wolf. In keeping with this program, Mrs. Miglietta has, among other things, opened the large carriage house, an attractive building adjacent to the house, as an art museum and as a center for social and cultural events.

As may be seen, this brick mansion's most arresting exterior feature is its colossal and highly ornamental entrance portico—an element that was distinctive of many of Russell Warren's house designs. It is an ample, two-story portico topped by a smaller or third-story portico, which carries the whole entrance treatment to the roof line. The roof is hipped and hidden by a decorative parapet rail. Four fluted Corinthian columns support the great entrance portico. The house is square-shaped, its corners ornamented with quoins. Tall French windows with heavy entablatures enhance its first floor.

One of the handsomest doorways in Bristol is found here in the De Wolf residence. It is framed with an elliptical fanlight and side-lights, and above it at the second-story level is an elaborate Palladian window. The mansion is situated on tree-shaded, landscaped grounds, a setting that brings out its rare vintage appearance.

On entering Linden Place, the visitor finds himself in an interior less ornamental than the exterior, but still very dignified. In the front part of the entrance hall is a groined vault supported by four Doric columns. At the rear of the hall, hidden from view as you first enter the passageway, is a splendid spiral stairway. In placing this to one side of the entrance hall rather than in the center, Russell Warren, it has been explained, followed the example of Charles Bulfinch, known in history as the first American architect. This fascinating stairway rises in a well three flights up to a glazed dome on the roof of the house.

All of the rooms in Linden Place are ample, airy, gracefully proportioned. There are ten fireplaces with mantels made of black or white marble and columns that support friezes of block panels. The walls of the principal rooms are white.

In the drawing room—its elegance emphasized by gold silk curtains and a ceiling medallion of Adam design—are several noteworthy items: a famous Claggett grandfather's clock, an oil portrait of Andrew Jackson attributed to Benjamin West (1738-1820) and a painting by Gilbert Stuart (1755-1828) of Charles De Wolf, father of the man who built the house. Four Queen Anne chairs grace the main hall and the dining room is dominated by a chandelier of crystal and doré bronze. Late nineteenth-century and twentieth-century sculpture is represented in Linden Place by three works by the great French sculptor, Auguste Rodin (1840-1917)—*Psyche*, *Roaring Lion* and *The Hawk and the Dove*—and two by Gutzon Borglum (1867-1941) who is best known for the gigantic faces he carved on Mt. Rushmore in South Dakota.

Perhaps the most interesting room in the house is the octagonal Glass Room, which protrudes on the side of the house opposite the carriage house. The Glass Room somewhat breaks the design of the house and its large vaulted windows appear incongruous to the rest of the house, suggesting it may have been a later addition. But it was designed by the architect as part of the original house and is reputed to have been the first Victorian Gothic room in this country.

Dominating the dining room is a magnificent crystal and doré bronze chandelier said to have come from Buckingham Palace.

THOMAS LEE HOUSE

East Lyme, Connecticut

"A SEAT OF JUSTICE"

For more than forty years during early colonial times in Connecticut, a room in the now-famed Thomas Lee House at East Lyme served as a local "Seat of Justice." It was presided over by Justice Lee, a son of Ensign Thomas Lee II, the colonist who built the Lee house about 1660. Now known as the Judgment Hall, this informal courtroom, with its stone fireplace and exposed ceiling, or "summer," beams, has been furnished as it was in the days when Thomas Lee III meted out justice to any lawbreakers in the region east of Saybrook, a region where the town of East Lyme later grew up.

Just as active in public life as the judge was his father, Ensign Thomas Lee II, founder of the prominent Lee family of early Connecticut. He was very young when he came with his family from England to America about 1641—only twenty-one years or so after the arrival of the Pilgrim Fathers in Massachusetts. He settled on land east of early Saybrook, land believed to have been secured earlier in England by his father, Thomas Lee I. The latter died at sea while accompanying his son to America.

It was on this land at what is now East Lyme that Thomas Lee II, built the two-story, clapboarded house which survives today as one of the oldest dwellings in New England. After becoming settled here, he soon was active in public life. His title of "Ensign" derived from the fact that he was a commissioned officer in the colonial militia. He also served as a town constable, an important position in those days, and was a member of the General Assembly in 1676. With his death in 1705, the family home passed to his son, Thomas Lee III.

All during the eighteenth century, the landmark remained in the Lee family. Last of the Lee owners was Dr. Thomas Lee, who conveyed the property to his sister-in-law, a Miss Holman. When she died, the old Thomas Lee House was, for the first time in 250 years, placed on the open real estate market. It was purchased by J. B. Rathbun, who promptly announced that the house would be demolished because it was no longer habitable.

At this point, members of the East Lyme Historical Society, under the vigorous leadership of the society's secretary, Miss Celeste E. Bush, launched a movement to buy and preserve the old Lee place.

Above: The handsome Queen Anne highboy in the keeping room was made from maple and cherry-wood around 1770.

Opposite: The historic Thomas Lee House, where generations of Lees resided, witnessed the reign of seven English sovereigns and was over a century old when the Declaration of Independence was written.

Above: The famed Judgment Hall contains a fascinating array of late seventeenth-century furnishings. The carved wainscot chair, however, is a heavy oak piece from about 1587. Below: The bed chamber in early houses such as this was seldom finished off as the parlor or other "public" rooms were.

Having limited means, however, the East Lyme group was generously aided by the Society of Colonial Dames, the Society of Colonial Wars, the Society for the Preservation of New England Antiquities and by several Lee descendants.

Thus it was that in 1914 the venerable Lee house became the property of the East Lyme Historical Society. Steps were immediately taken to repair the house under the direction of Norman Morrison Isham, an architect noted for his historical restorations. At a public reception in the house in 1915 the guest of honor was William Howard Taft, former President of the United States.

As with most early colonial dwellings in New England, the Thomas Lee house grew larger and larger with the passing years, having additional rooms to the west and a lean-to at the rear built onto it. Unlike many early colonists' homes, however, the Lee property was, in a sense, turned around to face north instead of south, its original position. This came about sometime after 1715 when the present Saybrook Road was laid out just north of the Lee house, and Justice Lee, being a local magistrate, wanted his house to face that highway. Accordingly, he built a new entrance door, a new staircase and a new chimney on the north side of the house and added a lean-to onto its south side. As seen today, the entrance door is topped by five small window lights, and a classic cornice enhances the front of the house. In keeping with its period, the house's clapboard sides are seasoned with linseed oil rather than painted.

Inside, the kitchen and the famed Judgment Hall come close to being completely furnished in pieces from the 1660-1760 period, while other rooms have a few later pieces. Most interesting is probably the Judgment Hall, primarily because it contains five rare seventeenth-century pieces. The heavy, throne-like wainscot chair in American-Jacobean style has a diamond pattern incised in the middle of the back panel which is surmounted by intricate carving that demonstrates superior craftsmanship. Also in this room in the same general style and period are a spice box, Bible box, an English-made court cupboard and a bride's chest.

A section of the walls in the Judgment Hall is covered with some of the wood paneling made of carefully hand-fitted, vertical, red-stained planks which dates from the early days of the house. The more conventional rectangular block paneling, as seen in the keeping room and other rooms, is painted Williamsburg gray and dates from around 1735.

Other notable interior features include the enclosed summer beam in the keeping room, which was the sitting room or parlor of that day; the two supporting brackets of "ship's knee" design in the kitchen; a window frame in the lean-to from the original one-room house that Ensign Lee built; and the staircase, with post and rail of white-oak, in the entry "porch" or vestibule. Such details of architectural and decorative interest, along with its historical associations, make the Thomas Lee House one of the most distinctive old houses on Long Island Sound.

Above: One notable feature of the interior is the enclosed summer beam above the fireplace in the keeping room. The conventional block paneling dates from 1735. Left: The massive dower chest in the Judgment Hall contrasts with the delicate table surmounted by an early American carved Bible chest.

HYLAND HOUSE

Guilford, Connecticut

ON THE OLD BOSTON POST ROAD

Through the diamond-paned casement window, sunlight illuminates an early book displayed in Hyland House.

During the early spring of 1916 a Guilford citizen, Clarence Norton, made known his plans to tear down one of Guilford's oldest houses and erect a garage adjoining its site. The house stood on Boston Street and dated from the far-off years when that street was part of the famous Boston Post Road. When Mr. Norton announced his plans, he had not yet purchased the house then owned by Gilbert Gates, a leading Guilford resident. Mr. Gates had purchased the house only two years earlier, in 1914.

Undoubtedly, Mr. Norton's proposal would have been fulfilled, and the old landmark would have disappeared, had it not been for the prompt intervention of a former Connecticut governor, Rollin S. Woodruff. He succeeded in convincing the owner of the house, Mr. Gates, that it was an historic landmark of the greatest importance in the annals of Guilford and the State of Connecticut, a landmark that should certainly be preserved. Thereafter, the Dorothy Whitfield Historic Society of Guilford bought the house and has maintained it as a noteworthy example of early colonial architecture.

Thus one of Guilford's most appealing landmarks was saved, a house almost as old and as interesting in many respects as Guilford's other famed domestic landmark, the Whitfield House, built about 1639 by the founder of the colony, the Reverend Henry Whitfield.

It was in 1660, only twenty years after the colony was founded, that George Hyland built the clapboarded house which was threatened with demolition 256 years later. The date of its construction is attested in a deed of 1719 of the Guilford Land Records. George Hyland had arrived in the Guilford Colony in 1651 and was an active leader in its affairs after building his home on the Boston Post Road.

George Hyland died in 1693 and left the house to his widow, Hannah, a daughter of Abraham Cruttenden. When the widow herself died in 1702, the Hyland property, which included a sizable tract of land besides the house, was divided among her four sons-in-law, one of whom, Thomas Hall, received that portion of the property on which stood the Hyland House. He later traded this land for other land with Colonel Samuel Hill, a leading Guilford real estate man,

Photo by Ruben-Cyr Agency

Unlike most early colonial dwellings, the overhang of Hyland House is chamfered with decorative molding. The leaded windows in diamond-pane design are reminiscent of Tudor England.

Above: This chest, dated 1710, with its original stenciled design reveals the whimsy of an early Guilford artisan. Below: Any meal was a cozy affair in front of the large brick fireplace.

who, in turn, traded this acquisition with Isaac Parmelee. At an earlier date Isaac Parmelee had married Elizabeth Hyland, one of George Hyland's daughters.

Then, in 1719, Isaac Parmelee sold to his son Ebenezer two acres of land, "it being part of the home lot formerly belonging to our honored father, George Hyland, where he last dwelt, with all the buildings, fences, timber, stone privileges, appurtenances and accommodations." A ship builder by trade and a skillful worker in wood and metal, Ebenezer Parmelee added the back portion, or lean-to, of the Hyland House in 1720, including within it another kitchen with a large fireplace.

An interesting chapter in the history of the old Hyland House began in 1773 when the now elderly Ebenezer and Anna Parmelee received, by the terms of a lately deceased neighboring woman's will, an indentured Negro servant girl named Candace. When twenty-two-year-old Candace entered the Parmelee home, she not only brought with her a winning personality and great energy but also a sizable "dowry" of household articles left to her by her late mistress. The articles included a bed and bedding, spinning wheels, furniture and wearing apparel. Candace remained with the family until after the death of Mrs. Parmelee in 1789. Thereafter, Candace, now thirty-eight years old, became a free woman and did household jobs around Guilford.

Four years after the death of his mother, Ebenezer Parmelee, Jr., sold the family home to his mother's cousin, Seth Cruttenden, who lived here until his own passing in 1830. As he had no heirs, his house was ordered sold by the Guilford probate court in the settlement of his estate. Thus it came into the possession of the Wildman family of Guilford and remained in that family for the next eighty years, until 1914, when its new owner, Gilbert Gates, was about to sell it.

The exterior of the two-story clapboarded Hyland House is stained red as were numerous buildings in seventeenth-century New England. It has that feature typical of so many early colonial dwellings, a hewn overhang, but its chamfered girts with bold molding is a treatment unknown elsewhere in Connecticut. Diamond-paned windows, a large central chimney, gable roof and a lean-to at the rear complete the picture of the Hyland House as a fine example of seventeenth-century architecture in New England.

Since acquiring this landmark, members of the Dorothy Whitfield Historic Society have furnished it throughout with antiques and pieces which recall the early colonial days in Connecticut. Among these are a Bible box on its own standard, an early Guilford chest with original painted decoration, kitchen utensils displayed around

the fireplace, a pencil-post bed covered with a resist-dyed quilt, a rare chair table, a spinning wheel and seventeenth-century plate ware. The interior of the house also has original door hinges in the butterfly, H and HL designs. In the east chamber, the fireplace is framed with a fine Bolection molding, a molding which projects beyond the wall's surface, while in the west chamber, simple pine sheathing is used on the fireplace wall.

Not to be overlooked in the long history of this house is that within it Ebenezer Parmelee, the boat builder and mechanic, constructed in 1727 the first town clock in Guilford—believed to have been the first town clock in America. It was placed in the belfry of the "Old Temple" on the Green and remained there until 1830 when it was transferred to the First Congregational Church, where it marked the time until 1892. It is now a prime exhibit in the state historical museum at the Reverend Henry Whitfield House in Guilford.

Fine relics of early eighteenth-century living at Hyland House include this delicate butterfly drop-leaf table.

Above: Material used in the construction of the old Morris dwelling was obtained primarily from the estate.
Right: The small dining room table is the gateleg variety fashionable in the eighteenth century.

54

PARDEE'S OLD MORRIS HOUSE

New Haven, Connecticut

"YE MANSION HOUSE"

Among members of the company of Puritans organized in London by John Davenport and Theophilus Eaton and who, in 1638, aided them in founding the Connecticut colony of New Haven, were Thomas Morris, a ship builder by trade, and his wife Elizabeth. When these colonists laid out a town of eight squares around a central one called the Commons (now known as "The Old Green"), Thomas Morris helped as much in this work as any of the other settlers. At that time the new town was given the name of Quinnipiac after the river on which it was located.

Within the eight squares, lots were assigned to the various proprietors who had a financial interest in the new settlement. Some of the colonists, however, were not in a position to invest as much in the project as the proprietors, and these, totaling thirty-two, were gratuitously given small lots by the governor of the colony, Theophilus Eaton. One of these thirty-two was Thomas Morris.

As a ship builder in what soon became a busy seaport community, Morris had plenty of opportunities to improve his worldly status. So he soon began to acquire land, especially in what was then known as Solitary Cove, a name later changed to Morris Cove. In 1671 he also purchased some tracts at a place near Solitary Cove called Oyster Shell Field. But Thomas Morris was destined not to remain owner of these tracts for very long, for he died two years later, his land holdings barely developed.

With his passing, the tracts were inherited by his three sons, John, Eleazar and Joseph. Then, in 1705, John sold his share of the inheritance to his brother, Eleazar, and moved to New Jersey. In his transfer of title, John described his property as containing "Ye mansion house now standing thereon." Since this is the first recorded mention of a house on the John Morris property, the old Connecticut dwelling now known as Pardee's Morris House must have been built sometime before 1705.

Most New Haven historians believe the house was erected in the period just after 1680. As supporting evidence, they point to the stone walls at each end of the frame house, walls which contain details displaying late seventeenth-century workmanship. Further evidence was offered in a heavy stone basin that, until twenty-five

The 1788 portrait of Captain Morris' daughter, Lorinda, exemplifies the primitive style of Rueben Moulthrop.

A main attraction of the home is the old shelter kitchen which harbored the homeless Morris family until their house was built.

years ago (when it was stolen), stood near an old well at the rear of the house, and which contained an inscription on its bottom reading "J. M., 1688." Thus it may be concluded that the landmark was completed by John Morris sometime between 1680 and 1688.

When Eleazar Morris left his will in 1717, he bestowed that part of his land holdings containing "Ye mansion house" on his son John. Because he had no children of his own, John left the property to two of his nephews, Daniel and Amos, sons of his brother James. Subsequently, Daniel sold his half interest in the Morris Cove farm to Captain Amos Morris who lived in the house for many years, rearing a family of twelve children in it. In 1767, Captain Morris added an ell which was needed to accommodate his large family.

During the Revolutionary War, British troops under General William Tryon invaded Connecticut, landing at New Haven and burning all houses on their line of march. One of these was the old

Morris House. The Morris family managed to save a few possessions by hiding them in caves in the woods, and when the British left the family returned to find that the house had not been completely destroyed. The stone end walls and stone chimneys remained, as did much of the heavy timber framework. Part of a charred lentil from this fire can be seen over the garden door at the rear of the house in the ell, now used as living quarters.

One outbuilding, an animal shelter, remained unharmed after the British raid. When Captain Morris and his family returned it is thought that they moved this shelter to the outside of the north wall, which was still standing, and lived here in one room while they rebuilt the main house. Now known as the shelter kitchen, this beamed room contains a stone sink and a fireplace with oven.

Today all rooms are furnished with early American antiques. The paneled hall in the main portion of the house runs from the west, or front, entrance to the garden entrance, which is used presently by visitors. It contains a round Chippendale table, dated 1789, a grandfather's clock from 1795 or before, and an early seventeenth-century Jacobean bench. The hall floor is faintly marked with octagonal-shaped stenciling. Four panes of bull's-eye glass are above each set of double doors which lead to the parlor and dining room at the front of the house.

In the parlor are Queen Anne and Chippendale chairs and an exquisite Queen Anne side table. The dining room contains a gate-leg table dating from the eighteenth century and banister—back chairs. Just off these rooms are two small closets, with windows in each, that are believed to have been powder rooms where the men could powder their wigs.

The large main kitchen contains an unusually large fireplace big enough to burn eight-foot logs and is believed to have been part of the original house. Beside it is a fine high-backed settle. A coach house on the grounds contains a valuable carriage, a gig, sled and early farm tools.

Without doubt the most outstanding piece of furniture in the house is the Governor Carver chair in Captain Amos Morris's study, a type which is among the earliest surviving chairs in this country. This sturdy piece came into the possession of the Morris family no later than 1690. Also in the study is a primitive-style portrait of Captain Morris done by Rueben Moulthrop, a well-known local artist. Two other portraits by him are elsewhere in the house.

When this New Haven landmark was offered for sale in 1915 after being held in the Morris family for almost 250 years, it was purchased by a leading citizen of New Haven, William Scranton Pardee. He had a life-long sentimental interest in the house because his first ancestor in Connecticut, George Pardee, who arrived in 1678, bought land at Morris Cove adjoining the Morris farm. When Mr. Pardee's will was opened after his death in 1918, it was found that he had donated the old Morris House to the New Haven Colony Historical Society, with a generous endowment for its maintenance.

Above: A study desk holds an 1850 toy kitchen in the children's room collection. Below: A Moulthrop portrait of Captain Amos Morris hangs in the study near a corner cupboard lined with lovely Delft ware and pewter.

BUTTOLPH-WILLIAMS HOUSE

Wethersfield, Connecticut

THE HOUSE WITH "YE GREATE KITCHIN"

All rooms in the Buttolph-Williams House have been restored and furnished with authentic colonial antiques of the late seventeenth-century era.

Aside from its fame as one of New England's finest examples of a late seventeenth-century house, the Buttolph-Williams House in Wethersfield, Connecticut, is additionally renowned for its "Ye Greate Kitchin." Few seventeenth-century dwellings standing in New England today have such a completely, authentically and attractively furnished kitchen—the heart of the house in colonial times—as the Wethersfield abode built by David Buttolph, a cordwainer or leather worker, in 1692.

Not the first of his family to settle in Wethersfield, oldest town in Connecticut, David Buttolph was a son of Lieutenant John Buttolph, who came to Wethersfield in 1676—forty-two years after the town was founded by Captain John Oldham and his group of "Adventurers" from Massachusetts. In addition to being a glover and trader, John Buttolph served as a lieutenant in the town's Train Band and also as a selectman. He died in 1692 leaving, among other bequests, two acres of land to one of his sons, David. At that time David was about twenty-four years old, had recently married, and was already the father of a child.

Now the owner of two acres of land, David Buttolph, in the same year his father died, is believed to have either bought the framework of another house and had it moved to his land or to have built a new house for himself. In either case, this is the house still standing today at Broad and Marsh streets—the oldest restored dwelling in age-old Wethersfield.

But David Buttolph did not remain here for long. Six years later, in 1698, he sold the house and moved to a Connecticut town named Symsbury. The purchaser of his house was Robert Turner, who, in 1711, sold the dwelling to Benjamin Belden, a felt maker. When, in 1714, Belden was licensed to keep tavern, he built an ell on the original Buttolph house where he sold rum and cider brandy. This ell remained attached to the house until a few years ago.

In 1721 the Wethersfield landmark was bought by Daniel Williams, and the house remained in his family for many years, giving to the dwelling its present hyphenated name, the Buttolph-Williams House. In 1862, however, it was sold to James Vibert, who drove the stage from Hartford to Middletown.

Above: During restoration of the old house, the four-inch
overhang with corbel and older white pine clapboards
were   discovered behind the nineteenth-century clapboards.
Left: An imposing nail-studded outer door
leads to the interior of the dwelling.

The Viberts lived here for an even longer period than the Williams family. The last Vibert occupant was Frank, a son of James Vibert, who lived to a ripe old age in the ell at the rear of the House and who cultivated a flower and vegetable garden that won the admiration of the Wethersfield townspeople. With Vibert's passing, the landmark passed into the hands of the Antiquarian & Landmarks Society of Connecticut, which in 1947 began work on its restoration and the furnishing of all of its rooms.

On viewing the exterior of this two-story "Pilgrim Century" house, one sees the familiar aspects of the Elizabethan mode of design as transplanted to early America—the large, central chimney, steep gabled roof, second-floor overhang, diamond-paned casement windows, and the clapboarded siding. Further evidences of this style were revealed during the restoration of the dwelling, such as the post and girt framework and the projecting brackets, or corbels, at the second-floor level of the posts.

An old nail-studded door leads to the interior of the house, where the visitor's first glimpse is that of an entrance "porch," or front hall, with a winding staircase leading to the second floor. The staircase has an attractive well-turned newel post and a molded handrail. All of the rooms in the house have white-washed walls and have been restored and furnished with colonial antiques of the late seventeenth-century era.

Among noteworthy items in the first-floor parlor, or Greate Hall, is a rare trestle-foot, gateleg table with its original leather hinges and a setting of fine seventeenth-century English Delft and two mid-drip brass candlesticks of English origin similar to one owned by an inhabitant of the Plymouth Colony. A New England oaken court cupboard displays pewter chargers and pewter candlesticks dated 1685. The parlor also contains an English brass lantern clock, a Connecticut sunflower-and-tulip chest bearing the date "1672," and numerous slat- and banister-back chairs, including one owned by the Chester family of Wethersfield in the seventeenth century.

Upstairs, in the bedroom above the kitchen known as the "kitchin chamber," is the finest chamfered summer beam and chimney girt in the house. On the bed in this room is a Connecticut blue and white resist coverlet dated 1717.

Of particular interest, however, is the kitchen. Warmed by a capacious fireplace with a pleasing mantel, it is a fascinating museum of the articles and accessories that helped to provide food and comfort for our colonial ancestors. Here is a varied collection of trenchers and other early woodenware, wrought-iron pieces, a rare seventeenth-century half-circle settle, a pair of high chairs, tables, benches, and the tools and utensils associated with the fireplace. Included in the latter is a jack and weights that was used for turning the spit in the fireplace. Although there are many articles in the kitchen, they are all attractively arranged, and there is no overcrowding of the exhibits. One could not find a more intimate glimpse into the domestic life of the first Americans than in the kitchen of the Buttolph-Williams House at Wethersfield, Connecticut.

Above: The heart of the house, "Ye Greate Kitchin," boasts a complete collection of woodenware, wrought iron and furniture from the pilgrim century.

Opposite top: Two items of Connecticut origin are the blue and white resist coverlet, dated 1717, and the pine six-board chest with gouge carving. Opposite bottom: Seventeenth-century mid-drip brass candlesticks of English origin rest on a rare New England trestle-foot gateleg table. Banister-back chairs complete the ensemble.

62

JOHN BOWNE HOUSE

Flushing, New York

A NATIONAL SHRINE TO RELIGIOUS FREEDOM

Almost immediately after John Bowne, an English settler in the Dutch colony of New Netherland, built his house at what is now Flushing, New York, in 1661, he defied the despotic Dutch governor of the colony, Peter Stuyvesant, by holding Quaker meetings in its kitchen. The governor had earlier issued an edict against all Quakers in his province, calling that religious group "an abominable sect." Described as "a conservative, quiet-spoken, plain but strong-minded man," John Bowne chose to ignore the governor's order.

As a result of this stand John Bowne was arrested in 1662 and brought before Governor Stuyvesant and the Colony Council at New Amsterdam, now New York City. Here, he recalled to the governor the famous Flushing Remonstrance, a document issued in 1657 by the colonists at Flushing, in which they protested the governor's religious intolerance and reminded him that his predecessor, Governor Willem Kieft, had promised them religious freedom. The Flushing Remonstrance has since become an outstanding document in American history.

But Governor Stuyvesant, impatient, irritable, autocratic, pounded his familiar wooden leg on the floor and ignored John Bowne's remarks. He ordered that the Englishman be fined "one hundred and fifty florins," and warned him "to abstain himself in the future from Quaker meetings," under the threat of a double fine and banishment from the colony.

Refusing to pay the fine or give up his right to religious freedom, John Bowne was immediately thrown into the New Amsterdam jail, served only bread and water, and later was sent out of the country "to wherever the ship shall land." The ship landed in Ireland, but when Bowne, assisted by Quakers, was able to get to Amsterdam, Holland, by way of England, his case was heard by the Dutch West India Company which controlled the New Netherland colony in America. Bowne became discouraged because the company gave him no satisfaction and ignored him after the first presentation of his plea. However, after he returned to America, he found that his plea had been successful. Although Bowne was never formally acquitted, the Dutch West India Company had sent a directive to

Above: This mysterious looking opening is actually the beehive oven in the kitchen, illuminated by a candle set in an ancient tin candlestick. The brick-lined oven is large enough to bake forty pies at one time.

Opposite top: John Bowne built the first section of his house, the kitchen, in 1661. The second addition—dining room and porch—was not made until 1680, while the last section was added by his son Samuel in 1696. Opposite bottom: Life at Bowne House in early Flushing is quaintly depicted in this historical sketch.

The fine mahogany secretary in the attractively furnished living room was built by a New York City craftsman around 1740. All of the original brasses, which came from England, still adorn the secretary.

Governor Stuyvesant stating that, "the consciences of men, at least, ought to remain free and unshackled."

John Bowne returned on March 30, 1664, to his home and family at Flushing, on the western tip of Long Island, and there, for the next thirty years, held Quaker services in his kitchen. These meetings were discontinued only after the Friends Meeting House was built at Flushing in 1694.

Not only did Bowne, who was a convert to the Quaker faith, welcome that religious group to his home, but here, too, he was host to some of the prominent settlers and visitors of seventeenth-century America. One of the most famous of these was George Fox, founder in England of the Quaker faith, who visited the Bowne home in 1672. Another guest was William Penn, founder of Pennsylvania and also a Quaker, who came in 1683.

With the death of John Bowne in 1695, the house was inherited in turn by a son, grandson and great-grandson. The latter's daughter, Mary, married Samuel Parsons, founder of a well-known Flushing nursery, and although they did not live in the Bowne House, years later their descendants came into possession of it.. And here it remained until 1946, when it was acquired by the Bowne House Historical Society, a group organized by Justice Charles S. Colden. The house has since been designated a historical landmark by the Landmarks Preservation Commission of the City of New York.

Today Bowne House resembles a New England "salt box" type of early dwelling. At first it was a simple, two-story, gabled house centering on an ample chimney that served the fireplace in the kitchen, then the most important room in the house. In 1680, however, John Bowne added a dining room, and in 1696, a year after he died, his son, Samuel, constructed a living room and built a new entrance porch. The bedrooms are lighted by three dormers in the steep-pitched roof. This roof was raised in 1830 and a north wing added to the house, a wing that contained a guest room, library and several more chambers.

In the house today are furnishings associated with each of the nine generations of John Bowne descendants. One article of unusual interest in the living room is a massive mahogany secretary, hand-carved and with its original brass hardware, said to have been made in New York between 1736 and 1750 especially for this room. Here, too, are portraits of Samuel Parsons and Mary Bowne Parsons, owners of the house in the early nineteenth century. One sleeping room in the dwelling is known as the William Penn Room and contains the four-poster, canopied bed in which the founder of Pennsylvania slept on his visit here in 1683.

In the dining room an object of particular interest is the highboy, a fine example of the William and Mary style, featuring trumpet legs. Here, too, is a tall eight-day clock, believed to have been made about 1735 by Anthony Ward in New York. Around the dining table are chairs of the early Queen Anne period. A handsome desk in the

library was made by a friend of John Bowne's from the wood of a fruit tree that grew on his grounds.

Oldest and most historic part of the house is, of course, the kitchen, the room where members of the Bowne family centered most of their activities and where the Quakers of Flushing and vicinity worshipped for more than thirty years. The capacious fireplace here was built by John Bowne large enough "to roast an ox in if he had a mind to do it." The kitchen is completely furnished with household articles and utensils of the seventeenth century. A framed tribute to his historic house, written by Justice Charles S. Colden, hangs over the kitchen fireplace.

The tribute contains these words: "In this room an oppressed people found sanctuary. Here lived John Bowne who suffered arrest, imprisonment, separation from his home, his wife and children and banishment to the Old World so that a then despised people might worship God in this room and in the New World, in the manner of their own choosing. Here was born religious freedom in the American way of life."

Above: Behind the dining table set with pewter stands the highboy which was a wedding gift from William Penn's daughter to Bowne's daughter.

PIETER BRONCK HOUSE

Coxsackie, New York

A DUTCH COLONIAL SHRINE

This typical Hudson Valley Dutch portrait, from about 1710, displayed at the Pieter Bronck House, is attributed to "The Schuyler Limner."

Focal point and principal object of interest in the colonial Dutch homestead at Coxsackie, New York, is the small, ancient, stone house built in 1663 by Pieter Bronck, son of one of the earliest colonists of New Netherland. The homestead, with its two old Dutch houses and various barns, outbuildings and roadways, is now the headquarters of the Greene County Historical Society. Not only is the Bronck settlement a shrine to descendants of that early Dutch family, but it is an outstanding memorial of this country's beginning years.

Founder of the family in America was Jonas Bronck, who arrived in New Netherland in 1639. That was only eighteen years after the colony was established, under the auspices of the Holland government, by the Dutch West India Company. Jonas Bronck, who brought his wife, young son, Pieter, and servants with him, is said to have been a man of some means with a good education. Included in what few personal belongings he brought to America was a small library of books—an unusual possession for migrating colonists.

But Jonas Bronck did not enjoy the New World for very long, for he died in 1643. His widow married Arent Van Curler, who later founded the city of Schenectady. He had arrived in New Netherland earlier to manage the vast Hudson River estate of his cousin, Kiliaen Van Rensselaer. When the newly wedded couple moved to Rensselaerwyck (now Rensselaer), where Van Curler had his headquarters, they took with them her stepson Pieter. During his boyhood days, Pieter Bronck showed signs of becoming a thrifty and energetic man.

When he grew up, Pieter went into the brewery business at Beverwyck (now Albany). Then, in 1661, he mortgaged his brewery to obtain cash for the purchase of land in the Catskill region on the west side of the Hudson River, below Albany. On his land part of the present town of Coxsackie evolved. By the terms of his patent from the Dutch government, Pieter Bronck was required to settle and build a house on his land within two years. So in 1663, Pieter completed the small, gabled, one-room-and-loft stone house that survives today as the original building and principal historic landmark of the Bronck homestead.

After Pieter died in 1669, his survivors continued to live in his small house, but gradually it became too cramped for his ever-

Above: The original Bronck home, the stolid one-room-and-loft at left, was built of fieldstone in 1663. The somewhat lighter brick building at right was added in 1738. Left: High on one gable end of the steeply pitched New House roof is a small shuttered opening used as a granary door.

The barn built on Bronck property around 1800 is thirteen-sided to signify the original states of the republic.

growing number of descendants. Soon after his son Jan was married, a stone addition was built in 1685 on the west side of the original house, containing a hall and main room with a loft above. Apparently, this enlargement served the family until 1738 when another new addition—actually a separate house later joined by a passageway—was built to the north of Pieter Bronck's small stone dwelling. This was a two-story edifice of brick construction, now called the "New House."

A separate dwelling, now known as the "Stepmother's House," was built nearby in the early 1800's. It received its name because here lived Elbertje Van Buren Bronck, second wife of Judge Leonard Bronck, first judge of the Court of Common Pleas of Greene County. It was built for her by the judge because of unfriendly relations between herself and the daughters of Judge Bronck's first marriage.

The Bronck homestead remained continuously in the family for the more than 275 years of its existence, until 1939 when it and the tract of land on which it stands was bequeathed to the Greene County Historical Society. The society has maintained all the buildings of the homestead since then.

Because it remained in the Bronck family for so long, the homestead, other than additions, has had few changes made to its exterior or interior. Furthermore, the Bronck descendants, quiet, conservative, substantial, were aware of the historical importance of their homestead and took steps to preserve the atmosphere and physical details of the house as a typical Hudson Valley Dutch home of seventeenth- and eighteenth-century America.

Unlike most of the early colonial houses of New England, which faced south, the 1663 house originally faced west toward an Indian footpath which was the principal route of travel before commercial traffic began using the Hudson River. Sometime later the house's entrance was changed to the east side to face the river as it now does. Staunchly built of native stone, it has an unusually high-pitched gable roof with a chimney at its west end. The four windows on it have small-paned casements with heavy paneled shutters. At each gable end there are two obliquely set windows of the bull's-eye type, which provide light for the loft under the high-pitched roof.

As with nearly all of the earliest Dutch houses, there is no front porch, or to use the Dutch word, "stoop." That feature was to come a bit later with the 1820 modernization of the New House, built in 1738. Connected with the old house by a covered brick passageway, this later building has as its most dominant feature a commodious stoop stretching clear across its facade. It also has two dormers in a roof as steeply pitched as the parent house. High on one gable end is a small shuttered opening that was used as a granary door. It should be added here that the brick work of the New House is of a salmon-pink color and provides a pleasing contrast to the gray stone work of the original dwelling.

All of the rooms in both houses are attractively furnished with colonial Dutch pieces and antiques, many of them Bronck family heirlooms. Especially noticeable in the original house's first-floor

Above: Of particular interest in the dining room are the 1820 modernization of the fireplace and mantel built in 1738, and the "carpenter's knees," upper left, which brace the ceiling beams. Left: A French toilet set is grouped below a large mirror decorated with reverse painting on glass.

common room, with its ample fireplace and paneled walls, are the unusually heavy beams that form its ceiling joists and the fifteen-inch planks that form its flooring.

The most interesting room in the 1663 house is the common room, or as it is frequently called, the Pioneer Room. The settle bench, or hutch table, beside the fireplace is a Bronck family piece that can be used as either bench or table. The fine old Dutch *kas* in this room is not a family piece but came from another local Dutch family. All of the woodwork trim in both houses is of exceptionally high quality.

In the hallway of the 1685 addition to the stone house are Bronck family portraits and an oil showing the house and its surroundings in the 1820's. Perhaps the most exquisite room in the entire dwelling is the West Room of the 1685 addition. It contains three paintings by the Hudson River School artist, Thomas Cole (1801-1848), as well as some personal possessions from his studio in nearby Catskill, New York. The natural wood paneling on the west or fireplace wall of this room is the finest paneling in the house and probably dates from 1792 when the 1685 addition had to be rebuilt due to storm damage.

Where the first Bronck dwelling has an atmosphere of solidity, of heaviness, the 1738 addition is somewhat lighter in tone, due to new construction methods and new building materials. In this New House may be seen most of the Bronck family furnishings, pieces and heirlooms, especially in the parlor, dining room and two second-floor bedrooms. The interior construction here, such as the curved "knee brackets" which support the ceiling joists, testifies to the handiwork of ship's carpenters. Of interest, too, are the Dutch doors, with their variety of decorative iron hinges.

Surrounding the original Pieter Bronck dwelling and its New House are some dozen other buildings, a few of historic interest, preserved on the grounds by the Greene County Historical Society and most of which contain exhibits. Among these are the thirteen-sided barn, built about 1800, which symbolizes the thirteen original American states; the restored Dutch Barn, with its exhibits of farming tools and equipment; a trading post named after Pieter Bronck; the historical society's library building, with its extensive source material on early Green County history; and the old Bronck family cemetery, where are buried Judge Leonard Bronck and other members of the family.

Thus in the heart of the legended Catskill country there survives a worthy memorial to Pieter Bronck and to his father—the Dutch colonist whose name was bestowed on the Borough of the Bronx in New York City, one of the most populous and best-known metropolitan neighborhoods in America.

Below: A valued article in any Dutch family was the traditional *kas* shown in the common room. The black ball front feet characterize the proper Dutch cupboard of the period.

Above: An early canopied bed dominates the bedroom which also features a Windsor cradle and Chippendale-style mirror. Left: The parlor, decorated in the fashion of the Victorian period, includes a rare combination piano and organ in a rosewood case.

SCHUYLER MANSION

Albany, New York

A "GREAT HOUSE" OF THE EMPIRE STATE

If the Schuyler clan was one of the most prominent of colonial New York families of Dutch origin, no member of the clan brought it more fame than did General Philip John Schuyler of the American Revolution and one of the Founding Fathers of the republic. For this reason, the mansion that General Schuyler built in 1762, and that still stands at Albany, New York, has high rank as one of the "great houses" of the Empire State. Along with its historical associations, the Schuyler residence, now owned and maintained by the New York State Education Department, is of interest as a fine example of colonial Georgian domestic architecture.

Noted as much for his hospitality as for his military, diplomatic, legislative and other history-making accomplishments, General Schuyler, assisted by his sparkling wife Catherine, a member of the celebrated Van Rensselaer family, entertained in his Albany mansion many of the greatest men of the American Revolutionary era. Not least among them was his close friend and superior officer, General George Washington. Others who enjoyed the Schuyler hospitality were Benjamin Franklin, Lafayette, Charles de Talleyrand, Thaddeus Kosciusko, Aaron Burr, Baron von Steuben, John Trumbull, Alexander Hamilton, and Generals John Knox and Nathaniel Greene.

Perhaps the most unusual guest at the Schuyler table was General John Burgoyne of the British Army. But it was as a prisoner of war that the English commander, known to his troops as "Gentleman Johnny," enjoyed the lavish hospitality of the Schuylers. In 1777, Burgoyne and his forces were defeated by the Continental Army at Saratoga, and he himself was taken prisoner and placed in the custody of General Schuyler. The British commander said afterwards that General Schuyler took him "to a very elegant house and, to my great surprise, presented me to Mrs. Schuyler and her family; and in General Schuyler's house I remained during my whole stay in Albany, with a table of more than twenty covers for me and my friends, and every other possible demonstration of hospitality."

It was in this mansion, which General Schuyler called "The Pastures" because his large estate overlooked green pasture land sloping down to the Hudson River, that the general's daughter, Elizabeth, was married to Alexander Hamilton. This was in 1780

A watercolor sketch by Phillip Hooker in 1818 shows the hexagonal porch which was added to the "great house" sometime after Schuyler's ownership.

Opposite : Philip Schuyler Mansion, facing the New England hills, is of rose-red brick with a white painted wood railing enclosing the double hip roof.

Above: The slender rope-turned balusters, each in a different twisted pattern, reproduce almost exactly those in the earlier Hancock House of Boston. Below: The New England Chippendale block-front secretary is surmounted with a broken-arch pediment. The interior of the fine mahogany piece is elaborately carved and features hidden document drawers.

when Hamilton was serving as secretary and aide-de-camp to General Washington. The parlor where the marriage ceremony was held is now known as the Hamilton Room. And it was in this mansion, too, that General Schuyler, in 1804, received the tragic news of his son-in-law's having been killed in a duel with Aaron Burr, the political leader and Presidential aspirant.

General Schuyler, a staunch Federalist, was living here when he played a leading role in the Continental Congress of 1779-1781, and when, later, he served as New York's first United States Senator, an office to which he was re-elected in 1797. When the general's wife, who was known to her many friends as "Sweet Kitty Rensselaer," died suddenly in 1803, it was a loss deeply mourned by General Schuyler. Then came word, in the following year, of his son-in-law's fatal duel. Already ill when this news came, General Schuyler died in his Albany mansion four months later, on November 18, 1804, in his seventy-first year.

Although historians usually note that the General "built" his mansion in 1762, it was actually the creation of his close friend and army colleague, General John Bradstreet, working in cooperation with Kitty Schuyler. This collaboration came about because of General Schuyler's absence on a military mission to London. Before he left, however, plans for the house were drawn, and while in England he purchased builders' hardware, carpets, draperies and wallpaper for his new residence. When he returned in the summer of 1762, the mansion on the Hudson was almost completed.

What he saw was a stately, two-and-a-half-story, colonial Georgian mansion of rose-red brick, a building material much favored by the prominent Dutch families of the Hudson River countryside. All exterior ornamentations of wood, such as the pedimented dormers on the low-pitched roof, the handsome Chippendale balustrade just above the cornice, the window frames and all outside shutters, were painted white, providing a most pleasing contrast to the rose-red brick facade. What General Schuyler did not see, however, on his first glimpse of the house, was its present hexagonal, or six-sided, entrance porch, an element that was added to the house late in the eighteenth century. A watercolor sketch that the Albany artist and architect, Philip Hooker, made of it about 1818, reveals that it was on the house early in the nineteenth century. At that time the mansion was evidently owned and occupied by a Mr. Bryan, since the artist identifies the house as the "Bryan Place."

When General Schuyler drew up plans for his new home before departing for London, he arranged for the Boston master carpenter, John Gaborial, to undertake all woodworking phases of the project. It would seem that John Gaborial was not only a carpenter, but also something of an artist. This is apparent in his handling of the Schuyler entrance hall, one of the most elegant in New York. Featured here is the handsome staircase, with its spiral, or rope-turned spindles, a form of ornamentation then new in the colony. A pilaster-supported doorway, with a decorative fanlight of leaded panes above it, divides the rear portion of the entrance hall.

A visit to the rooms of the Schuyler Mansion, all of them now furnished with eighteenth- and nineteenth-century antiques, bears out the observation made nearly two hundred years ago by General

Above: The Hamilton Room, where Betsy Schuyler married
Alexander Hamilton in 1780, is luxuriously decorated and
furnished to reflect the splendor and gaiety of the
Schuyler family era. Left: A delicate six-legged Sheraton
sideboard attributed to John Seymour (1790-1810) stands behind a table and chairs of the same style. The oil
on canvas is a full-length portrait of Alexander Hamilton.

75

The cherry chest-on-chest, of Salem origin, is decorated with carving in the rising sun pattern and three spirally turned flame finials on the top section.

Burgoyne regarding the mansion's elegance. The rooms are painted in the rich blues, reds, yellows and greens that Kitty Schuyler originally ordered, and have on display numerous Schuyler family items, including furniture, books, oil portraits, glassware, silver and even articles of clothing. Many of the textiles were made by Franco Scalamandré of New York City, following old designs, and presented to the mansion by him in 1950.

One of the handsomest rooms in the house is the northeast parlor, which is located to the right off the entrance hall. The crimson worsted damask draperies against the white walls and gray woodwork, the double row of dentils in the molded ceiling cornice and the pilaster-supported mantel over the marble-faced fireplace, all contribute to the distinction of this room.

Across the hall is the famous Hamilton Room, notable for its wood paneling, marble-faced fireplace and decorative French chandelier with black iron frame and crystal pear-shaped prisms. Blue and ivory damask curtains have a Chinese motif which was popular in wealthy American homes in the mid-eighteenth century. The satinwood furniture of Adam design is upholstered in light blue satin. The Persian rug is a Kirman.

The dining room, decorated in gold and white, contains a mahogany two-pedestal American Sheraton-style dining table, dating from around 1800, and American Sheraton chairs with the name of their first owner, "P. Gansevoort," iron-branded on the backs. Colonel Gansevoort was in command at Fort Stanwix in 1777 when the Americans first flew the Stars and Stripes in battle. The garniture of blue delftware vases, circa 1759, on the mantel is appropriate in this house which belonged to a family of Dutch ancestry. Across the back hallway from the dining room, on the Pembroke table facing the door to General Schuyler's study, is a mahogany dispatch box which once belonged to the famous John Hancock of Boston.

On the second floor in the northeast corner is the large bedroom, called the Burgoyne Room, where Burgoyne was "entertained." An interesting piece here is the six-legged Queen Anne walnut day bed, dating from 1730-1750. With bright blue woodwork and white toile drapes, the Burgoyne Room is one of the most vivid in the house. The walnut-veneered, oak, Dutch baroque bookcase in the upper hall is the mansion's oldest piece of furniture. It was made in Amsterdam, Holland, sometime between 1660 and 1700.

It was in 1911 when, after previously serving for a time as an orphan asylum, the old Schuyler Mansion was purchased by the New York State Education Department and work was started on the repair and restoration of this outstanding Hudson River landmark, seat of a man whom Daniel Webster said was "second only to Washington in the service he rendered the American colonies."

Above: Festoons of brass-beaded nails decorate the front rail of the Sheraton sofa seat. A narrow, carved central backpiece is raised nearly an inch above the rest of the mahogany frame.

Left: Catherine Malcolm, youngest child of General Schuyler, and her daughter, is one among many fine portraits at the mansion. The chair is a black-painted Windsor with fixed writing arm.

The north library at Seward House contains a fascinating array of objects
from around the world, as well as a life-like bust of Lincoln.

WILLIAM H. SEWARD HOUSE
Auburn, New York
HOME OF A GREAT STATESMAN

One day in May, 1860, William Henry Seward, then a leader of the new Republican party and one of the most prominent of Americans, left his seat in the United States Senate to spend a short time in his residence at Auburn, New York. During this stay, he fully expected to be notified that the Republican National Convention in Chicago, which opened on May 16th, had nominated him for the Presidency of the United States. To his surprise—and to the surprise of the entire country—the nomination went instead to a comparatively unknown Illinois lawyer named Abraham Lincoln.

Such is one of the chapters in the long and colorful history of the Seward House in the central New York town of Auburn. Still standing on its original site and now more than 150 years old, the residence is a worthy memorial to one of America's greatest statesmen, the man who, as Secretary of State under President Lincoln, skillfully guided this country's foreign relations during the crucial years of the Civil War. Before the war, Seward had served as a New York State Senator, as governor of the state, and as a United States Senator for twelve years.

The Seward house was built in 1816-1817 by Seward's father-in-law, Judge Elijah Miller. Seward, a junior law partner of the judge, married the judge's daughter Frances in 1824. Before the marriage, Judge Miller, a widower with two daughters, stipulated that his future son-in-law should live in the house with the family. This was agreed to by the young lawyer, and it was his home for nearly fifty years, during the time he achieved his greatest renown as an anti-slavery leader, one of the founders of the Republican party, a United States Senator, Presidential aspirant, and finally as Secretary of State in the cabinets of President Lincoln and President Johnson.

It was during this period, too, that he entertained in his Auburn residence some of the most distinguished men of his era. Among them were Presidents John Quincy Adams, Martin Van Buren and Andrew Johnson, and General Ulysses S. Grant, George Custer, Admiral David Farragut and Henry Clay. Here, too, was his permanent home when, in 1850, he made his famous anti-slavery declarations that "The Constitution devotes the Domain (i.e., the territories) to liberty. But there is a *higher law* than the Constitution which devotes it to the same noble purpose," and that there was an "irrepressible conflict" between the North and South over the slavery question.

According to this early print of the Seward House, it was situated on large, tree-shaded, landscaped grounds in Auburn, New York.

Above: The signing of the Alaskan treaty, for which
Seward was largely responsible, was depicted
by painter Emanuel Leutze in 1867. Right: The
colonial cradle (foreground) in the nursery
was used by Judge Miller's mother; the newer
crib and stool by Seward's grandchildren.

Unfortunately, William H. Seward was not in his Auburn residence on that fateful night in 1865 when an assassin's bullet took the life of President Lincoln, and one of the assassin's accomplices at the same time nearly took the life of Secretary of State Seward. Although severely wounded by stabbing in his Washington home, he survived the attack and lived to serve as Secretary of State under President Johnson. Mrs. Seward was ill in Washington at the time of the attack, and when the news was brought to her she was so shocked that she died two months later. A year afterwards, Seward's daughter, Fanny, who witnessed the attack, also died.

Saddened by these events, his health gradually fading, William H. Seward resigned his post as Secretary of State in 1869 at the close of President Johnson's administration. He retired to his Auburn residence and there, in the north library, spent the remainder of his days dictating his autobiography or writing his travel memories. Seward died on a couch in his library on the afternoon of October 10, 1872, at the age of seventy-one.

After his death, the Seward mansion was occupied by a son, General William Henry Seward II, who had served in the Civil War and who then was head of the Auburn banking house of William H. Seward & Company. When he died in 1920, the historic landmark became the property and home of William Henry Seward III. At his death in 1951, the house passed into the hands of The Foundation Historical Association of Auburn, a group formed to preserve Seward's residence as a memorial to one of the greatest Secretaries of State in American history.

When Judge Miller built this two-story house in 1816-1817, it was designed in the then popular Federal architectural style. One of the workmen on the house was a sixteen-year-old apprentice painter and carpenter named Brigham Young, who in later life became the principal leader of the Mormon Church and the founder of Salt Lake City. The woodwork he may have carved can still be seen today in the parlor fireplace.

Originally, this mansion was considerably smaller than it is today. It was in 1847 that the north tower and a spacious rear wing were added to it. Although the tower was designed in the Italianate style, resembling a square Tuscan tower, it does not clash with the Federal mode of the original house; in fact, the two styles blend quite harmoniously. The house was further enlarged in 1870, when Seward built onto its south side a large drawing room, dining room and several additional bedrooms.

At that time, too, he installed the magnificent spiral staircase that enhances the mansion's entrance hall. Made of manzanita and laurel wood, it was sent as a gift to Seward by the California Pioneer Society, which was grateful to him for his "successful efforts on the Senate floor in 1850 to have California admitted to the Union as a free state." The hall also contains a bust of Seward created in 1930 by the noted American sculptor, Daniel Chester French (1850-1931). Because of similarities of pose and expression, it is believed that the bust was inspired by a photograph of Seward made in 1860 by Mathew Brady, the celebrated Civil War photographer.

In all of the rooms of the house are displayed Seward family furnishings, as well as mementos, gifts, books, letters and documents

The Miller bedroom contains the possessions of Judge Elijah Miller, builder of Seward House. On the bed lies his beaver hat, as he left it.

A family gallery of portraits line one wall of the drawing room. The large ornate clock above the bookcase was hand-carved by a Swiss soldier.

associated with the life and times of President Lincoln's brilliant Secretary of State. Most of the household furnishings and ornamental details reflect the Victorian era, the period in which Seward carved out his history-making career. But here, too, are furnishings and mementos of the earlier Federal period, the era in which Judge Miller and his family lived, the time when Seward first met the judge's daughter and married her in 1824. These articles are in what is known as the Miller Bedroom, which features a fireplace with andirons, fire screen and bedwarmer acquired in 1817; a four-poster bed with original canopy and quilts; a rocking chair that belonged to Judge Miller's mother; the judge's spectacles, favorite fireside chair, lantern and his last beaver hat. The bedroom also contains an oil portrait of the Auburn jurist painted in 1843 by Chester Harding (1792-1866).

In the elegant parlor, or Gold Room, with its interesting Brigham Young fireplace, may be found the fragile, gilded furniture that William Seward brought from his Washington house after leaving office in 1869. During his last days, he used this room as a bedroom because failing health made it difficult for him to negotiate stairways. The piano here was a gift from Judge Miller to his daughter, Mrs. Seward. Among the oil portraits in the parlor are those of Admiral Farragut and Presidents Jefferson and John Quincy Adams. A great admirer of President Adams, Secretary Seward made him the subject of his first book, *Life of John Quincy Adams, Sixth President of the United States,* published at Auburn in 1849.

A large group of family portraits and a collection of more than two thousand books are the main features of the drawing room, an

The home of one of America's most distinguished statesmen is a pleasing combination of Federal- and Tuscan-style architecture. William Henry Seward lived here for almost fifty years.

Courtesy Foundation Historical Association, Inc.

The colorful dining room has gold draperies, butternut wood-work and Chinese-red wallpaper. In the niche at left sits an alabaster Buddha, one of three presented to Secretary Seward in Siam in 1871.

Opposite top: *Portage Falls*, 1839, an oil by Thomas Cole, hangs above an early American Steinway piano in the drawing room. The Oriental carpet loomed in Turkey has been in the room since 1870. Opposite bottom: The Gold Room is exquisitely furnished with the fragile gold-leaf furniture used on the State occasions held frequently in Seward's Washington, D. C., residence.

apartment offering an attractive fireplace with a decorative mirror overmantel, draped windows, arched doorways and an Oriental carpet loomed in Turkey. The paintings in the room include portraits of Seward and his wife, painted at Auburn in 1843 by Henry Inman (1801-1846) after Seward's second term as Governor of New York. One of the most appealing objects in the drawing room is a statuette of Seward's wife, seated at a small writing table in her garden. It was the work of John Rogers (1829-1904), popular sculptor of the Victorian era, whose Rogers Groups decorated nearly every well-to-do home in America at that time.

In what is called the North Library, where Seward died, several thousand more books are stacked on shelves. Assigned to "a place of honor" here by Seward is a bust of President Lincoln. While writing or dictating in this room, Seward sat in the "secretary chair" which he used as Governor of New York, as a senator in Washington and as Secretary of State.

An outstanding exhibit in the dining room is the sixty-place set of china presented to the Sewards by Prince Napoleon Joseph Bonaparte, nephew of Emperor Napoleon, while on a visit to the Seward home in Washington in 1861. Part of the set is arranged on the dining table and part is on display in a handsome corner cabinet. The dining room also contains an oil portrait of Seward's daughter-in-law, Anna Wharton Seward, made by Emanuel Leutze (1816-1868), most famous of American historical painters, and a portrait of Thurlow Weed, who besides being editor of the Albany *Evening Journal* was one of the founders of the Republican Party and Seward's chief political mentor.

In the nursery, the toys of the Seward children are on display and in the Victorian Bedroom, the dresses, shoes and bonnets worn by Mrs. Seward. The Display Room contains assorted Seward memorabilia and gifts, including a desk used by a member of the first United States Congress, and the Civil War Room presents, among its numerous relics and exhibits, a number of letters to Seward from the White House and signed "A. Lincoln."

One more room remains to be mentioned—the Diplomatic Gallery. Highlighted here is another canvas by Emanuel Leutze, a large painting titled *Signing of the Alaska Treaty*. It shows Secretary of State Seward about to sign a document that marked one of the greatest accomplishments of his career—the purchase by the United States from Russia of Alaska. Secretary Seward was the chief sponsor of the project, but he had numerous opponents who jeered at the idea, calling it "Seward's Ice Box" and "Seward's Folly." Nonetheless, Secretary Seward signed the treaty by gaslight at four o'clock on the morning of March 30, 1867. Originally called Russian America, the territory had its name changed, by order of Mr. Seward, to Alaska

Thus, for the payment of $7,200,000, the Seward "ice box" turned out to be a treasure chest, especially after the discovery of gold there during the 1890's. Since then, Alaska, now the forty-ninth state of the United States, has, with its mines, fisheries and forests, produced wealth more than a hundred times its original purchase price. And so it is that William Henry Seward, a man of many accomplishments, is best known today as the "Father of Alaska."

Photos by Frederick Young-Cyr Agency

The simplicity of Stenton Mansion's exterior admirably illustrates the Quaker life style.
The Georgian house is built of red brick laid in Flemish bond with black headers and white trim.

STENTON

Philadelphia, Pennsylvania

HOME OF PENNSYLVANIA'S GODFATHER

If William Penn was the "Father of Pennsylvania," the role of godfather of that state may well be attributed to James Logan, who came to the colony as Penn's secretary and who rose to become the power behind the throne in provincial affairs for nearly half a century. For that reason, the fine Georgian mansion that Logan built for himself at Germantown in 1728 is now one of the most historic houses in the state. It ranks high as an outstanding example of early eighteenth-century architecture in America. Since 1910, the mansion has been maintained by The National Society of the Colonial Dames of America in the Commonwealth of Pennsylvania.

Logan named his 511-acre country estate after the town in Scotland where his father was born. During the American Revolution, the mansion served successively as a brief headquarters for General Washington and the British commander, General William Howe. General Washington came here just before the Battle of the Brandywine in September 1777, and it was from the Stenton Plantation House that General Howe directed the Battle of Germantown in October 1777. At that time the mansion was owned and occupied by James Logan's grandson, Dr. George Logan, who later was elected a United States Senator from Pennsylvania.

When, after an absence of fifteen years in England, William Penn came back to his American colony in 1699, he had with him his twenty-five-year-old secretary, James Logan, an unusually brilliant scholarly and capable young man with legal training. And when, later in the year 1699, William Penn had to return to England on urgent business, he appointed James Logan as attorney for the proprietor of the Pennsylvania Colony—a position Logan was to retain for the rest of his life. As it happened, William Penn never again saw his province in the New World, dying in England in 1718. Thereafter, James Logan grew in power and influence in Pennsylvania as administrator for Penn's heirs.

Although Logan was a member of the Provincial Council for most of his mature life, having at one time, for a two-year period, served as governor of the colony, and although he also served one term as Mayor of Philadelphia, he was adverse to holding public office, preferring to work behind the scenes, to let public office holders do his bidding. As with the founder of the colony, James Logan was a

A decorative archway on the north side of the handsomely paneled entrance hall leads to the large staircase.

Gold damask draperies and window seat cushions enhance the rich décor of the parlor, which is the only completely paneled room in Stenton Mansion.

Quaker, had a broad tolerance for all religious creeds, was highly educated, knew the ways of men, possessed unusual tact and diplomacy, and had a wide knowledge of Indians and frontier life in that part of early America.

One of his greatest achievements was the preservation of peaceful relations with the Indians, especially with the Iroquois tribe, whose territory Logan regarded as a buffer zone between his colony and the French in Canada. For their part, the Indians respected and trusted Logan over the years, and thus colonial Pennsylvania was spared any difficulties with them. His last council fire with the Indians took place in 1742, when he entertained eighty-eight chiefs on the grounds of his Stenton Plantation. He was nearly seventy years old at the time.

But James Logan had other reasons to maintain peaceful relations with the Iroquois and similar tribes. As with so many public officials of colonial America, Logan was also engaged in private business—in his case, the fur business. He was at one time Philadelphia's largest operator in the fur trade and had to maintain a friendly attitude towards the Indians. It was his engagement in this trade that brought him a sizable fortune and made possible the building of the stately Stenton Mansion at Germantown. He later invested in land purchases and in time was the owner of some 18,000 acres in various parts of Pennsylvania and New Jersey.

Incidentally, it was James Logan who, while engaged in the fur trade, gave to America its most familiar vehicle of pioneer times, the Conestoga Wagon. After buying a capacious, sturdy wagon in 1717 to transport pelts from his headquarters on Conestoga Creek to his warehouse in Philadelphia, and with the acquisition of later vehicles, he referred to them in his account book as "Conestoga Wagons." And in this way was born the wagon that, hooded with white canvas and drawn by a bell-ringing team of six horses, transported freight throughout inland America.

As if being a long-time colony administrator for the Penn family and that colony's leading fur trader were not enough, Logan was also an outstanding scholar, linguist, author, mathematician and scientist. With so many interests, he has been likened to an eighteenth-century American version of the Renaissance man, a versatile type of many talents and preoccupations. When only thirteen years old in England, he had a sound command of Latin, Greek and Hebrew. He later learned French, Italian and Spanish.

In these languages, he corresponded with some of the leading scholars and scientists of Europe and America, and also wrote various scientific books as well as many essays on ethics and philosophy. In addition to this activity, Logan served on the first board of trustees of the College of Philadelphia, now the University of Pennsylvania. One of his closest friends during his last years was Benjamin Franklin. This little-known but richly accomplished man died in 1751 at the age of seventy-seven.

With his death, the Stenton Plantation House at Germantown passed to his son, William. In addition to devoting himself to Indian welfare, as had his father, William Logan was a merchant and served as attorney for the Penn estate and as a member of the Provincial Council. He died in 1776 and Stenton was inherited by his

Photos: Edmond J. Murray

son, Dr. George Logan. It was Dr. Logan's capable and talented wife, Deborah, who found the neglected correspondence of William Penn and James Logan, and who transcribed it for posterity.

All told, the Stenton Plantation House was continuously owned and occupied by six generations of the Logan family. In 1900, it was transferred to the municipality of Philadelphia, and ten years later it was given into the custody of The National Society of the Colonial Dames in the Commonwealth of Pennsylvania. Since then, the society has restored and furnished the mansion with period pieces, many of them Logan family heirlooms, in keeping with the years when James Logan was master of the house, and the succeeding two generations which occupied the house in the nineteenth century.

Now standing in a six-acre landscaped park, Stenton Plantation House is regarded by architectural historians as one of the finest

To the right of the main hall is the room which housed Logan's magnificent two-thousand-volume library. An early scroll-type map of the Philadelphia area and the celestial globe below Logan's portrait give some indication of his varied interests.

Edmond J. Murray

The regal Philadelphia walnut bed in the first-floor
Lodging Room is enhanced by canopy
and curtains in an elaborate floral pattern.

Courtesy National Society of the Colonial Dames of America in Pennsylvania

Opposite: The back porch opens onto the sunny brick walk
leading to the original outbuildings, including kitchens and
an orangery, which have been preserved in their entirety.

examples of Georgian house design. A three-story edifice, with its
hipped roof and six dormers constituting the third story, the
mansion is of red brick construction with white trim. The brickwork
is laid in Flemish bond in which each row alternates headers (the
ends of the bricks face the wall) and stretchers (the lengths of the
bricks are parallel with the wall). At Stenton the headers are black.
Two chimneys provide a fireplace for every room in the house.

Although it lacks the rich ornamentation of some colonial
Georgian dwellings, Stenton Mansion achieves its great effective-
ness through a perfection of proportion in both mass and detail.
Stenton's basic simplicity is well exemplified by the plain, but pleasing, doorway. It consists of three semi-circular stone steps that lead
to a white entrance door with a transom and slightly curved head
above it. There is no other ornamentation at the entrance door.

Also of unusual interest at Stenton Mansion is the fact that its
outbuildings, all of them part of the original Plantation of Stenton,
still exist in their entirety. At the rear of the house are kitchens, an
orangery, and carriage house, all of which are connected with the
main house by covered passageways paved with brick. The rambling
boxwood garden, although not original, provides an appropriate
setting for the eighteenth-century buildings.

After passing through the door of the mansion, visitors come upon
a wide entrance hall, paved with brick in a herringbone pattern,
with walls handsomely paneled from floor to ceiling. Double doors
in the hall open to a parlor on the left and the library on the right.
On the north side of the hall an archway leads to an ample staircase.

The parlor, perhaps the most interesting room in the house, is
punctuated by matching gold damask draperies and window seat
cushions. Between two of the windows hangs a walnut Chippendale
mirror with a detached phoenix finial surmounting the crest. Beneath is an elegant Queen Anne mahogany tray-top table from Ireland. Elsewhere in the parlor are six Philadelphia Chippendale chairs
and a valuable chest-on-chest in the same style.

An outstanding feature at Stenton is James Logan's library. When
James Logan was master of this house, his library was regarded as
the finest private collection of books in America. He bequeathed its
2,000 volumes to the City of Philadelphia. Later, his son, William,
added 1,300 volumes to the gift, and together the collection formed
the foundation of Philadelphia's famous Loganian Library.

Among the four bedrooms in the house, the Lodging Room is
typical—containing a four-poster canopy bed of walnut, made in
Philadelphia, a Philadelphia Chippendale mahogany easy chair
and a Sheraton-style fancy side chair.

There is some evidence that James Logan would have preferred
a more elaborate and richly ornamented mansion, but that he was
restrained by his wife, the former Sarah Read of Philadelphia, whom
Logan married in 1714. She genuinely believed in the principles of
simplicity and self-control advocated by the Quakers. It is perhaps
to her then, as well as to her gifted and accomplished husband, that
some credit for the unostentatious distinction of Stenton must go.
But whatever the causes, the primary fact remains that it is one of
the nation's most distinguished colonial dwellings.

JOHN HARRIS MANSION

Harrisburg, Pennsylvania

LANDMARK ON THE SUSQUEHANNA

It is doubtful if any other house in central Pennsylvania is as richly historic as is the old John Harris Mansion in the state capital at Harrisburg, a gray stone edifice built in 1766 by the founder of the city on the Susquehanna River. During the two hundred years of its existence, the Harris house has sheltered more well-known men and women and been the scene of more significant events than any other dwelling in that part of the state. Since 1941, this landmark, the oldest building in Harrisburg, has been the home of The Historical Society of Dauphin County, whose members have restored and furnished the mansion as it was in the days of John Harris and of succeeding notable occupants.

Another name for this house might well be the Cameron mansion, for during the Civil War, Simon Cameron, Secretary of War in the first cabinet of President Lincoln, lived here. Cameron was also a long-time powerful leader of the Republican Party in Pennsylvania, an ambassador to Russia and a four-term United States Senator. He resided here for more than twenty-five years and, during that time, held many important conferences, and entertained many celebrated individuals, in the historic landmark south of the State Capitol.

At an earlier period in the nineteenth century, the Harris house was owned and occupied by Thomas Elder, grandson of the "Fighting Parson of Paxton." At one time he was Attorney General of Pennsylvania. Thomas Elder lived in the house for eighteen years, until his death in 1853.

Elder had purchased the mansion in 1835 from Robert Harris, a son of the founder of Harrisburg, paying $5,000 for the dwelling and a portion of its site between River and Front streets. After becoming owner of his parental home in 1805, Robert Harris played influential roles in the military, business and political life of the city on the Susquehanna. He was a United States Congressman for four years in the 1820's.

The story of the Harris family in this part of Pennsylvania begins half a century before the building of the John Harris Mansion. About the year 1712 there came to the wilderness region of the Susquehanna a fur trader, John Harris, father of the builder of the mansion. Here, the elder Harris settled on land he had acquired from the

Above: An impressive full-length portrait of the powerful Senator Simon Cameron (1799-1889) is a prominent feature of the drawing room.

Opposite top: The stone mansion built for the founder of Harrisburg remained in the Harris family for over half a century. Opposite bottom: A massive Victorian sideboard crafted in the Eastlake tradition is set with a silver-plated tea service of the same period.

The early form of desk found in the Kelker Bedroom holds a letter box which contained ink, sand and quills. Portraits from the Kelker family are displayed above.

Provincial Council, established a fur trading post, operated a ferry across the river, and became the first settler of today's Harrisburg. In time the place acquired the name of Harris's Ferry.

After his marriage to a niece of Edward Shippen, first Mayor of Philadelphia, a justice of the State Supreme Court and later president of the Provincial Council, the pioneer fur trader and ferryman became the father of six children. The eldest of these, born probably in October 1727, was John Harris, Jr. In the meantime, the elder Harris acquired more and more land around his log trading post. At the time of his death in 1748, he was the owner of eight hundred acres, embracing the site of today's central Harrisburg.

With the death of the first settler, his oldest son, John Harris, Jr., took over management of the trading station, ferry and his father's land investments. Although he had plans to develop this strategic river crossing site on the Susquehanna, the younger Harris was interrupted in carrying them out by the French and Indian War, during which his log trading post was converted into a palisaded fort. After the war ended in 1763, John Harris once more took up the development of the family plantation at Harris's Ferry.

One of his plans was to build for himself and family a comfortable stone mansion, a house to be detached from the trading post and ferry on higher ground above the Susquehanna. And so it was that John Harris, Jr., with stone quarried from his own land and with the assistance of masons, carpenters and other workmen, completed in 1766 the residence that stands today as one of the most important historic landmarks of central Pennsylvania. It was erected ten years before the outbreak of the American Revolution.

After the close of the War of Independence in 1781, a conflict that John Harris strongly supported with provisions for General Washington's army, money to finance the war, and the sacrifice of a son, the proprietor of Harris's Ferry set about realizing another one of his plans—to lay out a town he felt sure would become a county seat and perhaps the capital city of the Commonwealth of Pennsylvania. So in 1785 he had his son-in-law, William Maclay, draw up a plan for the proposed town. Incidentally, Maclay later was elected the first United States Senator from Pennsylvania.

Included in the new town's plan was the founder's gift of two lots for a courthouse, two lots for a jail and four acres for a park (now part of Capital Park). The founder wanted the new town to be named Harrisburg. Some state officials, however, objected, claiming the town should be called Louisbourg because of its location in Dauphin County. When John Harris heard this, he exclaimed, "You may Louisbourg all you please, but I'll not sell an inch more of land except in Harrisburg." John Harris died that same year at the age of sixty-four.

As mentioned, the stone mansion remained in the Harris family until 1835 when it was sold to Thomas Elder. After Elder's death in 1853, the house was sold to the Reverend Beverly Waugh, a Methodist minister, who was also a teacher of mathematics and English literature. When the state legislature chartered the Pennsylvania Female College, the Reverend Mr. Waugh was appointed principal of the new college, and he conducted the first classes of the college in the one-time Harris home.

Above: A valued piece in the Kelker Bedroom is the Philadelphia Chippendale block-front chest-on-chest. Of late eighteenth-century vintage are the Louis XV architectural bed and marble-topped table. Left: Another popular item in Victorian America was the Renaissance bed.

With the passing of the minister-teacher in 1863, the mansion was sold to Senator Cameron, who occupied it until his own death in 1889. It was inherited by his daughter, Mrs. Margaretta Cameron Haldeman, and it remained in the Cameron-Haldeman family until 1941 when it was deeded to the Dauphin County Historical Society.

The gray mansion, which overlooks the Susquehanna River and the site of Harris's Ferry, is two-and-a-half stories high and is designed in the late Georgian style. Slender white columns support a first-floor porch occupying the entire front of the house. In its high-pitched roof are three dormers that provide light for the top story.

As might well be expected with so many different owners during its two centuries of existence, the John Harris Mansion has undergone numerous changes and alterations, both on its exterior and its interior. When the Reverend Mr. Waugh established the Pennsylvania Female College here in 1854, he reported that the mansion had been "thoroughly refitted" for use as a women's college, including the "introduction of gas, water and hot air furnaces."

Extensive alterations were also made by Senator Cameron after he bought the mansion. In order to conform to the Victorian style of that time, an era of high ceilings, long windows, heavy draperies and ornate decorations, the senator had the first floor of the mansion lowered about three feet, a move that called for the regrading of the grounds outside of the house. He also removed a partition in order to make the two south rooms into one large drawing room, to which he added a bay window. Senator Cameron built a wing at the rear of the house, containing not only a kitchen and pantries but a dining room, conservatory and various conference rooms. In addition, the enclosed stairs were removed and the present graceful curving stairway was built.

Despite these changes and alterations, however, members of The Historical Society of Dauphin County have succeeded in restoring and furnishing the mansion with many household articles, heirlooms and pieces reflecting the home life of its builder, John Harris, and the various owners and occupants who followed him.

In the reception room is a grandfather's clock which belonged to John Harris. It was made around 1780 by Isaac Thomas of Chester County, Pennsylvania. The dining room contains a large, ornate Eastlake-style Victorian black walnut sideboard, dating from between 1870 and 1880, which was owned by the Cameron family. On exhibit in the dining room are a set of blue and white French porcelain, circa 1864, and a set of Chinese Export china from the Revolutionary War period.

The largest, and in many ways the most impressive, room in the house is the drawing room. Elaborate foliate rococo forms, typical of the second decorative phase of the Victorian period in the mid-nineteenth century, are found in the wallpaper, cornice and a pair of gold, bronze and crystal chandeliers with shades by Tiffany's. There are two fireplaces with arched, white marble mantels and near one of them is an impressive full-length oil portrait of Senator Simon Cameron. Other pieces in the room include a small handsome writing table in the American variation of the Regency style, distinguished by shell ornamentation and animalistic legs; and in the area of the bay window which Senator Cameron added, is an American

The Victorian vogue is also reflected in the reception room furnishings at Harris Mansion.

Included in an interesting exhibit of kitchen
utensils is the white-painted settle
bench (left) which opens into a hutch table.

Empire horsehair sofa, an American Empire melodian with lyre legs
and a grouping of John Rogers (1829-1904) chalkware figures.

The most interesting room on the second floor is the William A.
Kelker Bedroom, named for a prominent local citizen of the brown-
stone era. The imposing eighteenth-century Philadelphia block-front
chest-on-chest is the most valuable piece here. The Queen Anne desk
is from an earlier period, circa 1720-1750. The Louis XV architectural
bed, Boston-style rocker and the marble-topped Empire-style column
table in the middle of the room all date from between 1820 and 1865.

Other rooms of interest are the complete Victorian Bedroom
originally purchased in 1841 for another residence and the kitchen
with its collection of rockers, utensils and a white-painted settle
bench which opens into a hutch table. Special exhibits found elsewhere in the mansion are a delegate's chair of the design used by
members of the Continental Congress and made in 1794 for the
United States Supreme Court, a hymn book made and hand-illumi-
nated in 1732 by Sisters at the Ephrata Cloister, and Indian relics
found at the site of historic Harris's Ferry.

Above: Delicate ornamentation relieves the austerity of Lemon Hill, a plastered brick home from the Federal period. Right: An architectural detail typical of the area is the rear piazza overlooking the Schuylkill River.

LEMON HILL
SWEETBRIER

Philadelphia, Pennsylvania

Two Fairmount Park Historic Landmarks

Among the twenty-three famous old mansions and residences in Philadelphia's renowned Fairmount Park stand two of singular distinction and appeal, both architecturally and historically. They are known as Lemon Hill and Sweetbrier. Both houses are situated on their original sites above the Schuylkill River, as are most of the houses, all built before 1850, in Fairmount Park. Both Lemon Hill and Sweetbrier have been carefully restored and furnished with period pieces.

Associated with the site of Lemon Hill is one of the great figures of American history—Robert Morris. As the "Financier of the American Revolution," Morris, in Philadelphia, raised the money to support General Washington's army during the War of Independence. In this work he was ably and generously assisted by another prominent Philadelphia financier and patriot, Haym Salomon. Robert Morris was also a leading member of the Second Continental Congress, a signer of the Declaration of Independence and founder in Philadelphia of America's first national bank. When President Washington offered him the post of Secretary of the Treasury, Robert Morris declined it in favor of Alexander Hamilton.

In linking the name of Robert Morris with the late eighteenth-century mansion known as Lemon Hill, state historians do not mean to imply that he was the builder and occupant of the residence. Due to lack of any documentary evidence, it is uncertain as to whether Lemon Hill was built by Morris or by a later owner and occupant of the site, Henry Pratt, son of the noted American portrait painter, Matthew Pratt. What is definitely known about the house is that it dates from around 1800 when Morris was still alive and the Federal style of architecture—the style of Lemon Hill—first became popular.

Also definitely known is that the estate identified as Lemon Hill for the past 170 years was originally the estate of Robert Morris, who called his place "The Hills." It was in 1770, five years before the outbreak of the American Revolution, that Robert Morris purchased a fifty-five-acre tract of land from the William Penn estate,

The winding staircase, invisible from the front doorway, is recessed from the spacious central hall.

Like most of the rooms, this bedroom displays furniture in vogue in the early 1800's. The fine bow-front chest of drawers and four-poster bed are mahogany. A camphor-wood trunk and cloth-covered hat box stand ready for use.

a tract that contains the site of today's Lemon Hill. Later he enlarged this tract to three hundred acres, and, after naming it The Hills, built a country manor house and laid out a farm on it. The outbuildings here included a large greenhouse which contained, among its exotic plants, a group of lemon trees, the first such in Philadelphia. This gave rise to the later name of Lemon Hill.

During the American Revolution, when Morris and other members of the Continental Congress were forced to flee from Philadelphia because of the imminent approach of General Howe and his British troops, the Morris estate on the Schuylkill River was taken over by the invading army. When he returned to The Hills after the army left, Morris found his manor house in such a dismantled condition that he had to rebuild portions of it.

He was living here when, in 1789, President Washington offered him the cabinet post which he declined. Thereafter, Robert Morris gradually retired from public life, a situation brought about by the growing precariousness of his personal financial affairs. He was soon heavily in debt as a result of unfortunate land speculations in the West; his creditors grew in number, and finally he was forced to "hide out" at The Hills to avoid arrest. Eventually, Robert Morris was apprehended in 1798 and confined to the debtors' prison in Philadelphia—the man who was the "Financier of the American Revolution." There he remained until 1801, and he died in obscurity five years later.

Among those who purchased portions of the Morris estate at a sheriff's sale in 1799 was Henry Pratt, a business acquaintance of the ill-fated financier. A successful Philadelphia merchant, Henry Pratt was the grandson of Henry Pratt, a noted Philadelphia goldsmith, and the son of the painter Matthew Pratt. That portion of the Morris estate containing the site of the financier's country manor house was in the Henry Pratt purchase, but whether or not Pratt acquired the manor house, or built a new house on its site, is not known. In any case, when Henry Pratt took up residence in 1799 on his newly acquired land overlooking the Schuylkill River he named the place Lemon Hill and so it has been known ever since.

As with Robert Morris, Henry Pratt was interested in horticulture. He added more gardens, greenhouses and shrubbery to his country place, and in time it became widely known as Pratt's Garden. After his death in 1838, however, the place fell into neglect, and it was eventually proposed to convert the estate into a cemetery. But when more than two thousand Philadelphia citizens signed petitions to have the city buy the land for a public park, Lemon Hill was saved. It was purchased by the city in 1844 and for a number of years was leased as a German beer hall and outdoor garden. Then, in 1855, it became a part of Fairmount Park when that name was officially chosen for the city's new recreational area on the Schuylkill River. Since then, the house has been furnished with period pieces by members of Chapter II of the Colonial Dames of America.

It was in 1926, shortly after he had been appointed director of the Philadelphia Museum of Art, that Fiske Kimball, one of America's foremost architectural historians, moved into the Lemon Hill mansion and lived there until his death in 1955. He restored

From the upstairs hall, the Palladian window is a striking background for the Empire-style, caned settee and matching chairs. A Gilbert Stuart portrait of William Shippen hangs over the mantel. Right: Viewed from the recessed staircase, the entrance hall reveals an excellent portrait of Henry Pratt by Henry Inman.

and renovated portions of the white brick house. Noting that an overly ornamental Victorian porch which had, in 1872, replaced the mansion's original front steps was out of key with the house's simpler Federal style of architecture, Kimball had it removed for the present graceful flight of steps, an element more in harmony with post-Revolutionary domestic architecture. Other suggestions of the Federal style to be found here are the handsome fanlighted door-way and the impressive Palladian window at the second-floor level.

In the entrance hall, with its gray and white flooring of marble laid in checkerboard pattern, may be seen an English Hepplewhite hunt board, and, above it, an oil portrait of Robert Morris painted anonymously but copied after the 1795 original of Morris by the distinguished portrait painter, Gilbert Stuart. From the entrance hall a recessed, winding staircase leads to the mansion's second floor.

The most attractive and elegant part of the house is its first-floor, elliptical drawing room, displaying Louis XVI style of furniture from the Philadelphia of the 1790's. Two wooden mantelpieces here curve to echo the oval shape of the room. A mahogany commode on one side of the room is a continental piece of the Louis XVI period, and, according to tradition, was originally the property of Robert Morris. A sofa, twelve matching armchairs and an Aubusson rug complete the drawing room furnishings.

Photos: Courtesy Philadelphia Museum of Art

Above: The elegance of the elliptical drawing room is unsurpassed. The light blue of the drapes is repeated in the Aubusson rug and complements the exquisite pieces. Right: Robert Morris, whose portrait is also in the entrance hall, was known as the "Financier of the Revolution." He died penniless in 1806.

If it is not known exactly when Lemon Hill was built, there is no uncertainty about Fairmount Park's other unique residence, Sweetbrier. It has been firmly established that Sweetbrier was erected in 1797 and that its builder was Samuel Breck, a wealthy merchant, cultivated gentleman and public-spirited citizen of Phildelphia during the post-Revolutionary era. Among Breck's many outside interests were art, gardening, literature, music, agriculture and writing. He shared these interests with his wife, Jean, who was the daughter of John Ross, builder of another noted Philadelphia mansion, The Grange.

As master and mistress of Sweetbrier, the Brecks made their country home into one of the leading social centers of the Philadelphia area. In addition to many prominent Philadelphians of the day, they entertained such prominent foreign personalities as the Vicomte de Noailles and the Marquis de Lafayette. The latter was a guest of the Brecks during his second American tour. Breck once described his country manor as "a fine stone house, rough-cast, fifty-three feet long, thirty-eight broad, and three stories high, having outbuildings of every kind suitable for elegance and comfort."

As time went on, however, the Brecks found that living in the country was becoming more and more unsuitable to them. Then came the tragic illness and death of their only daughter, Lucy. Thus in 1838 they sold Sweetbrier and moved into a town house in Philadelphia. Their former residence on the Schuylkill River was assured of preservation when, in 1867, it was included in Fairmount Park. It was used temporarily as a restaurant. Then, in 1927, the Junior League of Philadelphia, working in cooperation with the Fairmount Park Commission, restored Sweetbrier to its original state, furnished it with period pieces, and opened it to the public.

Sweetbrier is one more fine example of the Federal style of architecture that appeared on the Eastern seaboard at the beginning of the nineteenth century. Here may be seen a pleasing, dignified residence with a facade harmoniously balanced between straight lines and curves. The latter may be noted in the semi-circular arch of the fanlighted entrance door, in the second-floor Palladian window, and in the two dormers that project from the house's hipped roof. The entrance door is enhanced by two engaged Doric columns supporting a simple, classic entablature.

As with many Federal houses, the entrance hall of Sweetbrier does not have a stairway in its center; instead the stairway is in a recessed area on the left side of the hall. This arrangement provides a clear vista of the passageway from the front to the rear of the house, and effectively reveals a columned, fluted archway in the hall and the attractive fanlighted rear door opening on the garden.

Doorways on either side of the hall lead to the north and south parlors. Perhaps the most elegant of these is the south parlor. In this room may be found evidences—the delicate carvings, the applied molded decorations on the mantel—of the classic interior designs created by the English decorator, Robert Adam, but interpreted in Philadelphia by Robert Wellford. The mantel here, as in the north parlor, is not original to the house, but both are of the Breck period.

Below the oil, *The Town of New York*, in the hall at Sweetbrier is a yoke-front chest of drawers flanked by ball-and-claw-foot chairs in the Chippendale style.

Courtesy Philadelphia Museum of Art

Above: Sweetbrier Mansion was constructed in the neo-classic Adam style. Right: The classical styling prevails throughout the gracefully proportioned interior.

The Adam influence is again felt in the two gilded, oval-backed English chairs of the late eighteenth century.

Some of the furnishings in the drawing room suggest the French influence. Among these are the early nineteenth-century Aubusson carpet, the small marble-topped Louis XVI sewing table and the ormolu candelabra on the mantel. Other furnishings include a Sheraton chair with handsome back, carved urn and three feathers, and a Pembroke table. On the wall is a vertical rectangular mirror with a painted panel landscape surmounted by ball cornice and a gracefully carved eagle.

The south parlor is noted for its tasteful combination of English- and French-style décor as well as for the beauty of its lines.

Above: Amstel House was probably built in 1730, but
the service wing shows evidences of an earlier
construction date. Right: An interesting item in the
dining room is a pair of bell candlesticks. The bell
was rung to signal church service and the candle
was then used at the altar. The American-
made table and chairs are Chippendale.

106

AMSTEL HOUSE

New Castle, Delaware

THE HOME OF DELAWARE'S FIRST GOVERNOR

It is now widely known as Amstel House—the early eighteenth-century brick house at the northwest corner of Fourth and Delaware streets in the historic old city of New Castle, Delaware. This name derives from the fact that New Castle was called New Amstel when the Dutch occupied the area in the middle of the seventeenth century. But this same dwelling could well have been called the Van Dyke House, for in it lived Nicholas Van Dyke, first Governor of Delaware after the American Revolution. It is now maintained as a public museum by the New Castle Historical Society.

Among the distinctions of Amstel House is that it was visited by President Washington on April 30, 1784, when Governor Van Dyke's daughter, Ann, married Kensey Johns, Sr., member of a prominent New Castle family. It is said that another and later guest in the house was the Marquis de Lafayette, who came during his return visit to the United States in 1824-1825.

Curiously enough, Amstel House is not Dutch in style nor was it built by an early Dutch settler. Its builder was an English colonist, Dr. John Finney, and the date of its construction is believed to have been 1730. That was many years after the Dutch had lost this Middle Atlantic region to the British, who re-named the early New Amstel settlement New Castle. After building his house, Dr. Finney practiced medicine in New Castle through the middle years of the eighteenth century, during the period when Delaware was one of the original thirteen colonies. With the outbreak of the American Revolution in 1775, the settlers in the region west of Delaware Bay convened at New Castle and formed Delaware State.

By that time, however, Dr. Finney was dead, having passed away in 1774. His brick residence was rented from the Finney heirs by Governor Nicholas Van Dyke, who remained in the house with his family until 1785. A descendant of one of the early Dutch settlers of the region, Governor Van Dyke brought to the house its greatest fame. A year after the governor's daughter married Kensey Johns, Sr., in 1784, the Finney house was occupied by the newlyweds, and Kensey Johns, Sr., was still living there when he became Chancellor of Delaware.

The unpainted staircase in the lower hall is hand-carved and was assembled entirely with wooden pegs.

Above: The Sheraton breakfront with elements of Gothic styling incorporates a sunburst pattern inlaid in white wood. Below: Oil paintings of Ann Van Dyke and Kensey Johns, Sr., hang in the drawing room where their marriage, attended by Washington, occurred in 1784.

In 1904, the dwelling was purchased and occupied by Professor Henry Hanby Hay of Girard College, Philadelphia. After extensive research into the landmark's past history, Professor Hay resolved to call his residence Amstel House, even though it had no association with the early Dutch settlement of New Amstel. He felt that his name, rather than Van Dyke House, would help to avoid confusion with another old Van Dyke residence opposite Amstel House, one built by the governor's son, Nicholas Van Dyke, Jr., who became a United States Senator from Delaware. Still another Van Dyke vintage mansion in the neighborhood was owned and occupied by the senator's son, Kensey Johns Van Dyke.

It was in 1929 that the New Castle Historical Society acquired Amstel House, and, after refurnishing it with period pieces, has since maintained it as an historical museum. The house commands interest, aside from its historical associations, by reason of various structural details dating from colonial times. Here, for example, is an unusually broad facade, giving the house a squarish appearance. This impression is accentuated by the wide wooden shutters on all of the windows and the low spread of the gable roof. A classic, pedimented entrance door, somewhat narrow for the size of the house, is at the center of the house front. Both doorway and window frames are painted white.

On entering the residence, the visitor finds himself in a dignified entrance hall that bisects the house and leads to a broad stairway ascending to the second floor. On one side of the hall is the parlor or drawing room. For the most part, its walls and ceiling are white, however, the handsome paneling, which covers the entire side wall opposite the door from the hall, is finished in a deep blue-green color. Here are hung oil portraits of Ann Van Dyke and her husband, Kensey Johns, Sr. In this room, too, may be seen the fireplace hearth containing an inscription to the effect that President Washington "here attended the wedding of Ann Van Dyke, on April 30, 1784, to Kensey Johns, Sr."

The Washington who came to the Van Dyke wedding reception that April day was not the "cold, severe-looking" man of the famous Gilbert Stuart portraits. In a letter written soon after the event, Justice James Booth said: "The Great Man stood upon the hearthstone and kissed the pretty girls—as was his wont." Another account states that he "not only kissed them at the hearthstone, but he renewed the proceeding at his departure, for he stood on the steps, held the bride's cheeks between his hands, and bestowed the parting kiss upon the doubtless radiantly happy and pretty upturned face."

Also of interest in the parlor are two cupboards on either side of the fireplace mantel, said to have once concealed secret panels in which the master of the house was supposed to have kept the wines and cigars he provided for his guests. The cupboards contain a fine collection of English and Dutch Delft and Chinese Export porcelain. The room is otherwise elegantly furnished with eighteenth-century period pieces partially donated by Mrs. Coleman du Pont, a descendant of Governor Van Dyke. Included are three mahogany tilt-

top birdcage tables—one with ball-and-claw feet, the others with snake feet—and a tall clock made by George Grow of Wilmington, Delaware, before 1770.

The dining room has several fine pieces, including a sizable mahogany dining table, dated 1760; six New York Chippendale chairs; the English mahogany tier table of the same date; and a Sheraton-style English mahogany breakfront inlaid in white wood, circa 1770.

A choice example of the curious old American custom of window-pane writing with a diamond may be found in Amstel House. On a window pane in the second-floor bedroom to the left of the staircase one can read the inscription:

> "Around her head ye angels constant vigil keep,
>   And guard fair innocence her balmy sleep."

Since the inscriber of these lines did not include his initials, nor is it known whether the lines were original with him, much conjecture has resulted over this bit of window-pane writing. Although some have suggested that the lines might apply to a baby girl, others feel that they were intended for a new bride in the house and that the inscriber was Kensey Johns, Sr.

White-painted parlor walls accent the rich blue-green finish of the single paneled wall. Two cupboards on either side of the fireplace are said to have concealed the wine and cigars served to the master's guests.

The sedate colonial residence of John Dickinson originally
had a hipped roof. When this was ruined by
fire in 1804, it was replaced by the gable roof.

JOHN DICKINSON MANSION

Dover Vicinity, Delaware

"THE PENMAN OF THE REVOLUTION"

Some five miles southeast of Delaware's capital city of Dover stands the old colonial home of John Dickinson, known in American history as "The Penman of the Revolution." An early writer once said of him: "In the literature of that struggle, his position is as preeminent as Washington in war, Franklin in diplomacy and Morris in finance." And Thomas Jefferson asserted that "his name will be consecrated in history as one of the great worthies of the Revolution." In addition to Dickinson's unique role as the author of important Revolutionary documents, pamphlets, laws and manifestos, he served as an early governor of both Delaware and Pennsylvania.

Built more than two centuries ago, the John Dickinson house would have been destroyed had it not been for prompt action on the part of the National Society of the Colonial Dames of America in the State of Delaware. It was in 1952 that the society, realizing the historic importance of the house, donated $25,000 to the State of Delaware for its purchase and preservation, and the state matched this gift. Since then, a special committee has furnished the landmark with period pieces, some of them from the Pennsylvania-Delaware region. The house is now maintained as a public museum.

Although he served as governor of both Delaware and Pennsylvania (the chief executive of the two colonies was then known as President), John Dickinson did not come from either of them. He was born on November 2, 1732, in Talbot County, Maryland, the son of Judge Samuel and Mary (Cadwalader) Dickinson. At that time the family lived at Crosiadore, one of Maryland's leading estates. Subsequently, John's father acquired a large tract of land in Kent County, Delaware, and when John was eight years old, the family moved into a brick mansion built by his father in 1740 on the Delaware land, the house that now is one of the outstanding historic landmarks of Delaware.

Here John Dickinson grew to manhood. Here, too, was raised his younger brother, Philemon, who, as a militia major general in the American Revolution, attained almost as much fame as John. At the end of the war, Philemon was a Delaware delegate to the Continental Congress. Then, from 1790 to 1793, he served as a United States Senator from New Jersey.

The integrity of the man is successfully communicated in this portrait of Dickinson attributed to Charles Willson Peale. The painting is displayed on the west wall of the dining room.

Courtesy Delaware State Archives, Hall of Records

Covering the bed in the main chamber is a spread depicting General Washington and thirteen patriots, one of whom is John Dickinson, "The Penman of the Revolution."

After spending his boyhood days in the country mansion near the St. Jones River, John Dickinson left the estate and went to Philadelphia to study law under John Moland, Esq., one of the city's ablest attorneys. Young Dickinson then departed from America and pursued further law studies at the Middle Temple in London. He returned in 1757 and began the practice of law in Philadelphia. He also became interested in politics and soon was writing political pamphlets, then the widest means of communication on public issues.

Dickinson's unusual abilities were quickly recognized. In 1762 he was elected to the Pennsylvania General Assembly, to which he was re-elected in 1764. When the Stamp Act Congress was held in 1765, it was John Dickinson, a delegate, who prepared for that body *The Declaration of Rights Adopted by the Stamp Act Congress.* That marked the beginning of his career as a pamphleteer. From that time until the creation of the Declaration of Independence, John Dickinson wrote many of the most important documents of the pre-Revolutionary era.

His influence grew even wider than before with the publication, in 1768, of his famous *Letters of a Farmer in Pennsylvania* and, in the same year, *A Song for American Freedom.* Both dealt with the colonists and their rights as free men. Later he drafted the "Petition to the King" and "Address to the Inhabitants of Quebec" adopted by the Congress of 1774. With the outbreak of the American Revolu-

Photos: Courtesy Delaware State Archives, Hall of Records

Above: An oil of Samuel Dickinson, John's father, graces the handsomely furnished parlor. Left: The dining room also displays many fine pieces which are typical of the Dickinson era.

Displayed in the parlor are an English bracket clock owned by Dickinson, a tilt-top table set with a Salopian tea service and a Chippendale sofa.

tion, however, John Dickinson exchanged his pen for a sword, and served as a colonel in the Continental Army and later as a brigadier general in the Delaware Militia.

During the war, while the British held Philadelphia, Dickinson took his family to the safety of his boyhood home in Delaware. Later he was elected a delegate to the Constitutional Convention of 1787 and in that body he advocated the plan of two senators for each state. He followed this up with a series of letters, signing himself "Fabius," which greatly helped to win public support for the new Constitution. And it was through his influence that Delaware was the first state to ratify the new Constitution on December 7, 1787.

Although in his later years John Dickinson lived in Wilmington, he nonetheless maintained, as a plantation, his boyhood home in the Dover vicinity. Here he continued his interest in public affairs and carried on part of his voluminous correspondence with friends and statesmen. He died in Wilmington, 1808, at the age of seventy-six, and was buried in the Friends Meeting Yard in Wilmington.

With his death, the home in which he grew to manhood was inherited by one of his daughters, Sally. She was unmarried, and at her own death, the property passed to the children of his sister, Mrs. Albanus Logan. In the years following, the landmark was occupied by tenants of the Logan family and successive owners of the property, until 1952 when the house was acquired by the Delaware chapter of the National Society of Colonial Dames of America.

Regarded as a fine example of lower Delaware eighteenth-century, plantation architecture, the two-story Dickinson Mansion has its brickwork laid in Flemish bond. Originally, the house had a hip roof, but this was ruined when fire attacked the upper part of the dwelling in 1804. In repairing and restoring his country manor, John Dickinson added to it a gable roof. At an earlier period, a dining room wing and a kitchen wing were built onto the house. Re-creation of the original Dickinson gardens has been undertaken by various Delaware garden clubs.

All rooms in the house have been furnished with pieces of the Dickinson era. Some of these are family heirlooms. One such is John Dickinson's bracket clock, which hangs in the parlor. An unusual item in the entrance hall is a handblown glass lantern suspended from a hook in the ceiling over the bottom of the staircase. On the stair landing is a fine tall case clock with a rocking ship movement, made by Duncan Beard, a Delaware clockmaker, around 1780. The small library contains John Dickinson's Chippendale chair, a Queen Anne secretary-desk and a collection of books and pamphlets written and owned by him.

An oil portrait of Dickinson, attributed to Charles Willson Peale (1741-1827), hangs on the west wall of the dining room. On the sideboard under the portrait are two glass hurricane globes once owned by General Philemon Dickinson. In the china cabinet on the east wall are pieces of the Dickinson family silver, including a coffee pot with the Dickinson coat of arms and Judge Dickinson's cruet stand with the coat of arms on the stand and each caster and the family crest on each bottle.

114

Courtesy Delaware State Archives, Hall of Records

In addition to the bracket clock, the spacious parlor contains a Chippendale sofa and a tilt-top table set with a Salopian tea service. One end of the room is paneled, with a fireplace in the middle and arched china cabinets on each side with glass-paned doors. The cabinets contain Canton and Nanking china and early English porcelains which the Dickinsons would have known. A portrait of Samuel Dickinson, John's father, hangs over the fireplace.

Here, then, is a fitting memorial to "The Penman of the Revolution." Two other memorials to him are located at Carlisle, Pennsylvania. These are Dickinson College, chartered in 1783 and now ranked as one of the best of America's smaller colleges, and the Dickinson School of Law, occupying a handsome Georgian-style building built in 1917.

Significant pieces among the family silver include a coffee pot, Judge Dickinson's cruet stand, and a pair of sauce boats, all marked with the family crest.

Photos: Courtesy Kirby Lithographic Co., Inc.

SOTTERLEY

Hollywood Vicinity, Maryland

SEAT OF THE PLATER, BRISCOE AND SATTERLEE FAMILIES

When, in 1910, a prominent New York resident, Herbert L. Satterlee bought the historic old plantation house in Maryland known as Sotterley, he acquired a dwelling that was named after Sotterley Hall, ancient seat of his ancestors in England. By a curious coincidence this colonial residence was built and occupied for nearly one hundred years by members of the Plater family, a family whose ancestors had also lived in the venerable Sotterley Hall in England.

At the time of the Norman Conquest, the Satterlees were living in the manor house at Suffolk, England. Then, during the Wars of the Roses, after Edward IV defeated his rival, Richard Neville, the Earl of Warwick, many estates of the earl's followers were confiscated by the king. So it happened that in 1471 the Satterlees were expelled from Sotterley Hall and replaced by the Plater family. Although ancient Sotterley Hall was razed more than two centuries ago and replaced by an elegant Georgian residence, there still survives in Suffolk the old Sotterley Church.

Located some sixty miles east of Washington, D. C., and three miles from the town of Hollywood on the Patuxent River, the Maryland plantation house of Sotterley is one of the state's principal historic landmarks and is open to the public as a period museum.

Work on the construction of Sotterley is believed to have been begun about 1720 by James Bowles, early owner of the plantation on which it was built, who died seven years later. However, it remained for George Plater II, who married Bowles' widow in 1729, to complete the mansion as it is known today. At that period the Bowles plantation consisted of more than a thousand acres of land in Tidewater Maryland and the colony was then being administered by Charles Calvert, the fifth Lord Baltimore.

In completing the St. Mary's County house, George Plater II used many indentured servants, some of them gifted craftsmen, to convert a simple plantation house into a charming and unique eighteenth-century mansion. One of the most skillful of these indentured servants was Richard Boulton, who created the house's unusual Chinese Chippendale stairway and shell alcoves in the drawing room. He was the subject of various legends. It is said that on the

The portrait of Louisa Pierpont Morgan, daughter of J. P. Morgan and mother of Mrs. Ingalls, who initiated the Sotterley Foundation, was painted by H. Walker in 1886.

Opposite top: The red-painted pine paneling in the small parlor complements the Chinese motif of the Chippendale staircase in the central hall. A secret passage leads from the closet to a bedroom directly above. Opposite bottom: The dining room, added before 1797, has antique mahogany chairs with Chinese-lattice backs.

117

118

day Richard Boulton's term as a bonded servant was ended, he gathered up his tools and walked off, leaving unfinished a small piece of molding on the banister of the staircase—a tiny strip that remains unfinished to this day. Another story is that Boulton was freed by the master of the house so that he might remain to design and execute the handsome shell alcoves in the drawing room.

A lawyer by profession, as was his father, George Plater II was appointed to numerous public offices in the colony, including that of a naval officer and collector of customs. Just before his death, he was named provincial secretary, second in importance to the governorship. Meanwhile, he acquired more and more land and at the time of his death owned some 16,000 acres in Tidewater Maryland.

When George Plater II died in 1755, his house and plantation on the Patuxent River were inherited by his son, George Plater III. Following in his father's and grandfather's footsteps, the third George Plater also became a lawyer and public office-holder. Tradition has it that it was this George Plater who bestowed the name Sotterley on the house in which he was born and raised. Later in his career, George Plater III represented Maryland in the Continental Congress of 1777-1778 and again after the Revolution, from 1788 to 1791. On the latter date, he was elected Governor of Maryland, but served only one year because of his death in 1792.

With his death, Sotterley was inherited by a son, George Plater IV. When he died in 1802, his heir, George Plater V, was only five years old. George Plater V led a tragic life. As a child, he was cared for by his uncle, John Rousby Plater. When approaching maturity, the fifth George Plater developed an uncontrollable urge for gambling. By the time he became of age, Plater is said to have been hopelessly in debt. According to tradition, he lost his remaining equity in Sotterley through a dice game in 1822 with Colonel William Somerville, a brother of his late stepmother.

Having no interest in Sotterley, Colonel Somerville promptly sold it to a man named Thomas Barber. It was Barber's stepdaughter, the wife of Dr. Walter Hanson Stone Briscoe, who, with her husband, became in 1826 the next owner and occupant of Sotterley. The Briscoe family, whose ancestors first came to Maryland with the *Ark* and the *Dove* in 1634, was to remain at Sotterley for almost as many years as the Platers.

A descendant, Elizabeth Briscoe Cashner, decided to sell the house in 1910. As it happened, the Right Reverend Henry Yates Satterlee, bishop of Washington, D. C., had visited Sotterley earlier and become very much engrossed with its history and its connection with the name of his ancient family seat in Suffolk, England. This interest was shared by his cousin, Herbert Satterlee, the New Yorker, who, as earlier noted, bought Sotterley in 1910.

Mr. Satterlee restored the old house, rehabilitated its grounds and gardens, and acquired several hundred acres of land bringing the plantation back to its original boundaries. By the time of his death in 1947, the place was as completely restored to its eighteenth-century appearance as it could be. In 1961, the estate was deeded by his daughter, Mrs. Mabel Satterlee Ingalls, to the Sotterley Man-

On the landing of the Chippendale staircase hang portraits of Herbert Satterlee's grandparents. The Massachusetts-made, mahogany-cased clock dates from around the turn of the eighteenth century.

Opposite: The history of pastoral Sotterley dates from a land grant by Lord Baltimore to a deputy of Maryland's first governor. The long, low frame building is situated on a meadowed vista overlooking the blue Patuxent River which flows beyond.

Sotterley's stately and richly appointed drawing room, or Great Hall, has two shell alcoves, probably executed by Richard Boulton, a skilled servant of George Plater II.

sion Foundation, which is sponsored by The Society for the Preservation of Maryland Antiquities.

Situated at the top of the old "rolling road" down which hogsheads of tobacco were rolled to waiting vessels in the Patuxent River, the old mansion is a long, low house of frame construction, two stories high, with a gable roof surmounted by an ornamental cupola bearing the date "1730." Most conspicuous feature of the exterior is the mansion's famed one-hundred-foot-long portico, paved with Newcastle flagstones imported from England sometime before 1727. It provides a sweeping view of meadows dotted with grazing sheep and the blue Patuxent River beyond. At one side of the house is located the restored garden, which features an antique sundial resting on a pedestal bearing the coats of arms of the Plater, Briscoe and Satterlee families.

The rather plain exterior of Sotterley gives little suggestion of the magnificence of its interior rooms. This atmosphere is immediately sensed in the central entrance hall where the remarkable Chinese Chippendale staircase ascends to the second floor. It is one of the few of its kind surviving from colonial times. The Chinese motif is continued overhead by a Chinese teakwood lantern and by a mirror with an extraordinary carved gilt frame. A dramatic bird-in-flight figure decorates each side and the entire frame is surmounted by an intricately wrought pagoda ornament. The pine paneling here and in all of the original downstairs rooms is one of the most expressive aspects of Sotterley's interior. Vigorously executed, it is painted a variety of colors—white in the entrance hall, pale yellow in the Great Hall, bright red in the small parlor— setting the tone for each room.

The outstanding feature of the mansion's drawing room or Great Hall is the pair of handsome shell alcoves, believed to have been designed and executed by Boulton, on either side of the fireplace. Within the alcoves are displayed a pair of early Sheffield silver candelabra. On the walls is a set of four cut-crystal candle holders with S-shaped arms dripping with prisms. Two tall Queen Anne mirrors, both of rare workmanship, are also in this fine old room.

Of special interest in the dining room, which was added to the original house prior to 1797, are the antique mahogany chairs with Chinese-lattice backs, repeating the motif of the Chinese Chippendale staircase in the central entrance hall. The dominant colors here are various shades of green found in the wallpaper and the Hong Kong rug, handmade to order for the room. The unusual wallpaper with its palm tree columns and bamboo-trellis chair rail is curiously reminiscent of some of the decorative designs at the Brighton Pavilion in England.

On side tables under portraits of Governor Plater and his wife are a pair of urn-shaped sandalwood knife boxes of fine workmanship. Equally interesting is the Royal Crown Derby set of dessert chinaware on the dining table. Made around 1820, each piece has a different flower depicted on it, with identification on the back. The set includes two large, beautifully decorated containers, probably intended to hold sherbert, which are divided into two sections, the bottom half to be used for ice or hot water.

Associated with the small parlor (or sitting room), with its red-painted paneling, is the legend that it might have been here where George Plater V played the losing dice game which brought an end to the Plater family reign at Sotterley. Under the window is a finely crafted old English card table, inlaid with mother-of-pearl. A secret passage from the closet of this room leads to the middle one of three bedrooms above, which is otherwise accessible only through one of the other two.

When this storied colonial mansion was certified by the Historic American Buildings Survey of the Department of the Interior as possessing "exceptional historic and architectural interest," it was the culmination of the efforts and foresight of primarily four individuals who lived over a 225-year period—James Bowles, who selected the site and started the building; George Plater II, who created the beautiful dwelling we have today; Herbert Satterlee, who rescued the place from probable ruin; and Mabel Satterlee, who made it possible for present and future generations to enjoy Sotterley.

Above: The noteworthy Chinese Chippendale staircase in the entrance hall is also the work of craftsman Boulton. Below: Wallpaper with a palm-leaf motif is a fitting recent addition to the dining room. The portrait above the Hepplewhite sideboard is of John Paul Jones.

Above: The facade of the house is characteristically Georgian in appearance, beautifully proportioned with its pedimented carved doorway and keystoned lintels which surmount the windows. Right: The portion of Widehall which fronts the Chester River is meticulously landscaped with formal lawns and gardens.

WIDEHALL

Chestertown, Maryland

MANSION OF A MERCHANT PRINCE

The old Chestertown, Maryland, mansion known as Widehall is one of those dwellings which impresses even the casual observer, its mass is so beautifully proportioned, its workmanship so accomplished, its state of preservation so pristine. To the student of American architecture and the decorative arts, Widehall is unsurpassed as a surviving example of its time and place. This is not only because of its great age, its rich historical associations and its distinguished architecture, but also because of its remarkable restoration and its splendid refurnishing, work that was started more than half a century ago by members of the Hubbard family of Chestertown and is carried on even today by Widehall's present owner, Wilbur Ross Hubbard.

Although the Hubbard family acquired this handsome Georgian town house overlooking the Chester River only as "recently" as the early twentieth century, its members are generally credited, by what they did on this dwelling, with being pioneers in the colonial house restoration movement on the Eastern seaboard. It was Mr. Hubbard's mother who first started work on the authentic restoration of Widehall. At that time she had no examples to go by—no Colonial Williamsburg, no Winterthur, no American Wing of the Metropolitan Museum of New York. Today, Widehall is acclaimed as the first "restoration" in Chestertown, an historic old community now famed for its numerous restored mansions of colonial vintage.

Not only is Widehall a tribute to the efforts of the Hubbard family, but it is also a memorial to its builder, Thomas Smyth, who has been termed the "Merchant Prince of Chestertown." He was one of the great public figures of Maryland history in the days before and during the American Revolution. Two other noted public figures who became later owners of Widehall were Governor Robert Wright of Maryland and United States Senator Ezekial Chambers. A number of successive owners lived at Widehall until 1909 when it was acquired by the Hubbard family.

It is generally believed that Thomas Smyth built his mansion about 1770. At that pre-Revolutionary period Chestertown was one of the most flourishing communities on the Eastern Shore, an im-

WIDEHALL, Chestertown, Md.

Widehall was built sometime between 1665 and 1670 by Thomas Smythe, wealthy Kent County ship owner. Dedicated restorative work has made it one of Chestertown's finest homes.

Above: Formal elegance is the keynote of the drawing room with Chippendale and Queen Anne furnishings and antique needlepoint valances. Below: The elaborate Philadelphia Chippendale highboy is considered the home's finest piece.

Photos: Courtesy Wilbur Ross Hubbard

portant port of entry, and the home place of many merchants, importers and shipowners. Old land records of the area show that Thomas Smyth was the wealthiest merchant in Kent County. He was also a shipowner whose sailing vessels were in the British West Indies trade.

As with so many businesmen during the republic's formative years, Thomas Smyth played a leading role in public life. A few days after the Chestertown Tea Party of 1774, similar to the more famous one in Boston, Thomas Smyth was unanimously elected chairman of the local Committee of Correspondence. He later became the first head of Maryland's revolutionary provisional government and served in this capacity until 1776 when the state's first constitution was framed and its first governor elected. Thomas Smyth was also a benefactor, one of the founders and first treasurer of Chestertown's Washington College, opened in 1782.

In the years after the Civil War the owner, or owners, of Widehall attempted to up-date the residence by adding highly ornamental Victorian details to its facade and to other sides of the house. Being out of harmony with the handsome Georgian architecture of the mansion, these details were removed by members of the Hubbard family, who restored the house to its original appearance. As it stands today, this Eastern Shore residence is one of the finest and most imposing colonial Georgian "town houses," as opposed to plantation houses, in Maryland.

Situated adjacent to the old Customs House, a landmark (also owned by Wilbur Ross Hubbard) surviving from the great days when Chestertown was a port of entry, Widehall is a three-story building of brick construction with a hip roof and dormer projections. It has two fronts, one on the street, the other on the river. The river front has an enormous porch with Ionic columns (later than the period of the house), a porch affording a magnificent view of the lawn and gardens running down to Chester River.

The main entrance, or "town house front," is on Water Street. It is approached up stone steps to a flagstone terrace which is accentuated with brick columns surmounted by stone capitals, then up another flight of stone steps to the lovely pedimented doorway supported by fluted pilasters. The brickwork is unusual, for the front is all header bond. All of the windows have keystoned lintels and the whole front facade has the balanced symmetry of Georgian architecture.

The interior is even more elaborate, with every detail thoughtfully conceived. The most arresting view in the house is in the spacious entrance hall where one sees the graceful mahogany stairway through a series of tastefully executed arches. Details of the wood carving in each room are different from those in all the others, but a feature of all the first-floor rooms is the broken pediment above each doorway and overmantel.

The living room is enhanced by mahogany chair rail and mahogany window sills. All of the windows in the house have inside shutters. In the rest of the house the shutter handles are brass, but in this room they are sterling silver, as is the door lock and keeper.

Architectural excellence, a rich blend of color and fine antique pieces contribute to the beauty
and elegance of the dining room. The slanted Wall of Troy design is unique to this room,
but the broken pediment above the overmantel is an outstanding feature of all the first-floor rooms.

Above: An English bed in the Hubbard bedroom has the original needlepoint bedhangings once owned by the Earl and Countess of Sussex. Opposite: The graceful mahogany staircase is approached through a series of spacious arches in the home's entrance hall.

The outstanding piece of furniture in this room is a Maryland secretary desk of the Hepplewhite period. This desk still contains its original label showing it to have been made in Baltimore about 1790.

The dining room is especially beautiful with the unique slanted Wall of Troy design around the cornice and the fan cupboards flanking the fireplace. On the butterfly shelves of these cupboards is a set of armorial Chinese Export porcelain bearing the coat of arms of the Ross family of Scotland, from whom the owner is descended. Also in this room is silver bearing the same coat of arms and an unusually fine Hepplewhite sideboard.

All the rooms are carpeted with antique Oriental rugs. The drawing room and halls are filled with furniture of the Chippendale period, much of it made by the fine craftsmen in Philadelphia, the most noteworthy being the elaborately carved Philadelphia Chippendale highboy on the second floor.

On the leisurely, time-hallowed Eastern Shore of Maryland there are many noteworthy historic houses, but few as charming as Widehall, for it is more than a virtual period museum. Its stately rooms and well-groomed lawns are alive with the pleasant sounds of entertainment and sociability as frequently today as they were at their inception two centuries ago.

Above and right: Dr. William Thornton, winner of the competition for design of the Capitol, also designed the Octagon for its owner, Colonel John Tayloe. Work on the mansion was completed in 1800 and it immediately became a center of official and social functions in Washington, D.C.

THE OCTAGON

Washington, D. C.

An Unusual Design by an Unusual Architect

One of the most unusual public figures of the post-Revolutionary era designed and supervised the construction of one of the most unusual houses standing in Washington, D. C., today. Trained as a physician rather than an architect, Dr. William Thornton created the six-sided residence now nationally known as the Octagon House. He also designed the main portion of one of the most renowned edifices in the world today—the Capitol Building in Washington.

Built about the same time as the White House, the Thornton-designed residence at New York Avenue and Eighteenth Street ranks in historical and architectural interest with such other Washington landmarks as the Decatur House, Blair House and Petersen House, the house where Lincoln died. Now being restored and refurnished as it was in the early nineteenth century, the Octagon House will be opened to the public in 1970.

Its historical associations are impressive. During the War of 1812, it served President James Madison as a temporary "White House" after the British burned and sacked much of Washington, including the home of the President in 1814. It was in the Octagon House that President Madison ratified the Treaty of Ghent in 1815 and here, too, his wife Dolley reigned for a time as one of the most glamorous of Washington hostesses during the early days of the republic.

In the 170 years of its existence, the Octagon House, nearly always a center of official or unofficial social activities, welcomed more distinguished guests than any other private home in the District of Columbia. Among those who passed through its inviting front door were, in addition to President Madison, such other chief executives as Jefferson, Monroe, Adams and Jackson. Here, too, may have come Stephen Decatur, Admiral David Porter, Daniel Webster, Henry Clay, Marquis de Lafayette, John Randolph and John C. Calhoun.

What brought so many to the Octagon House, what made it a leading social rendezvous of the nation's capital, were the hospitable, engaging and cultivated personalities of its host and hostess, Colonel John Tayloe and Mrs. Tayloe. When Colonel Tayloe, the then proprietor of Mount Airy, one of the oldest and most famous of Virginia estates, decided early in 1797 to build a town house, he chose

Every fifth one of the slender balusters on the Octagon's stairway is of iron, joined to handrail and carriage, which undoubtedly was the primary reason it survived the years of neglect which followed the Tayloe occupancy.

The dining room of the Octagon is furnished much as it would have been in Tayloe's day. The cornice, a reproduction of the original, was copied in the President's Office when the White House was restored several years ago.

Philadelphia as its site. But his close friend, President Washington, persuaded him to select the new national capital as a more suitable site than Philadelphia, by conveying to the colonel a vivid picture of the future of the capital city, as Washington envisioned it. And so Colonel Tayloe built the Octagon House in Washington, completing it by 1800, the year after President Washington died.

After purchasing a V-shaped lot at New York Avenue and Eighteenth Street for $1,000 in the new capital city as then laid out on paper by the planner Major Pierre Charles L'Enfant, Colonel Tayloe was confronted with the problem of finding an architect who could design a town house suitable for his curiously shaped lot. Eventually he settled on Dr. William Thornton, the physician-architect, a man who was nothing if not ingenious. It may have been that Dr. Thornton was recommended to the colonel by President Washington, who, a few years earlier in a competition for the design of a national capitol building, had selected Dr. Thornton's as the winning design.

Born in the West Indies, educated in England, Dr. Thornton received his medical degree at Edinburgh and came to the United States in 1793. He is recorded as later devoting himself to many activities other than the practice of medicine—invention, horse racing, city planning, painting, writing, scientific research, philosophy, and, of course, architecture. Still later in his versatile career, Dr. Thornton was appointed first clerk of the United States Patent Office, and, afterwards, commissioner of pensions.

With the completion of their odd-shaped town house in 1800, the Tayloes began life there as leading social figures of the national capital. A curious fact about their mansion is that it is not octagonal, or eight-sided, in form; it has only six sides. The true octagonal house was invented in the middle of the nineteenth century by Orson Squire Fowler, author of *A Home For All; or, the Gravel Wall and Octagon Mode of Building* (1849). However, the Tayloe residence gave the illusion of being octagonal, so its owners called it Octagon House, a name that has endured to this day.

After 1855, when Mrs. John Tayloe died, the Octagon House was no longer used by the family as a town house. In 1865, it was converted into a private school for girls. Then, from 1866 to 1879, the government rented it for use by the Hydrographic Office. Subsequently, the Octagon House was leased to a number of families, and it is very likely that the old landmark would have fallen into ruin had it not been for Glenn Brown, longtime secretary of The American Institute of Architects. As early as 1889, he suggested that the Octagon House would make an ideal national headquarters house for his organization. Ten years later, The American Institute of Architects took formal possession of the mansion together with its stable, smokehouse and garden.

Three years later the organization exercised its option to buy the property for $30,000, and extensive repairs were made, including restoration of the interior rooms and halls. Membership in the organization increased to such an extent that a newer and larger headquarters building was built in 1940 adjacent to the Octagon House, making it possible to convert the mansion into a public museum.

A three-story residence of brick construction, the Octagon House has a graceful and unusual facade whose distinctive feature is a semi-

circular central unit built into the street corner apex of the V-shaped house. A flight of stone steps in this unit leads up to an attractive entrance portico, embellished with two Ionic columns. Because of the unusual floor plan here, most of the interior rooms of the house are either circular or rectangular in form. A large circular entrance hall features black and white marble flooring and two black iron heating stoves, both believed to be original with the house.

To the left of the entrance hall is the dining room, refurnished with period pieces by the family of John W. Cross (1878-1951), a distinguished Fellow of The American Institute of Architects. Both the dining room and the drawing room, on the right hand side of the entrance hall, feature rare Coade stone mantels, with deeply undercut sculptural trim. They were imported from London in 1799 and bear the maker's name. Both rooms also have cornices that are reproductions of the original ones.

An impressive stairway leads to the second floor, which contains perhaps the most popular room in the house—President Madison's study, now called the Treaty Room. In this circular study above the main entrance to the house President Madison ratified the Treaty of Ghent in 1815, ending the War of 1812 with England. Among the outstanding exhibits in this room is the pivoted, circular table on which the treaty was signed. It has wedge-shaped drawers marked A to Z which President Madison used for filing purposes.

Behind the house is a garden which harmoniously joins the mansion with the smokehouse and the headquarters building of the AIA. Outside the back door of the Octagon is the brick-lined entry to a mysterious tunnel which curves around the house and reaches eighteenth Street where it is sealed off. It is thought that perhaps the tunnel may have originally extended to the Potomac River which was then close by.

Above: The Octagon was spared the British torch in 1814 and later became the residence of President and Mrs. Madison. In the Treaty Room, the President's study, he signed the Treaty of Ghent in 1815. Below: The large drawing room contains a priceless, exquisite Coade stone mantel with undercut sculpture, perfectly preserved.

Above: Historic Claymont Court, commanding a fine
view of the Blue Ridge Mountains, is still a
productive one-thousand-acre livestock farm.
Right: The attractive entrance foyer, which leads
to the living room, contains an English
gaming table with unusually heavy animal feet.

CLAYMONT COURT

Charles Town Vicinity, West Virginia

HOME OF WASHINGTON'S GRAND-NEPHEW

Of the eight West Virginia country houses built by the younger brothers of President George Washington, or by their descendants, the one considered grandest of all is Claymont Court, erected in 1820 by Bushrod Corbin Washington, grand-nephew of the President. It is the focus of what has come to be known in West Virginia as the Washington Country, where all eight residences lie among the green hills at the northern end of the Shenandoah Valley. In this lovely and historic region the Shenandoah River cuts through the Blue Ridge Mountains to unite with the Potomac River at Harpers Ferry.

When Claymont Court was built in 1820, which was about the same time as the other Washington homes were erected, there was no State of West Virginia. All of this region, as far westward as the Ohio River, was part of the Commonwealth of Virginia. It was not until the Civil War, in 1863, that West Virginia was formed out of the western part of the Old Dominion State. In building their houses at the northern end of the Shenandoah Valley, General Washington's kinsmen located them in the vicinity of Charles Town, founded in 1786 by Charles Washington, youngest brother of the first President (and not to be confused with Charleston, the capital of West Virginia). Still standing today is Happy Retreat, a mansion built at Charles Town by Charles Washington, and Blakeley, built by John Augustine Washington II, Bushrod's brother.

It was after Bushrod and John Augustine had married two sisters, Anna Maria and Jane Charlotte Blackburn, that the brothers decided to build country homes near each other in the Shenandoah Valley. Claymont Court and Blakeley are separated by a stream, Bullskin Run, along which, starting in 1748, young George Washington had served as a surveyor for the great landowner, Lord Halifax. On returning home, George expressed such warm enthusiasm for the Shenandoah Valley area that his older brother, Lawrence, bought several thousand acres of it from Lord Halifax. At the same time Lord Halifax presented his young surveyor with a gift of five

A porcelain rococo Meissen clock is located beneath a portrait of Martha Washington in the ballroom.

Below: The elegance
of the formal dining area is enhanced by a Hepplewhite
banquet table and chairs. The pierced cross
bracing between the legs of the chairs is distinctive.

hundred acres in the same region. Later, George Washington bought a thousand more acres in the valley, acquiring it, says tradition, on the installment plan.

When Claymont Court was completed two miles west of Charles Town at a reported cost of $30,000, it stood forth as a showplace of the countryside. In fact, some of the earlier settlers in the region were amazed by its magnificence. Many even called it "Washington's Folly." In 1838, shortly after Bushrod Washington was elected to the General Assembly, his imposing mansion was accidentally attacked by flames and burned completely to the ground.

Part of a letter written by a Mr. Bedinger, whom Bushrod had defeated in the race for the General Assembly, tells of the fire at Claymont Court. "Thus has been destroyed," wrote Mr. Bedinger, "the Mansion which but a few years since Cost More than thirty thousand dollars. I am sincerely Sorry for this loss as he is an innocent good man. And I deplore his weakness and folly in erecting such an expensive building, but—Pride & Ambition too often lead to great follies."

Described as a man with "grand ideas," and also as a person with substantial wordly means, Bushrod Washington lost no time in rebuilding Claymont Court just as it existed originally. Here he lived in the years following, entertaining his many friends and supervising the development of his estate of more than one thousand acres, making it one of the finest livestock farms in that part of Virginia.

With his death in 1851, Claymont Court passed to his son, and, later, to his grandson. Both of these heirs continued the tradition of hospitality begun at the mansion by Bushrod Washington and his wife. But this way of life came to an end with the outbreak of the Civil War in 1861 and the formation of the new State of West Virginia. Thereafter, Claymont Court came into the hands of a number of successive owners and finally was acquired by the famous author and humorist, Frank R. Stockton. Stockton, who is best remembered for *The Adventures of Captain Horn, Rudder Grange* and "The Lady or the Tiger?" lived there until his death in 1902.

Despite its numerous proprietors since the Bushrod Washington heirs relinquished its ownership, Claymont Court has been kept in good condition and many of its rooms have been furnished with appropriate pieces. In recent years, the one-thousand-acre estate has specialized in the breeding of Hereford cattle. Among the numerous outbuildings here is a five-hundred-foot show barn.

The estate also contains two old slave-quarter buildings, which have been converted into two six-room guest lodges, and seven tenant houses and five silos. A two-mile winding driveway under massive oak trees leads to the great lawn that fronts Claymont Court. In this attractive setting, the manor house presents an impressive example of early eighteenth-century domestic architecture, remindful of some of the imposing plantation houses of the Old South. It is a two-and-a-half story edifice with a large central unit and two smaller wings on either side. A two-story gallery at its front affords a panoramic view of the estate and of the Shenandoah Valley.

The rooms of the mansion are outstanding for their elegance and for their reflection of a gracious way of life during the early eighteenth century. The handsome foyer—which contains a stately grandfather's clock with solid gold face that once belonged to the Washington family—leads to the beautifully furnished living room, the library, the formal dining room and perhaps the most impressive room in the house, the Gold Room (or ballroom).

A portrait of George Washington, attributed to Gilbert Stuart, in its original gold-leaf frame hangs over one of the two fireplaces in the ballroom. Nearby is a Hepplewhite china cabinet and a matching settee dating from the early eighteenth century. The room also contains a large French Aubusson rug and Meissen clock and candlesticks dated 1710. Below the first floor an English basement contains a massive kitchen, an informal dining room, a recreation room and various utility rooms. The interior of Claymont Court, no less than its exterior, bears out the claim that it is the most impressive of the eight Washington houses in this part of West Virginia.

Above: Included in the ballroom's impressive collection of antique furniture are a French-style gilt library table with marble top and shell carving (center) and a Hepplewhite breakfront cabinet with matching settee (left). Right: Possibly the loveliest piece is an American version of the Louis XV style chest of drawers. The serpentine front and hand-carved wood give it an almost delicate appearance.

Above: Ludwell-Paradise House, the first Williamsburg landmark acquired for restoration, retains its original facade. A different type of brick was used on each floor to achieve a pleasing pattern in Flemish bond with glazed headers. Right: The stable has been reconstructed on its original foundations near the garden.

136

LUDWELL-PARADISE HOUSE
Williamsburg, Virginia
AN EARLY RESTORATION IN COLONIAL WILLIAMSBURG

When John D. Rockefeller, Jr., and the Reverend W. A. R. Goodwin began their monumental project of restoring historic old Williamsburg in 1927, the first colonial landmark they acquired was the Ludwell-Paradise House on Duke of Gloucester Street. Here was an early eighteenth-century mansion that the late Dr. Goodwin, rector of Williamsburg's Bruton Parish Church, long had his eye on as part of his dream to preserve and restore the venerable second capital of early Virginia. And it was the late John D. Rockefeller, Jr., who brought to reality the minister's dream.

What these two far-sighted men found in the Ludwell-Paradise House was a more than two-hundred-year-old residence, well preserved, two stories high, of red brick construction. It was probably built by Philip Ludwell III, member of one of the most prominent families of early colonial days in Virginia, sometime after 1737. When the George Wythe mansion was built in Williamsburg a few years later, the Ludwell and Wythe dwellings ranked as two of the leading "great houses" and social centers of the colonial capital.

The living room furniture, a pleasing mixture of antiques and reproductions, complements the handsome décor of this eighteenth-century town house.

It was in 1700 that Philip Ludwell II, of the famed Green Spring plantation near Williamsburg, purchased the lot on Duke of Gloucester Street where the Ludwell-Paradise House now stands. His father was Philip Ludwell I, who had married Lady Berkeley, widow of Sir William Berkeley, Governor of the Virginia Colony and long-time proprietor of the Green Spring estate. After this marriage, Philip Ludwell became owner of Green Spring plantation. It was at this country place that Philip Ludwell II grew to manhood and became a figure of importance in Jamestown.

Needing a town house, Philip Ludwell II acquired the lot on Duke of Gloucester Street. It is believed that he built a dwelling here sometime between 1710 and 1716, the period when he was serving as deputy auditor general of the Virginia colony. When, however, this property was inherited by his son, Philip Ludwell III, in 1737, the elder Ludwell's original house was razed and replaced by the two-story brick edifice standing on the lot today.

In this house Philip's second daughter, Lucy, later became something of a character in the colonial capital. But at the time Philip Ludwell III died in 1767, his daughter lived in England as the wife

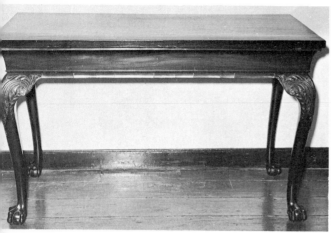

Above: The English Chippendale table, circa 1760, found in the living room, has ball-and-claw feet typical of the style. Below: Replacements and materials from deserted eighteenth-century buildings in the area were utilized in the interior.

of John Paradise, a scholar, linguist and member of Dr. Samuel Johnson's celebrated circle of literary friends. Mrs. Paradise was an unusual personality, eccentric, quick-tempered, emotional. She is supposed to have caused quite a stir in London society by throwing hot water from her tea urn into the face of a gentleman guest who annoyed her by talking too much. During the American Revolution and for some years afterward, the Paradises remained in England. John Paradise is believed to have been a strong supporter of the Crown during the War of Independence.

Because of this, the Commonwealth of Virginia confiscated various properties owned by Mrs. Paradise in her native state. When Dr. Samuel Johnson heard of this, he is said to have lifted his eyebrows and quipped, "Paradise's Loss." Although the Paradises tried to recover these properties during a visit to Virginia in 1788, they were unsuccessful and returned to England.

After the death of her husband in 1795, Mrs. Paradise continued to live in London for the next ten years. She then returned to her native Virginia where she lived in the residence on Duke of Gloucester Street built by her father. At that time the house was owned by her two nieces, Mrs. Portia Hodgson and Mrs. Cornelia Hopkins. One legend has it that while living here Mrs. Paradise entertained callers by riding in a coach that had been reassembled on a large back porch and that was slowly rolled back and forth by a servant. In 1812 she was committed to the Williamsburg insane asylum where she died a few years later.

In 1818 the Ludwell-Paradise House was sold to a relative, James Lee. After Lee's daughter and sole heir married Parkes Slater, the house remained in the hands of Slater descendants, until 1926 when it was conveyed to John D. Rockefeller, Jr., and the Reverend Mr. Goodwin as a first step in the restoration of Colonial Williamsburg. At that time the brickwork of the house was found to be in excellent condition, but the interior needed some repairs and replacements. To effect these, the architect-restorers purchased suitable materials from various unoccupied eighteenth-century houses in Tidewater Virginia.

Architecturally sophisticated for its day, the Ludwell-Paradise House is a fine example of early colonial Georgian design. Its two-story facade is well proportioned and notable for its central entrance door, the arrangement of its eighteen-pane windows, its Flemish bond brickwork and its denticulated cornice. A low hip roof and end chimneys complete the facade design. Although the house was probably originally intended to have a second floor as deep as the first, with four full rooms, the plans were changed and the depth of the second story was reduced by half. Thus the rear portion of the first floor is covered by a lean-to roof. The residence, now privately occupied by the Rudolph Bares, Jr., family, is furnished with a number of antiques and reproduction pieces of the eighteenth-century era in Williamsburg. In the living room are several Chippendale pieces, circa 1760-1780, including a secretary, corner chair and a fine side table. The room also has a Sheraton side chair made in Philadelphia about 1790.

Although the house itself is the original edifice, its outbuildings, located in a long narrow garden at the rear, are reconstructions built

on the foundations of the old structures. Here may be found the kitchen, woodhouse, stable, well, privy (called the "necessary house"), smokehouse and storehouse. The garden itself is a restoration and features a fine dwarf box collection as well as holly, spring bulbs and summer flowering shrubs. The garden is open to the public.

When the late Mrs. John D. Rockefeller, Jr., decided in 1935 to move her famed collection of American folk art to Colonial Williamsburg, she chose the Ludwell-Paradise House as the most suitable building for its display. In 1957, however, the Abby Aldrich Rockefeller collection was moved into a building of its own in Colonial Williamsburg.

In order to make an authentic restoration, the paneling in the dining room was completely stripped for a close study of interior detail.

Above: Scotchtown was once the residence of two eminent
Americans: Patrick Henry and Dolley Payne Madison
Below: The parlor is richly decorated in gold and muted
green. The Queen Anne drop-leaf table beneath the portrait
of Dolley Madison dates from the mid-eighteenth century.

140

SCOTCHTOWN

Ashland Vicinity, Virginia

HOME OF THE "ORATOR OF THE REVOLUTION"

It may seem odd that the name Scotchtown should be applied to a single house, but such has been the case with an estate near Ashland, Virginia, ever since pre-Revolutionary times when it was the home of Patrick Henry, the great American statesman, author of the Bill of Rights, Governor of Virginia, and the "Orator of the Revolution." The name arose from the fact that the house was originally built by a Scotsman and around it stood something of a "town" of estate outbuildings—an office, kitchen, warehouse, washhouse, blacksmith shop, and, below the hilltop site of the house, some thirty cabins and a mill.

Another famous occupant of Scotchtown was a young lady, Dorothea Payne, who later became Dolley Madison, wife of the fourth President of the United States and most celebrated First Lady in American history. Her father, John Payne, a Quaker, acquired Scotchtown and moved into it with his family, a few years before Henry bought the place. Recollections of her life on the Hanover County plantation just north of Richmond are plentiful in Dolley Madison's *Memoirs*. John Payne sold Scotchtown in 1771 and later moved with his family to Philadelphia.

It was in 1771, four years before the outbreak of the American Revolution, that Patrick Henry purchased the plantation house and the 960 acres surrounding it. Of Scotch descent himself and a native of Hanover County, Patrick Henry must have been familiar with Scotchtown since his boyhood. It was the sort of country place he had always wanted, where he could enjoy his books, his violin, and his favorite sports of fishing and hunting. Here, too, he could entertain his many friends from the colonial capital at Williamsburg. A capable lawyer as well as a brilliant orator, Patrick Henry was then serving in the Virginia House of Burgesses.

While the orator had not yet become owner of Scotchtown when he made one of his famous statements—the assertion that "If this be treason, make the most of it!"—he was living in the plantation house at the time of most of his later celebrated remarks. It was from this house he rode down to Richmond for the second Continental Congress, where he delivered the ringing words: "Is life so dear, or peace so sweet, as to be purchased at the price of chains

According to Jefferson, the eloquent Patrick Henry "through a long and active life had been the idol of his country beyond any man who ever lived."

The dining room, principally furnished in the Queen Anne style, has wide-plank flooring covered by an elaborate Oriental rug.

Opposite top: An American Chippendale wing chair upholstered in red silk damask is a splash of color in the off-white library. Opposite bottom: Light gray paneling offsets the rich mahogany finish of the table and chairs in the hall. The mirror above retains its original glass.

and slavery? Forbid it, Almighty God! I know not what course others may take; but as for me, give me liberty or give me death."

At Scotchtown, Patrick Henry lived the comfortable life of a country gentleman, although he was active in most of the fateful events leading up to the War of Independence. Here, also, he and his wife raised their three boys and three girls. Mrs. Henry, however, died in the spring of 1775. A year later, Patrick Henry was elected the first governor of the new Commonwealth of Virginia. Before moving to the Governor's Palace at Williamsburg and while still residing at Scotchtown, Patrick Henry married his second wife, Dorothea Dandridge, a granddaughter of Colonial Governor Alexander Spotswood.

After settling at Williamsburg in 1777, Governor Henry sold Scotchtown to Colonel Wilson Miles Cary, a wealthy landowner. As occupant of the plantation house during the American Revolution, Colonel Cary had not only General Lafayette as a visitor in May 1781, but also, a month later, the general's British pursuer, Lord Cornwallis. Another prominent visitor was Baron Ludwig von Closen, who afterwards wrote of the place: "This plantation, which is called *Scotchtown,* is charmingly situated in the midst of a plain 6 leagues from Porter. The house is spacious and handsome, extremely well furnished, and delightfully well ordered. In a word, it is one of the most pleasing establishments in America."

Scotchtown was built by Colonel Charles Chiswell, who came from Scotland to the Virginia colony during the late seventeenth century and who afterwards served as clerk of the colony's General Court. It was in 1717 that Colonel Chiswell was granted a tract of land in what is now Hanover County amounting to nearly ten thousand acres. A resident of Williamsburg, he evidently decided to build a country home on his large tract, which was then a wilderness area. The colonel is believed to have built Scotchtown sometime after the land was granted to him in 1717.

Records show him living on his plantation as early as 1732. In that year he was visited by William Byrd II of Westover, member of the famed Byrd family of Virginia, leading planter, colony official and author. In his book *Progress to the Mines*, Byrd mentions this visit: "I arrived about two o'clock, and saved my dinner. I was very handsomely entertained, finding everything very clean, and very good."

After Chiswell's death in 1737, the property passed to his son, John, who had married Elizabeth Randolph, member of another prominent Virginia family. John Chiswell served in the Virginia House of Burgesses for thirteen years. A daughter of the John Chiswells married John Robinson, speaker of the House of Burgesses, treasurer of the colony, and a man of considerable wealth.

When John Chiswell attempted to raise tobacco on his Scotchtown acreage, the project failed, and once more he found himself, as one account has it, "chronically short of cash and land poor." He later borrowed money in order to join his son-in-law, John Robinson, in a lead mining company. Then, in 1760, John Chiswell

A delicate pencil-post bed is the focal point of the white bedroom. The decorated dower chest in front is American, made of walnut.

transferred ownership of Scotchtown to John Robinson in a move to help meet his financial obligations.

With the death of John Robinson in May 1766, it was discovered that the speaker of the House of Burgesses had been deeply in debt to the Virginia colony. Thereafter, the administrators of the Robinson estate sold Scotchtown in order to meet Robinson's debts. It was a few years later (1771) that Patrick Henry bought Scotchtown.

In 1824, the plantation was sold to Captain John J. Taylor, and it remained in the possession of Taylor descendants until June 26, 1958, when it was purchased by the Hanover County branch of the Association for the Preservation of Virginia Antiquities. The house was restored and furnished with eighteenth-century period pieces, including a cradle and some china which belonged to Patrick Henry.

In design, Scotchtown is not so ornamental as many other colonial houses of Virginia. It is, however, well proportioned and presents a pleasing appearance. Of frame construction, with clapboard siding, the house has a central entrance portico of classic design, a modillioned cornice and a high-pitched gable roof. The hipped ends of the roof provide a decorative touch to the house's over-all pattern.

A central entrance hall is wainscotted in heart pine painted gray and the room doors are of walnut, with heavy hinges. The hall contains a marble-topped Queen Anne tea table, dating from 1720-1750; a Queen Anne settee from a slightly later period, with turned stretchers and cabriole legs; and a Chippendale block-and-shell grandfather's clock, probably made in Rhode Island.

The parlor is dominated by a fireplace which slants across one corner, is flush with the wall and thus has no mantel. It has a marble inner facing and is surrounded by muted green-painted wood paneling which reaches to the ceiling; the remainder of the room is wainscotted. Most of the furniture in the parlor is Philadelphia Chippendale, or a variation, including a small table with birdcage detail; the two straight-backed, straight-legged chairs which accompany the table; and a wing chair in one corner. The gold damask upholstery of this chair and a sofa across the room have given the name Gold Room to the parlor. Over the wing chair hangs an interesting Philadelphia walnut mirror with gilded shell crest.

The large and handsome library has a fireplace matching the one in the parlor except that the paneling and wainscotting are off-white. Over the fireplace hangs an oil portrait of Patrick Henry, a fine copy of a Thomas Sully work, which conveys powerfully the young patriot's fierce determination and pride. Among the outstanding pieces of furniture in the room are a Philadelphia Chippendale straight-legged mahogany wing chair of eighteenth-century design, upholstered in bright red silk damask, and an exquisite Queen Anne walnut lowboy with cabriole legs, dating from 1720-1750.

The most attractive bedroom is known as the Blue Room, which contains a fine example of a Philadelphia-made fan-backed Windsor

The blue bedroom is attractively decorated with blue
and white drapes that match the canopy
of the large Hepplewhite tester bed.

chair with splayed legs and bobbin-turned members. The attractive
blue and white drapes match the canopy of the large Hepplewhite
tester bed and the bedspread. All the floors in Scotchtown are wide
plank and most of them are partially covered with fine Oriental rugs
of varying sizes, including two Kirmans in the parlor.

As might be expected of a residence standing out in the open
countryside for more than two centuries, Scotchtown has numerous
legends and traditions attached to it. Among these are suggestions
of an Indian raid, of a duel that left a "bloodstain" in the entrance
hall and of a "dungeon" (once a wine cellar) in which a husband
is supposed to have chained his wife. And then there is the tale
about the dashing British cavalry officer, Major Banastre Tarleton,
who is said to have performed the physically questionable feat of
riding his horse up the steps of Scotchtown and through its central
entrance hall, departing from the hall's rear entrance.

For most of those interested in Scotchtown, however, its principal
association remains one of historical fact—owner and occupant Patrick Henry, who may have entered the realm of legend, but who
was a real person, as this charming dwelling reminds one so well.

ROLFE-WARREN HOUSE

Jamestown Vicinity, Virginia

THE HISTORIC "FIFTY-FOOT BRICK HOUSE"

Pocahontas, wife of the enterprising Englishman, John Rolfe, is a colorful, legendary figure of America's past.

Opposite: This quaint colonial brick home, designed after an English country manor, was built in 1652. The land was originally presented to John Rolfe and his bride, the Indian princess Pocahontas, by her father Chief Powhatan.

Across the James River from Jamestown, Virginia, near a high bluff, stands one of the oldest houses in America, a house built on land associated with the renowned Indian princess, Pocahontas, who married the early English colonist, John Rolfe. This "Fifty-foot Brick House," as it was known in colonial records, was erected in 1652 on a tract owned by Thomas Rolfe, only child and son of the first heroine in American history, a daughter of the powerful Indian chief, Powhatan. Now known as the Rolfe-Warren House, the historic brick dwelling is maintained as a public museum by the Thomas Rolfe Branch of the Association for the Preservation of Virginia Antiquities.

Originally, its site was on land claimed by the great Powhatan Confederacy of Indians. When the English colonists arrived on the shore of the James River in 1607 and founded Jamestown, first permanent English settlement in America, they immediately built a palisaded fort for protection against the Indians. This settlement was started thirteen years before the arrival of the Pilgrims in New England. Among the Jamestown colonists was Captain John Smith who, although not governor of the colony, revealed himself to be a capable leader amid the uncertainties of life in the New World.

As time went on, however, Chief Powhatan and his tribesmen grew increasingly resentful of the white settlers on the James River, a situation that led to sporadic conflicts. In the midst of one of these, Captain John Smith was captured by Chief Powhatan and was about to be executed when, according to the popular legend, his life was saved through the intercession of the Indian chief's daughter, Pocahontas. Whether this actually occurred is a matter that historians and scholars have not been able to verify.

After his release, Captain John Smith returned to Jamestown. One of his first projects for the betterment of the colony was to construct a "New Fort" at a location "opposite Jamestown," that is, across the James River on Gray's Creek, for the additional protection of the settlers. Old records of Surry County list this site as "Smith's Fort Plantation." The fort was completed in 1609 on ground now occupied by the Rolfe-Warren House. Some remains of the breastworks of the fort are still discernible near the house.

Above: The display of late seventeenth-century furniture reconstructs the life of the earliest settlers. Below: Fluted pilasters, part of the remarkable wood paneling in the north room, lead to an attractive cornice at the ceiling. A rare Elizabethan armchair, circa 1603, stands near the window.

Then, in 1610, there arrived in Jamestown the English colonist, John Rolfe. An enterprising individual, Rolfe was the first Englishman to introduce the regular cultivation of tobacco in America, starting this work at Jamestown in 1612. Finding a ready market for his tobacco in England, Rolfe helped greatly to improve the economic status of the colony and became the father of the vast American tobacco industry of today.

It was during this period that John Rolfe met and fell in love with the Indian princess, Pocahontas. With the permission of her father, Chief Powhatan, and the governor of the colony, Rolfe, in 1614, married the Indian princess who had been converted to Christianity and baptized Rebecca. As a result of this marriage, not only was peace restored among the Indians and the colonists, but Chief Powhatan presented to the couple, as a dower gift, the land across from Jamestown where Smith's Fort had stood.

When John Rolfe visited England with his wife in 1616 Pocahontas was cordially received by London society. The couple were about to return home when she became ill and died. Rolfe came back to America, but left their only son, Thomas, to be raised and educated in England by paternal relatives. Just when John Rolfe himself died is not exactly known, but he is believed to have lost his life in the great Indian massacre of 1622.

It was in 1635 that Thomas returned to America and laid claim to the land south of the James River that had been willed to him by his father. At a later period, through Thomas Rolfe's daughter, Jane, who married Robert Bolling, a family was established that became one of the leading first families of the Old Dominion. One member of this family, in later years, was Mrs. Edith Bolling Galt Wilson, second wife of President Woodrow Wilson.

Located in what is now Surry County, the Smith's Fort Plantation tract was sold in 1652 by Thomas Rolfe to Thomas Warren, a burgess representing Surry in the colonial legislature. Although it is not known definitely whether Rolfe or Warren built the Fifty-foot Brick House now standing on the site, it has been determined that the dwelling was erected in 1652 and that, according to old Surry County records, Thomas Rolfe was commonly on the property "before & after & whilst ye said house was building." The house is located two miles north of the town of Surry, Virginia, on Route 31—the Rolfe Highway.

Thomas Warren retained ownership of the place until his death in 1669. The several successive owners included, it is said, a "penurious farmer" in the mid-1880's who sold souvenir bricks from the house to tourists.

The historic dwelling at Smith's Fort Plantation would have fallen into complete decay had it not been for the generosity of John D. Rockefeller, Jr., who, in 1928, purchased the house and presented it to the Association for the Preservation of Virginia Antiquities. At that time, when Mr. Rockefeller was also engaged in restoring nearby Colonial Williamsburg, he stipulated that the association restore and refurnish the house as a public museum.

It was two Colonial Williamsburg architects, Singleton P. Morehead and A. Edwin Kendrew who, in 1934, undertook the task of returning the Rolfe-Warren House as nearly as possible to its original condition. They observed that "the appearance before restoration was that of a house on the verge of ruin." They also discovered, however, that the interior woodwork was largely intact.

In reference to its design, the house has been justly acclaimed as a masterpiece of early colonial architecture—symmetrical, well balanced, harmonious and without undue ornamentation. It is said to have been modeled after an English gentleman's country seat. Resting on a high basement of English bond brickwork, the house's main portion is of ruddy brick laid in Flemish bond. It is one and one-half stories high with a steeply pitched roof containing three narrow dormers. A modest porch leads into the building's central entrance hall.

Of particular interest in the interior is the north living room. Here, on the fireplace wall of the room, is a remarkable design of wood paneling, consisting of fluted pilasters on either side of the fireplace that lead up to an attractive cornice at the ceiling. Also on either side of the fireplace are two arched cupboards with butterfly shelves.

All rooms in the house are furnished with rare seventeenth- and eighteenth-century pieces. Among these are a formidable-looking English oak linenfold chest, dating from about 1640; a rare, late Elizabethan gros point armchair, from about 1603; a lacquered mirror, circa 1690; and a seventeenth-century Bible box and Bible, dated 1622. Here, too, are a child's chair, circa 1640, from the Rolfe ancestral home in England, and a large dough tray, dated 1611, from the Rolfe family.

Included on the grounds of the Rolfe-Warren House, an area of about twenty acres, is a replica of a small colonial garden planted in native shrubs and flowers by the Garden Club of Virginia. The quiet and fertile countryside of Surry County makes a fine setting for this house which is closely associated with the place Englishmen first put down in mainland America the roots of their heritage.

Above: The simple, unadorned wood paneling was found to be largely intact throughout the house. Below: A graceful ornamental chair, also representative of the 1600's, complements the arched cupboard with butterfly shelves built into the north room paneling.

THE MOORE HOUSE
Yorktown, Virginia
WHERE THE REVOLUTION ENDED

This brass telescope from eighteenth-century London might have been used to sight "the enemy." Now it rests on a drop-leaf Pembroke table in the parlor.

Opposite: During the siege of Yorktown, the Articles of Capitulation, which virtually ended the War of Independence, were drafted amid considerable debate at Moore House.

One of the most important historic shrines in America today is a small, unpretentious, frame dwelling at Yorktown, Virginia, now nationally known as the Moore House, because it was the scene of perhaps the most dramatic moment in American history. It was here that officers of the American and British armies drafted the Articles of Capitulation under which the British surrendered, thereby bringing an end to the large-scale fighting in the American Revolution. It was an event that made possible the birth of a new nation.

As is well known, it was the three-weeks' seige of Yorktown by the American forces under General George Washington, who also had the assistance of French troops under Rochambeau, that brought about the surrender of Lord Cornwallis and his British soldiers on October 19, 1781. Although Yorktown was under heavy American gunfire during the seige and many of its buildings were destroyed or damaged, the Moore House managed to escape any direct hit. At that period the house was owned and occupied by a leading Yorktown merchant, Augustine Moore, and his family.

After three weeks of constant shelling, Lord Cornwallis found himself in a desperate situation. His army was sapped by casualties and disease, his ammunition was running low, his food supplies diminishing, and his hope of securing reinforcements by sea had vanished when French naval ships under Comte de Grasse blockaded the Chesapeake Bay approaches to Yorktown. In a word, Lord Cornwallis at last felt himself "bottled up" at Yorktown.

Following a consultation with his staff, he decided on surrender. Accordingly, about noon on Wednesday, October 17, 1781, he sent a drummer boy with a flag of truce to a point on his defense works. There followed a parley, and the young messenger delivered a communication from Cornwallis to General Washington. It read: "Sir, I propose a cessation of hostilities for twenty-four hours and that two officers may be appointed by each side, to meet at Mr. Moore's house, to settle terms for the surrender of the posts of York and Gloucester."

By suggesting "Mr. Moore's house" as a meeting place, Cornwallis immortalized the dwelling in American history. In his reply to the message, General Washington refused a twenty-four hour

The cupboard installed in the southwest corner of the dining room in 1938 was taken from Fanshaw-Old Hall in Wakefield, England. A Salopian tea set, pewter mugs and plates and a silver muffineer line the shelves.

cessation of hostilities, but did grant a two-hour cessation during which the British commander was to outline briefly his proposals in writing. This was done, and at 4:30 that afternoon General Washington received the terms under which Lord Cornwallis agreed to surrender. Satisfied, General Washington ordered a suspension of hostilities for that night.

On the morning of October 18 the American commander replied to the British commander's original request, agreeing to a meeting of two representatives from each side. During the afternoon of that same day, as an American officer, Lieutenant Ebenezer Wild, noted in his diary: "Two Commissioners from the allied armies (American and French) met two more from the British at Moors House (which is on the right of the American lines), where the articles of *Capitulation* were agreed on." The allied armies were represented by Lieutenant Colonel John Laurens (American) and Vicomte de Noailles (French) and the British by Lieutenant Colonel Thomas Dundas and Major Alexander Ross.

It is said that the fourteen Articles of Capitulation were not agreed upon until after considerable debate. When the work was completed about nine o'clock that evening, copies of the document were taken to General Washington and Lord Cornwallis. The next day, October 19, 1781, the Articles were signed by the two commanding generals, virtually ending the American Revolution. That afternoon the British soldiers marched out of Yorktown and laid down their arms in a field south of town, an area now called Surrender Field. Two years later the War of Independence was officially and legally ended by the Treaty of Paris.

Although Augustine Moore was owner and occupant at the time of the historic event, he was not the Moore House's builder. Old records show that he had purchased both the house and a five-hundred-acre plantation around it in 1768. He continued to live in the house until his death in 1788, Moore's widow until her own passing in 1797.

There does not appear to be any conclusive information about who built the house, although one historian suggests it may have been constructed sometime before 1750 and that its builder could have been one Lawrence Smith, who had inherited the land.

Moore's will provided that upon the death of his wife, Lucy, the house was to be inherited by General Thomas Nelson, commander of Virginia militia, a signer of the Declaration of Independence, Governor of Virginia and personal friend of Augustine Moore. However, General Nelson died before Moore's widow and at her death the house passed to Nelson's son, Hugh, who in 1818 sold the dwelling to other members of his family. Finally, in 1821, the property was transferred by the Nelson family to another purchaser. During the remainder of the nineteenth century and the early twentieth century there were many owners of the Moore House.

In the meantime, the old landmark was gradually falling into ruin and was finally abandoned as a family habitation. It is said that at

Above: A well-worn rug from the late 1800's features a needle-work design of geometric squares on an alternating red and blue background. Chintz curtains partially hide the slender turned posts of the four-poster rope bed. Left: Artifacts recalling the Revolutionary period are displayed on a round Queen Anne drop-leaf table in the famous Surrender Room.

A Bible lies open on the writing arm of the dignified American walnut secretary. The Windsor armchair is believed to have been in the house in 1781.

Opposite: The handsome wooden mantel with dentil molding is painted the beige-green color popular in the colonies. The ornately framed portrait of Illingworth also typifies the colonial period.

one period the house was used as a cow barn, and at another time as a shelter for transient farm workers. When, however, the Yorktown Centennial Association was formed in 1881 to observe the one hundredth anniversary of the seige of Yorktown, the association's first move was to acquire, restore and refurnish the town's most historic landmark, the Moore House.

After the house was made habitable, it was sold to a private family because the association did not have sufficient funds to maintain it on a permanent basis. Eventually, in 1931, 150 years after the seige of Yorktown, it was purchased by the United States Government and placed under the jurisdiction of the National Park Service. This was followed by the establishment of Yorktown Battlefield as a Colonial National Historical Park.

The Moore House is, of course, of colonial design. Not too large or too highly ornamental, it is of frame construction, a story and a half high, with a central entrance portico, colonial windows and shutters, and two balanced and well-proportioned end chimneys. An outstanding feature of its exterior, however, is the hipped gambrel roof with projecting dormer windows—a characteristic of many colonial houses. A modillioned cornice at the roof line provides a pleasing decorative touch. This type of cornice derives its name from its horizontal bracket which has an Ionic volute at the outer end and a larger, reversed one at the inner end.

Inside the house there are two large, four moderate sized and three small rooms, all furnished with authentic period pieces by the Daughters of the American Revolution and other patriotic societies. A wide central entrance hall runs the full length of the house and contains a pleasingly designed stairway, with a landing, ascending to the second floor. Below the first floor, there is a brick-walled basement with an outside entrance.

In the dining room to the left of the front door are eight items believed to have been Moore family property—a silver spoon, ladle, sugar bucket and tea-strainer spoon, and four hand-painted Chinese porcelain plates. The well-worn Windsor chair in the family parlor at the rear of the house is thought to have been here in 1781.

The comfortable room in the northwest corner of the house, to the right of the entrance, is known as the Surrender Room. It is here, according to tradition, that the Articles of Capitulation were drawn up. Three pieces in this room have Moore family associations: a clear English wineglass with a conical bowl and drawn stem; an eight-inch brass candlestick with square base encircled by a beaded design; and in the middle of the room, a mahogany American Chippendale tilt-top tea table, dating from 1760-1775, on which the Articles may have been drafted. The small fireplace in the corner has a handsome but simple wooden mantel, with dentil molding, which is painted a subtle shade of beige-green favored in colonial times, as is the wainscot molding around the walls of the room, placed about two feet off the floor. Over the mantel hangs an oil portrait of an Englishman named Illingworth by Pompeo Batonni (1708-1767). The elegant style of the painting and its ornate Georgian gilt frame are typical of the late colonial and Revolutionary period.

Besides being the "first brick home west of the Alleghenies," Colonel Whitley's home
has the distinction of being the only house in Kentucky known to have its owner's initials
patterned in brick over the front entrance. "E W," Mrs. Whitley's initials, decorate the back wall.

WILLIAM WHITLEY HOUSE

Stanford, Kentucky

FIRST BRICK HOUSE WEST OF THE ALLEGHENIES

One of the oldest houses in Kentucky, that state of many old houses, has a large, curious design on its brickwork facade, a design outlining the two letters "W W." The house is located in the central part of the commonwealth just off U. S. 150, between the towns of Stanford and Crab Orchard. Now an historic shrine and public museum maintained by the Kentucky Department of Parks, this dwelling is alone among houses in Kentucky having such lettering inlaid in the brickwork over its front entrance, an inscription that obviously was placed there when the house was built.

If this lettering seems unusual, it was an unusual man who ordered its design—the builder of the house, Colonel William Whitley, whose initials the two letters are. This distinctive ornamentation enhances the decorative aspect of the residence without detracting from its architectural design and symmetry. The two-story, brick Whitley house has an historic and architectural appeal matched by few other dwellings in the Commonwealth of Kentucky.

The man who built this landmark nearly two hundred years ago, an edifice also widely acclaimed as the first brick house west of the Allegheny Mountains, was one of the great figures in Kentucky and inland American history. A contemporary, associate and fellow-frontiersman of such other celebrated men as Daniel Boone, George Rogers Clark and Isaac Shelby (first Governor of Kentucky), Colonel William Whitley often welcomed these men into his brick home for meetings and conferences on wilderness problems. In his classic work, *The Winning of the West*, President Theodore Roosevelt stated that the Whitley House was, during Kentucky's early days as part of Virginia, a center of religious, political and social life of the Transylvania region and of the Wilderness Road.

A native of Amherst County, Virginia, where he was born in 1749, William Whitley journeyed westward to the Kentucky region in 1775, the year the American Revolution began. Soon he became active in the affairs of the wilderness region into which settlers were pouring under the leadership of Daniel Boone. By 1780, he was commissioned a colonel in the region's militia. In this role, he and his men protected from Indian attack the many settlers and travelers on the Wilderness Road and Natchez Trace through Kentucky. For this work, he was granted ten thousand acres of land in the area.

Colonel Whitley won additional renown, in the years just before Kentucky was admitted to statehood in 1792, as a leader in the region's civic, political and social life and as a philanthropist and writer.

A modillioned cornice adds to the charm of the home William Whitley built in pioneer Kentucky.

157

Courtesy Kentucky Department of Public Information

The rug before the fireplace conceals the blood-stained flooring, a memento of Indian attacks. Directly above this room was a hide-out used during the frequent raids.

Evidence both of Colonel Whitley's unusual character and his staunch patriotism came with the outbreak of the War of 1812. Unable to resist the call to battle, and despite the fact that he was sixty-four years old, William Whitley promptly enlisted as a private in the army and joined the forces of General William Henry Harrison against the British. And so it was that, at the Battle of the Thames in Ontario, Canada, fought in 1813, William Whitley was killed in action. A persistent legend asserts that it was Whitley who, through his superior skill as an Indian fighter, brought about the death in that battle of the famed Indian chief and British ally, Tecumseh.

The exact date that Colonel Whitley built his house is uncertain. One which has long been accepted is 1786, but one authority suggests that it was sometime between 1787 and 1794. During the early period the Whitley estate was known as Sportsman's Hill because it overlooked the site of what is thought to have been America's first horse racing track.

When Colonel Whitley built his "first brick house west of the Alleghenies," he also introduced into the region the Federal style of architecture. Although his residence is often identified as Georgian, it is actually a more simplified variation of the colonial, a version now classified as Federal. The Federal mode of design began on the seaboard about 1780, or just after the American Revolution, and spread westward through Pennsylvania and Ohio.

As with other Federal-style houses, the Whitley edifice is oblong in mass, two stories high, and with a gabled roof and chimneys at each end of the house. Four windows and a central entrance door are at the first-floor level and five windows at the second-floor level. The rose-colored brickwork was laid up in Flemish bond with dark headers and even darker bricks which form diamond patterns on the gable ends. A handsome modillioned cornice adds to the appeal of the house. In addition to the "W W" on the front of the house, the initials "E W" for Whitley's wife, Esther, are inlaid in the brickwork at the rear.

The interior of the house is more ornamental than its exterior. In each of its rooms are furniture and period pieces of the days when Colonel Whitley and his family lived in the house, which were restored to it after 1951 when the Kentucky Department of Parks acquired the landmark and converted it into an historic shrine.

Off the central entrance hall is situated the parlor, an elegant room with a spacious fireplace and elaborately carved wood paneling on one side of it. Above the mantel are thirteen small panels symbolizing the original thirteen colonies, an ornamental touch that gives additional evidence of Colonel Whitley's individualism. Since his sturdy brick house was also expected to serve as something of a fort in case of Indian attack, the colonel placed his first-floor windows at a higher level than usual to afford added security. He also attached inner supports of iron to the heavy, hand-carved wooden doors on the first floor.

Among the interesting exhibits in the second-floor bedrooms is a four-poster cord feather bed of the type that was used in Colonel Whitley's time. The attic, or third floor of the house, was used for

Above: Thirteen carved panels above the spacious fireplace symbolize the original colonies and give evidence of Whitley's patriotism. The elegant parlor also contains a portrait of the colonel. Right: A four-poster designed after the Queen Anne style dominates one of the upstairs bedrooms.

games and dancing, as well as for spinning and weaving. It is said that during the colonel's time the attic also contained a secret hiding place where women and children might find shelter in the event of an Indian attack.

An intriguing element of the interior, which once more reveals Colonel Whitley's flair for ingenious design, is the stairway leading upward from the entrance hall to the second floor. It consists of thirteen steps, with hand-carved eagles holding olive branches adorning the stringcourse of the staircase. The newel post is highly ornamented and shaped in the form of an Irish harp, an appropriate symbol for Colonel Whitley in view of his Irish ancestry.

GEORGE ROGERS CLARK HOUSE
Louisville, Kentucky
KENTUCKY'S FAMED LOCUST GROVE

A dusty path leisurely winds its way to the north porch of gracious Locust Grove.

Of the two Kentucky houses occupied by George Rogers Clark, the bachelor-conqueror of the Old Northwest Territory (now the states of Ohio, Indiana, Illinois, Michigan, Wisconsin and part of Minnesota), the only one still standing is the Louisville plantation house widely known as Locust Grove. It was in this Georgian residence that Clark spent the last nine years of his life, living with his brother-in-law and sister, Major and Mrs. William Croghan. The house, now restored and furnished with antiques of the Clark era, is maintained as a public museum by the Historic Homes Foundation, Inc., and Jefferson County.

By the time General George Rogers Clark came to live at Locust Grove in 1809 he had already achieved wide fame as a hero of the Old Northwest, as a rugged frontiersman who, with a handful of men, took over the strategic towns of Kaskaskia and Cahokia, in Illinois, and Vincennes, in Indiana, during the American Revolution, a feat that prevented the British from capturing the Old Northwest Territory. Not only was this Virginia-born man a military genius, but he was also an outstanding Indian fighter, a colonial government leader, a spokesman for Kentucky's first settlers, and founder of the settlement at the Falls of the Ohio River that now is the great city of Louisville, Kentucky.

During his final years at Locust Grove, however, George Rogers Clark did not live a retired life. A sociable man, one who enjoyed the company of his friends, General Clark often welcomed to the house some of the most prominent men of the time. Many of these distinguished visitors also came to see Major William Croghan, member of the celebrated Croghan family of early Ohio River days. The major's uncle was George Croghan, a native of Ireland who came to America before the American Revolution and won renown as a frontiersman, trader and Indian agent west of the Alleghenies.

Believed to have been built about 1790, just before Kentucky was admitted to statehood, Locust Grove had a guest list that included three future presidents, Andrew Jackson, James Monroe and Zachary Taylor, as well as Vice-President Aaron Burr. A frequent guest was William Clark, younger brother of George Rogers Clark and a leader of the history-making Lewis and Clark Expedition through Western America. Other visitors were John J. Audubon, the celebrated artist-ornithologist; John Wesley Jarvis, the portrait painter; and Cassius M. Clay, the American political leader and diplomat.

The conquerer of the Old Northwest Territory was still living at Locust Grove when word came to him that his nephew, George Croghan, had become a hero of the War of 1812. In command of only 160 men at Fort Stephenson, the twenty-two-year-old Croghan repulsed almost a thousand British and Indians who tried to attack the fort. He later became Inspector General of the United States Army. After his death in 1849, Locust Grove was inherited by his son, St. George Lewis Livingston Croghan, who lived in the plantation house until his own death in 1861.

George Rogers Clark died at Locust Grove in 1818 at the age of sixty-six. At first he was buried in the Croghan family graveyard, but later his body was removed to Cave Hill Cemetery in Louisville.

At the time he built his brick residence in the last decade of the eighteenth century, Major William Croghan, who had earlier served with distinction in the American Revolution, was one of Louisville's most successful merchants. He had his plantation house designed in what has been called the Kentucky version of Georgian architecture. It is a two-story dwelling with a gabled roof, chimneys at

Major William Croghan (1752-1822) surveys the parlor from his position above the mantel. To the left is a cherry secretary of superb craftsmanship decorated in seven woods.

The ornate wallpaper more than compensates for the simplicity of the ballroom. The eagle
mirror over the mantel was popular in the late eighteenth century. Through the convex
glass, every part of the large room was visible to the watchful hostess, no matter where she sat.

either end, and a dignified central doorway. The horizontal effect of its facade is accented by the water table at the first-floor level and the Greek band at the second-floor level. The rose-colored bricks used in its construction, laid in Flemish bond, were baked on the Croghan plantation, and the stones of its foundation came from nearby creek beds and hillsides. Also from nearby came the native walnut and poplar trees that provided interior woodwork trim.

As most of the original Croghan family furnishings were sold after the death in 1849 of the builder's son, Dr. John Croghan, the house has since been refurnished throughout with period pieces, principally of Southern origin and contemporary with the years when George Rogers Clark lived there. An original family item, however, is the Croghan family silver tea and coffee service, which was made, circa 1810, for the major by Jean Baptiste Dumoutet of Philadelphia and purchased from one of the major's great-great-granddaughters.

In the parlor, with its spacious fireplace and paneling of unpainted walnut, there are two fine old pieces attributed by tradition to the fabulous Kentucky cabinetmaker known only as Josiah. He settled in Green County, Kentucky, in the late eighteenth century and made many of the articles of furniture in pioneer Kentucky plantation houses. The cherry secretary in the parlor of Locust Grove, believed to have been designed by Josiah around 1800, is decorated with inlay, cross-banding and stringing, in seven woods.

There are two other pieces at Locust Grove attributed to Josiah—a serpentine chest and a cherry Pembroke table. In the parlor hang portraits of Major Croghan and his wife painted at Locust Grove in 1820 by John Wesley Jarvis (1780-1834), who was at the peak of his career as a portrait painter. A portrait of Colonel George Croghan, the major's son, hangs on the walnut-paneled wall above the fireplace in the dining room. A simple but tasteful Hepplewhite table of walnut in this room is of Southern origin, as is the cherry sugar chest.

In marked contrast with the earlier rooms he slept in as a frontiersman, surveyor, soldier and Indian fighter is the first-floor bedroom that George Rogers Clark occupied at Locust Grove. It is one of the most elegant rooms in the mansion. On one side stands a cherry four-poster bed, dating from the first years of the nineteenth century and found in Fleming County, Kentucky. An authentic Clark heirloom in this room, draped over a chair, is his fringed deerskin hunting coat. A collection of early terrestrial globes which would have delighted Clark is also on display here. Many of the globes, dated 1811 and 1812, were made by James Wilson of Bradford, Vermont.

Of particular interest in this bedroom is the oil portrait of George Rogers Clark hanging on the wood-paneled wall above the fireplace. It was painted at Locust Grove by Joseph H. Bush (1794-1865), a native of Kentucky and one of the best known of that state's pioneer artists. Bush later said that although this was his first portrait, he never achieved a better likeness.

Above: A water table and Greek band accent the horizontal effect of the brick facade. Below: A collection of early terrestrial globes is displayed in the bedroom once occupied by George Rogers Clark. His fringed deerskin hunting coat is draped over the rocker at right.

Above: "My Old Kentucky Home," a two-and-a-half story
Georgian-style dwelling, is named after the song by
Stephen Foster whom it inspired. Right: A wrought-
iron gate and low brick wall surround the
Rowan family burial plot.

"MY OLD KENTUCKY HOME"
Bardstown, Kentucky
THE HOUSE THAT INSPIRED STEPHEN C. FOSTER

Two years after his marriage in 1850 to a young Pittsburgh lady, Stephen Collins Foster, now immortalized as one of America's most popular song writers, and his wife paid a visit to his cousin, John Rowan, Jr., at Bardstown, Kentucky. They were prevailed on to remain at the Rowan home, known as Federal Hill, for almost an entire summer. The house survives today and is nationally renowned as "My Old Kentucky Home," because, according to tradition, it was in this place that Foster was inspired to write his best-known song. Today, the house is a museum and historic landmark in a state park maintained by the Commonwealth of Kentucky.

There are numerous other memorials in America to the man who composed not only "My Old Kentucky Home," but "Oh! Susanna," "The Old Folks at Home," "Massa's in de Cold, Cold Ground," and many other equally popular ballads. These shrines include the Stephen Collins Foster Memorial Building in his native city of Pittsburgh; Foster Hall at the Eastman School of Music in Rochester, New York; five bridges across the Suwannee River in Florida; and a monument at Fargo, Georgia. None of them, however, have the human interest appeal that pervades the house in Kentucky, believed to have inspired Foster to write what is now the official state song.

Foster was born of a Scotch-Irish father and English mother in 1826 and wrote his first published song at the age of sixteen. Though he had very little formal education, he early showed great talent in music. When he was twenty years old, he left Pittsburgh and went to Cincinnati where he worked for two or three years as a clerk. On returning, Foster married Jane McDowell, member of a prominent Pittsburgh family, and then the couple set out on their visit to Foster's cousin, John Rowan, Jr., at Bardstown, Kentucky.

A generous, sympathetic, carefree individual, but one who always seemed to be improvident, Stephen Foster turned out to be an unsuccessful husband and his marriage failed. In 1860, just before the Civil War, he went to New York where he lived for the remainder of his days, dying penniless in Bellevue Hospital after a fall in his room in a Bowery lodging house in 1864. Foster was then only thirty-eight years old. Up until a few days before his fatal fall, Foster continued composing. During a period of twenty years he had written about 160 songs.

The delicate Waterford crystal chandelier brought from Ireland is the oldest antique in the home.

At this handsome desk, Stephen Foster composed many of his well-known songs. Made of cherry and mahogany, it is distinguished by mirror doors and hand-carved, rope-style legs.

Aside from its association with Stephen Foster, the Rowan manor house at Bardstown stands as one of Kentucky's oldest and most historic residences. It was the seat of the Rowan family, members of which played vital roles in the state's early history. First of the family to arrive in the then Kentucky wilderness country was William Rowan, who came from Pennsylvania in 1783, nine years before Kentucky was admitted to statehood. He first settled in Louisville, then moved to the vicinity of Bardstown where he quickly became active in public affairs.

At Bardstown, William Rowan placed his young son, John, in Doctor Priestly's private school, one of the first schools in the commonwealth. Later John Rowan studied law and was admitted to the bar at Bardstown in 1795. It was about this time, too, that John married and brought his bride to a small brick house he had built on the family estate of 1,300 acres just east of Bardstown. That small brick house was to provide the nucleus for the present mansion.

After being appointed Secretary of State for Kentucky in 1804 and after his election to Congress in 1806, John Rowan decided on the construction of a manor house suitable to his station. Prior to 1818 he completed an addition to his original small brick house—the two-story mansion now celebrated as "My Old Kentucky Home." He called his place Federal Hill. With his election to the United States Senate in 1824, Rowan, of course, spent most of his time in Washington, and his Federal Hill manor house was used principally as a summer home and hunting lodge.

When Senator John Rowan died in 1843 at the age of seventy, the plantation house was inherited by his son, John Rowan, Jr. In 1848, John, Jr., was appointed United States Minister to the Kingdom of Naples, and it was he who welcomed his cousin, Stephen Foster, to Federal Hill.

All told, four generations of the Rowan family occupied the estate from 1795 to 1922, when it became the property of the Commonwealth of Kentucky. Two leading architects of the state, E. J. Hutchings and G. M. Grimes, then undertook the direction of the necessary restoration work on the house and laid out a park around it. The place is now officially known as My Old Kentucky Home State Park, and hostesses, costumed in antebellum dresses, conduct tours of the manor house and its landscaped grounds. In the park's amphitheater an engaging muscial drama, "The Stephen Foster Story," is staged each summer.

Most architectural historians agree that Federal Hill is one of the best examples in Kentucky of colonial Georgian architecture. It is three stories high, of brick and stone construction, and exceptionally well proportioned, both on its exterior and interior. The brickwork was laid in Flemish bond but without the dark headers associated with some of Kentucky's other early houses. An unusual feature of the front elevation is the two narrow windows on either side of the classic entrance portal, an arrangement that antedated the use

Above: Eighteen silver dollars were used to mint each mug of this unusual mint julep set. The stately candelabra flanking it were handed down through four generations of Rowans. Left: This sturdy tester bed has the distinction of being the largest in the house.

The three-corner cupboard made in England over two hundred years ago has decorative brass butter-fly hinges.

of sidelights flanking the entrance door itself and which originated in some of the early houses of Pennsylvania, where the Rowan family first settled.

The main hall contains the most valuable piece in Federal Hill, the cherry and mahogany desk used by Foster while he visited the home. A handsome arch, supported by delicately fluted colonettes, separates the hall into two sections. A stairway in the rear section ascends to the second floor where the family bedrooms are located. On the third floor are the library of Senator Rowan and a nursery. This rear portion also contains a bedroom and first-floor doorway opening on the Rowan semi-formal flower garden, which has now been restored. At a little distance from the garden may be seen the family burial plot, also a small log room built over a stone spring house in which Senator Rowan, according to tradition, played poker with Henry Clay and some of his other fellow-lawyers.

To the left of the front entrance is the parlor. All the mantels of the fireplaces at Federal Hill are outstanding examples of the wood-carver's art, and this is especially evident in the parlor, where the mantel has dignified classical lines emphasized by double columns on each side. Here, too, are displayed such other adornments as a rosewood piano more than a century old, a Duncan Phyfe table and a hand-carved what-not of black walnut, all representative of the early 1850's when Stephen Foster was a guest in the house. Of particular interest in the parlor, however, is an oil portrait of Foster, revealing an intelligent, thoughtful, sensitive, smooth-shaven man in his late thirties.

The elegant dining room, to the right of the entrance, primarily contains American Empire mahogany furniture, the armchairs distinctive with their boldly curved arms. However, the rarest piece in the room is the two-hundred-year-old corner cupboard. Made in England, it has brass butterfly hinges and king's crown carving. The sepia-tinted, pictorial wallpaper in the dining room is the nearest to the original of any in the house. This French Colonnade pattern, its pastoral scenes interspersed with classical buildings, typifies the kind of wallpaper that was popular throughout the Atlantic seaboard, as well as Kentucky, during the mid-nineteenth century.

In the downstairs bedroom is a clustered-column tester bed with crotch-grained veneer and mahogany finish which is probably of New Orleans origin, although some cabinetmakers in St. Louis did similar work. The oval-back, American Louis XV chair in this bedroom, a forerunner of the Belter style, is similar to chairs and sofas found elsewhere in the house.

In these rooms, as elsewhere, Federal Hill displays to an ample degree the distinctive qualities of architecture, décor and human association which make it a highly suitable memorial to the popular American composer who is best remembered for a song which pays tribute to the importance of these qualities.

Above: Dominating the first-floor bedroom is a magnificent
clustered-column tester bed covered by a century-
old princess plum quilt. Left: The parlor, furnished in
the style of the 1850's, appears much as
it did when Foster enjoyed the Rowan hospitality.

Photos: Bill Tracy, courtesy Blount Mansion Association

Above and right: William Blount's home became the center of social, political and military activity for the entire territory. The mansion and outbuildings were the first frame structures west of the Appalachians.

WILLIAM BLOUNT MANSION

Knoxville, Tennessee

SEAT OF "THE FATHER OF HIS STATE"

After President Washington appointed William Blount of North Carolina in 1790 to be governor of the just-created "Territory South of the River Ohio," the new governor built a comfortable frame home at what is now Knoxville, Tennessee, and there administered the affairs of his vast territory. In this house, too, he later took the lead in founding the State of Tennessee, a role that in some quarters earned for him the title of "The Father of His State." When statehood was achieved in 1796, William Blount was elected one of Tennessee's two first United States Senators.

Still standing in Knoxville is the Blount home, built more than 175 years ago and probably the oldest frame house west of the Appalachian Mountains. In a sense, it might be called the birthplace of Tennessee. The house is now a public museum maintained by the Blount Mansion Association.

That William Blount was an exceptional man, a competent public administrator and a skillful leader of men, was evidenced early in his career. He was born near Windsor, North Carolina, on March 26, 1749, into a family prominent in the colony's affairs. His father was Colonel Jacob Blount and his mother, the former Barbara Gray, a member of an early family. When Blount was twenty-two years old, he joined his father at the Battle of Alamance fought in May 1771. Later, during the American Revolution, William served as paymaster of the Third Regiment, North Carolina Line, of the Continental Army.

On reaching the age of thirty-one years, in 1780, William Blount became Speaker of the North Carolina House of Commons. Afterwards, he served in the Continental Congress of 1782-1783 and 1786-1787 and was a delegate of the North Carolina convention which ratified the United States Constitution. In the meantime he was active as a merchant and manufacturer in his native state.

During this early period, what is now Tennessee was part of North Carolina territory. When the first settlers of the territory attempted to form a new state to be called Franklin, their effort failed. Shortly afterward, North Carolina ceded the territory to the United States Government, and it was then (1790) that the government set up the new "Territory South of the River Ohio," which was followed

A 1681 edition of the English Decalogues is on display in the parlor along with spectacles typical of the period, a quill pen and Louis-Philippe snuff box.

Above: Of particular interest in the parlor is the Persian Kirman rug in which a fox-and-grapes design, illustrating Aesop's fable, is woven in shades of burgundy and blue against a buff background. Below: A graceful pencil-post bed brings elegance to the otherwise rustic pine-paneled master bedroom.

Photos: Bill Tracy, courtesy Blount Mansion Association

by President Washington's appointment of Blount as governor. The President had been urged to name Blount to this position by many prominent North Carolinians.

Foregoing the pleasures of life among the gentry of his native North Carolina and taking with him his wife and six sons and daughters, William Blount traveled westward over the rugged Appalachian Mountains and into the wilderness country of future Tennessee. It was while journeying through the middle of the region that William Blount came upon a settlement called White's Fort, a site that greatly impressed him. He decided that here should be the seat of his territorial capital, and he laid out a town at the place, calling it Knoxville in honor of his friend, General Henry Knox, then Secretary of War in Washington.

After completing his plan for the town, Governor Blount's next step was to build a comfortable home for himself and family. This house was completed in 1792. As one of the first frame houses west of the Appalachian Mountains, the Blount dwelling was in sharp contrast to the log cabins of early settlers of future Knoxville. At the rear of the house a small separate building served as Governor Blount's territorial office. Thus the house actually served as the capitol building of the "Territory South of the River Ohio." As such, it became the center of political, civil and military affairs. And with his gracious wife and now maturing sons and daughters with him, Blount made his attractive home the region's leading social center.

As administrator of the territory, Governor Blount, through the exercise of unusual tact and diplomacy, succeeded in ending the frequent Indian attacks on the settlements within his jurisdiction. When Blount was appointed governor by President Washington, he was also named Superintendent of Indian Affairs for the territory.

Governor Blount now proceeded to organize a territorial legislature. At its first session, held at Knoxville in February 1794, the legislature voted on various proposals Blount made for the territory's development. Among them was his plan to found a college at Knoxville. This was approved and the new institution was named Blount College, now the University of Tennessee. When the governor's daughter, Barbara, enrolled in Blount College, she became, according to local tradition, one of America's first five "co-eds."

In June 1795, when the census showed that the territory had a population of 77,632—more than enough for its admission into the Union—Governor Blount made the first moves in seeking statehood for his territory. He promptly called for the organization of a Constitutional Convention and the election of delegates to it. When the convention was held at Knoxville in January 1796, Governor Blount was elected its presiding officer. He was also named to the committee for the drafting of a state constitution. After the constitution was adopted, the governor called for the selection of state officials.

Tennessee was admitted into the Union on June 1, 1796, and one of the first acts of the new state's legislature was to name William Blount a United States Senator. At a later period he was elected to the Tennessee state senate and became speaker of that body, a post he held until his death on March 21, 1800, at the age of fifty-one years. Named after him is Blount County, south of Knoxville, and the town of Blountville.

Described by the well-known Tennessee historian, John Trotwood Moore, as "the most important historic site in Tennessee," the two-story frame house that Governor Blount built here in 1792 survives today by reason of the care and upkeep of the property shown by its various successive owners and occupants. It was purchased in 1926 by the Blount Mansion Association, and since then the mansion association has completely restored and refurnished the house as it was in Governor Blount's time.

A room that arouses particular curiosity among visitors to the house is the Governor's Office, the place where William Blount administered territorial affairs. It is authentically furnished with pieces that could have been found in any frontier office of the late eighteenth century. Another unusual room, now called the parlor, was where receptions and dances were held. When the festivities were over, it was converted into a comfortable family sitting and living room. An attractive fireplace enhances one end of the room, which is painted in its original rich cream color.

In the parlor stands an imposing scroll-top secretary with a secret drawer. It originally belonged to Colonel David Campbell, a contemporary of Governor Blount. This room also contains an Oriental rug with designs of Aesop's fable of the fox and the grapes, and, above the fireplace, an elegant chimney glass, or overmantel looking glass. The centerpiece of the dining room is a handsome American Hepplewhite table with banquet ends. Around it are English Chippendale chairs. One of the bedrooms in the house is known as the Pine Bedroom, because it is paneled in North Carolina pine which Governor Blount brought to Knoxville. Its furnishings include a graceful pencil-post bed made of poplar and a Dutch clothes press, called a *kas*.

The mansion is considerably enhanced by the attractive eighteenth-century garden, now maintained by the Knoxville Garden Club, which lies at the rear of the house.

Below: Typically colonial, the kitchen stands in sharp contrast to the comfortable dining room. A trestle-type table is set with pewter plates and horn drinking cups.

Above: John Vogler built his home in the symmetrical Federal style, an innovation for the 1819 Moravian religious colony. The clockface painted on the front entrance hood indicates a shop within. Right: Artisan Vogler gave even the functional brass door handle a creative flair.

174

JOHN VOGLER HOUSE

Winston-Salem, North Carolina

A MORAVIAN SHRINE

Among the numerous restored houses in the historic Moravian community of Old Salem at Winston-Salem, North Carolina, few are more venerated by residents and visitors alike than is the 150-year-old John Vogler House. This is not only because of its excellent state of preservation and its marvelous collection of early nineteenth-century Moravian furniture and household articles, but also because of the unusual personality of John Vogler himself, the man who built the house in 1819 and who lived there until his death in 1881 at the great age of ninety-seven.

The Moravian Church, one of the earliest and best-known religious denominations in America, was founded by the followers of John Huss in Moravia and Bohemia as far back as the middle of the fifteenth century. Its followers first came to America in 1734, their emigration financed by the German nobleman, Count von Zinzendorf, who became a member of the Moravian Church. He sent four groups to this country, two to Philadelphia and two to the vicinity of Savannah, Georgia. It was from the Pennsylvania communities that members of the church went out and founded religious settlements which, with the growth of America, evolved into several large and important cities. Also from these early Moravian colonies came spiritual, cultural, educational and social contributions to the texture of American civilization. They were particularly known for their love of music which enriched their daily lives in many forms.

In the South, for example, the Moravians founded the religious colony of Salem in the northwestern part of North Carolina, settling there in 1766. Out of that community came, after 1850, the town of Winston, and the two communities were united in 1913 to form the city of Winston-Salem—now famed for its many textile mills and tobacco factories. Still surviving there, however, is the restored section of the original Moravian settlement, now known as Old Salem.

In the North, Moravians established Bethlehem, now one of Pennsylvania's largest cities, as well as the town of Nazareth, where the residence of Count Zinzendorf, the Moravian leader, still stands.

One of the most devout followers of this religious group was John Vogler, as were members of his family. Vogler was born in Friedland, about six miles from Salem, in 1783. Here he early learned to be a

The somber portraits of Christina and John Vogler are set against gaily flowered red and blue wallpaper in the parlor.

Above: The quaint yellow-tile Moravian stove brought welcome warmth to the dining room. Below: Tools of the silversmith's trade are attractively arranged in the shop where Vogler once worked.

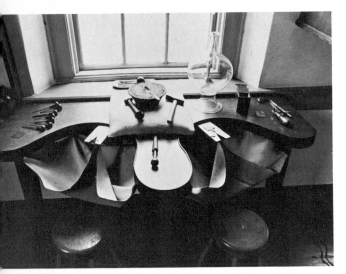

craftsman, a worker with tools, having been apprenticed to his uncle, Christopher Vogler, a gunsmith. After settling in the Moravian colony at Salem, he entered other handicraft fields, becoming a silversmith, clockmaker and general artisan. He made brass hardware, violins, surveyor's instruments, gunlocks and other items.

All of this work was done in a shop on the first floor of his house. When John Vogler first became interested in the repair and sale of watches and clocks, it seems he encountered some resistance on the part of Brother Eberhardt, a fellow Moravian and a clockmaker himself. After the brother complained to the local Moravian governing board about Vogler's new enterprise, the board ruled in favor of Vogler, saying that old Brother Eberhardt "does not attend to his work as well as Vogler, also that he often does not make these things at all, and otherwise is too high in his prices."

A further demonstration of John Vogler's versatility came after he visited Peale's Museum in Philadelphia and was impressed, among other things, with the silhouettes on display. Thereafter, Vogler became a silhouette artist of considerable skill. He is quoted as once saying, "Industry was never a burden to me and my hands generally could perform what the mind dictated."

Although a traditionalist in the Moravian faith, Vogler had a progressive outlook on the expanding American world around him, especially in the fields of industry and the mechanical arts. He watched with intense interest the birth and rise of Winston as a cotton and tobacco manufacturing center. Once, after inspecting a new cotton factory, Vogler observed, "This factory we pronounce a most excellent display of the genius and workmanship of man. . . . It is really elegant and has the sweetest machinery we have ever seen."

When he had sufficient means and the time came for him to build a substantial house in Salem, Vogler once more showed his progressive outlook by having it designed in the Federal style, which was then a building innovation for a Moravian religious colony. His house, completed in 1819, is a two-story building of brick construction and possesses all of the features of the Federal style—symmetrical lines, rectangular shape, central entrance door, window arrangement, gable roof and end chimneys. An unusual decorative touch is the clockface painted on the entrance door hood. Unusual too is the brass door handle, believed to have been made by Vogler himself.

Although the exterior of his house represents the then new Federal style of architecture, the interior follows the traditional pattern of Moravian domestic life. The rooms are furnished with Moravian pieces and household articles of the early nineteenth century, many of them belonging to the Vogler family.

Of particular interest in the dining room is a yellow tile stove designed and made by Moravian craftsmen. Here, too, is a peacock feather "shoofly," reminiscent of the days before screens came into existence. The table in the dining room is set for vesper, the Moravian mid-afternoon meal. In the kitchen may be seen, among many other useful utensils, a washing machine and a Dutch oven.

One of the most attractive rooms in the house is the parlor. Here, above a white-painted fireplace, hang oil portraits of John Vogler and his wife, Christina, painted by a local artist about 1830. In front of the fireplace are two Moravian "ear-wing" chairs. The blues and reds of the flowered wallpaper and hooked rugs in this room contrast pleasingly with the golden browns of the floor and furniture. And on a table near the master's chair and music stand rests a home-made violin, testifying to the genuine love of music that character-ized John Vogler and the Moravians in general. He once wrote of himself that he had made and played a "much praised" violin while still a young boy.

Right: The house is furnished primarily with original locally crafted Moravian pieces. Simplicity and grace mark the split-hickory rocker and straight chair made by Vogler. His walnut cradle, circa 1820, is in the foreground. Below: Two "ear-wing" chairs are drawn up to the fireplace in the colorful parlor.

ORTON PLANTATION HOUSE
Wilmington Vicinity, North Carolina
IN A MAGNIFICENT GARDEN SETTING

Photos: Hugh Morton

Eerie Spanish moss near the second-floor balcony veils a portion of the landscaped grounds at Orton.

Opposite: A luxuriant mound of red azaleas highlights the elegance of Orton Plantation House, built about 1735. The portico was added 105 years after the original section.

Situated at the center of one of the South's famous gardens, a park-like estate canopied by moss-hung live oaks, Orton Plantation House near Wilmington, North Carolina, is well deserving of such a handsome and colorful setting. Now a private home, it has been classified by most architectural historians as a singularly outstanding example of the Greek Revival style and is one of the best known of the many historic houses in the Cape Fear River country of North Carolina.

In the beginning, however, the Orton Plantation House was but a modest one-and-a-half-story building. When it was constructed, in about 1735, it did not have the imposing, two-story, classic entrance portico that now is its most impressive feature. The original builder was Roger Moore, sometimes known as "King Roger" Moore, who was a member of the distinguished Moore family of early North and South Carolina history and whose father was Governor James Moore of South Carolina. Roger was known as "King" both for his regal and "masterful personality" and for his "great generosity."

It was his brother, Colonel Maurice Moore, who led a group of younger members of North and South Carolina established families into the Cape Fear River country where, in 1725, they laid out plantations on land granted them by the Lords Proprietors of that part of the North Carolina colony. These plantations were devoted to the growing of rice of such high quality that it was frequently used as seed further south.

The first owner of the land that became Orton Plantation was Colonel Maurice Moore. But he did not retain ownership for very long, transferring title to it to his younger brother, Roger. And thus it was that, about 1735, Roger Moore built the one-and-a-half-story house on his plantation that evolved, over the years, into the majestic Orton Plantation House of today.

About this time, too, Roger Moore served on the eight-man Colony Council which advised the governor of the colony on public matters. Furthermore, he was a member of the four-man commission that fixed the boundary line between North and South Carolina. When his plantation home in the Cape Fear River countryside was completed, Roger Moore is said to have named it Orton after a town near the Moore ancestral seat in England.

Chippendale chairs flank this fine Sheraton side-board from the late eighteenth century. The legs feature spool-turnings followed by reedings.

With Moore's death in 1750, the property passed to his two sons, William and George. At a later date, the place was acquired by Richard Quince, a leading merchant of the nearby town of Bruns-wick. In addition to his commercial activities, Richard Quince was active in public life as a commissioner of the town of Brunswick, chairman of the Superior Court, a justice of the peace, a church warden and a judge of the Vice Admiralty. He died in 1778 and was buried in the church yard of St. Philip's Church adjoining Orton Plantation.

Of even greater prominence was the next owner of the Cape Fear River plantation house, Benjamin Smith, who purchased the property from Richard Quince, Jr., in 1796. When he was only twenty-one, Benjamin Smith served for a period as General Washington's aide-de-camp in the American Revolution. Later in life and after acquiring Orton Plantation, Benjamin Smith became increasingly active in politics and finally, in 1810, was elected Governor of North Carolina. Among his accomplishments as governor was the founding of the town of Smithville at the mouth of the Cape Fear River, a town now called Southport.

At a still later period in his life, however, the former governor lost much of his fortune through financial difficulties, including the endorsing of the note of a friend. Then in 1824 came the sale, at public auction, of his Orton Plantation, advertised as a plantation "containing 4,975 acres, more or less." The one-time Governor of North Carolina died a pauper in 1826 and his body was seized by creditors, which was the custom at that time. Later it was stolen by friends of the governor and buried in the grave yard of St. Philip's Church.

In that same year Orton Plantation became the property of Dr. Frederick Jones Hill, whose grandmother was a niece of Roger Moore, the mansion's builder. Besides his medical practice and his leadership in the field of public education, Dr. Hill must have been something of a connoisseur of architecture. It was he who, in 1840, enlarged the original one-and-a-half-story Orton mansion by adding a full second story and a gable roof, and by installing the magnificent entrance portico supported by four fluted Doric columns—a project that transformed it into the masterpiece of Greek Revival architecture that it is today.

In 1854 this most handsome of antebellum mansions was sold by Dr. Hill to Thomas Calezance Miller. The Millers remained here during the Civil War until it was overrun by Union troops who used it as a hospital. Just after the close of the war Thomas Miller died and the plantation came into the hands of several successive owners. About 1880, it became the property of Colonel K. M. Murchison, who had served with distinction in the Confederate Army and who, after the war, became a successful businessman.

With the death of Colonel Murchison in 1904, the Orton property descended to the colonel's son-in-law, James Sprunt. In addition to being the "Son" in the well-known cotton exporting firm of Alexander Sprunt & Son, in his later years of semi-retirement, he wrote several books on early Cape Fear history.

Above: The elaborately carved set in the north bedroom includes a
magnificent Hepplewhite bed with urn-and-spade foot design.
Left: The colorful formal gardens have made Orton
one of the South's most famous garden estates.

Above: A closer look reveals the intricate detail of the living room cornice. Below: As in most of the rooms, late Empire furnishings characterize the east bedroom.

Inasmuch as James Sprunt had presented the Orton property as a gift to his wife, the former Luola Murchison, it was he who encouraged her to add the two Greek Revival wings that contribute so greatly to the mansion's charm. This work was expertly undertaken in 1910 by Mrs. Sprunt's brother, K. M. Murchison, Jr., a prominent New York architect. He also aided his sister in the enlargement, design and planting of the estate garden that now is as much an attraction as the mansion. After Mrs. Sprunt's death in 1916 James Sprunt erected in the garden the small Luola Memorial Chapel, which also is a fine example of Greek Revival architecture.

In Orton's present version, the living room, which was the entire first floor of the original mansion, is located in its center. Measuring twenty-seven by forty-two feet, the room has dark gray marble mantels at each end. Over both are matching convex mirrors with gilded frames adorned with Pegasus figures rather than the usual eagles. The elaborate cornice and fine plaster work in the center of the ceiling were added in 1910.

To the south of the living room, in one of the 1910 wings, is the dining room with its concave dome, which is about twelve feet wide. A handsome crystal chandelier hangs from the ceiling and the walls display an impressive collection of the portraits of the Lords Proprietors of colonial North and South Carolina. A rare Daniel Quare clock, dating from about 1700, is against one wall. The Sheraton sideboard, from around 1800, has spool turnings followed by reeding; the posts project through the top and ends creating a turned-button effect.

The grounds and gardens surrounding the house are today more spectacular than ever. When James Sprunt died in 1924, Orton Plantation was willed to his son, James Laurence Sprunt. In 1934, he greatly enlarged his mother's garden, making Orton into one of the South's most famous garden estates. Its walks, terraces and pools abound with pine, cedar and magnolia trees, live oaks, camellia, japonica and azalea and other flowering plants.

Perhaps the loveliest of the gardens at Orton is the Scroll Garden on the lower terrace to the east of the house. Viewed from the charming white-painted belvedere to the north, the garden is outlined and punctuated with gracefully curved podocarpus hedges and features azaleas and pansies in the spring and ageratum and marigolds in the summer. Beyond are the rice fields, which now serve as a wild fowl sanctuary, and the broad Cape Fear River. The classic white-columned mansion, the colorful and varied gardens and grounds, and the uncluttered countryside surrounding the estate combine to present one of the most memorable sights to be found anywhere in the South.

Top: The dining room, occupying one of the 1910 wings, displays a collection of portraits of North and South Carolina's Lords Proprietors. Left: The first floor of the original house now comprises the living room. Matching dark gray marble mantels with unusual Pegasus mirrors above are at each end. The elaborate cornice and center of the ceiling are 1910 additions.

FORT HILL

Clemson, South Carolina

PLANTATION HOME OF JOHN C. CALHOUN

During the years when John C. Calhoun was serving as Secretary of War, Vice President of the United States, Secretary of State and United States Senator, he lived, when not in Washington, at Fort Hill, the large plantation house he owned at what is now the town of Clemson in his native state of South Carolina. His official duties in the nation's capital did not occupy all of his time. There were many intervals, each year, when he could relax on his thousand-acre plantation near Pendleton. It undoubtedly would have pleased him, had he lived long enough, to see that his plantation house, standing on its original site, is now part of the campus of Clemson University, a leading institution of higher learning founded by his son-in-law, Thomas G. Clemson.

The spacious plantation house where lived the man known in American history as "The Voice of the South" is now open to the public as a period museum and is maintained by the South Carolina Division of the United Daughters of the Confederacy. It was in 1825 that John C. Calhoun became owner of Fort Hill and its surrounding plantation. He proceded to enlarge the house and to add to it the white-columned porticos and other architectural details that are so attractive today. The original portion of the house was built about 1803 by the Reverend James McElhenny, who called it Clergy Hall. McElhenny was pastor of the nearby Old Stone Church, which still stands near Clemson. After Calhoun bought the place, he renamed it Fort Hill because it was the site of a small palisaded fort during the American Revolution.

Here, Calhoun was to live, when not absent in Washington, for the next twenty-five years, Here, too, he and his wife, Floride, were to raise seven surviving children out of a total of ten. And it was at Fort Hill that the Calhouns welcomed and entertained many of the most famous and glittering personalities of the antebellum era. Mrs. Calhoun was described as highly educated, a talented musician, a prominent leader of Washington and Southern society, and an ardent Episcopalian.

When John Calhoun moved into Fort Hill, he immediately focused national attention on it. He was then Vice President of the United States under President John Quincy Adams, and was re-elected in

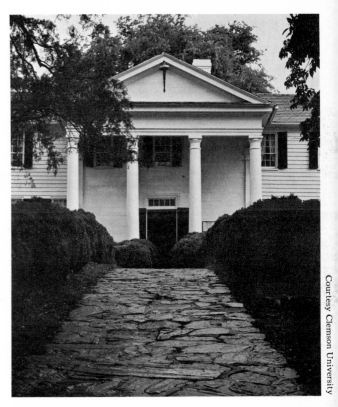

A hedge-bordered stone walk leads to the entrance of the imposing plantation home where the "Voice of the South" lived.

Opposite: Fort Hill, a rambling fourteen-room frame structure, is located on the Clemson University campus which was founded by Thomas Clemson, Calhoun's son-in-law.

Above: According to tradition, the carved eagles on the back of the George Washington sofa were a model for the design of the first American silver dollar. Above the sofa hangs a portrait of Anna Calhoun Clemson. Below: The sideboard was given to Calhoun by Henry Clay after one of Calhoun's speeches defending the Constitution.

1828, this time under President Andrew Jackson. He continued to make Fort Hill a showplace while later serving in the United States Senate, where he made such an impact on the history of this nation as a champion of states' rights and the Doctrine of Nullification.

A native of Abbeville, just south of today's Clemson, John Calhoun was born on a frontier farm in 1782, the son of Scotch-Irish parents. His father died while he was still a young boy and his early education was limited. He managed, however, to enter Yale University in 1802 and, after his graduation, studied law and became a practicing attorney in South Carolina. In 1811 he was elected to his first term in Congress, where the dynamic, good-looking Calhoun first gained a national reputation as one of the most eloquent of the War Hawks agitating for war with Great Britain.

From that time onward, John Calhoun remained in public life until his death in Washington in 1850 at the age of sixty-eight. He was buried in the churchyard of St. Philip's Episcopal Church at Charleston, South Carolina. His widow survived him by sixteen years, passing through the strenuous period of the Civil War. She died in 1866. At that time, however, she was living in nearby Pendleton, having relinquished occupancy of Fort Hill to her son, Andrew, in 1854. He remained here until his own death in 1865.

One of the most glamorous social events in the history of South Carolina was the marriage, in the parlor at Fort Hill, of a Calhoun daughter, Anna Maria, to Thomas Green Clemson, which occurred in 1838. Well-educated, talented in numerous other fields besides that of his profession, Thomas Clemson was a consulting mining engineer, having received his training in the city where he was born, Philadelphia. After he was appointed American chargé d'affaires to Belgium, he and his family lived in that country for some years. But after the death of John Calhoun in 1850, the family returned to America in 1852 and lived for a while in Maryland. Then, in 1872, Fort Hill passed into the hands of the Clemsons and thereafter it was their home. Here, Mrs. Clemson died in 1875 at the age of fifty-eight. Her husband continued to live in the plantation house until his own death in 1888 at the age of eighty-one.

In his will, Thomas Clemson provided for the founding of a college on the grounds of the Fort Hill plantation, and there Clemson University opened its doors in 1893. Since the year it was founded, the university has also maintained the historic Fort Hill plantation house as a memorial to the Calhoun and Clemson families, carrying on his work in cooperation with the United Daughters of the Confederacy of South Carolina.

Designed in the Southern Colonial style, the Calhoun house is an attractive white, two-story dwelling of frame construction, with a gable roof, end chimneys, and a large, central entrance portico of Greek Doric design rising to the full height of the two-story facade. The house is set in the midst of a spacious lawn and plantings of hundreds of luxurious English boxwood shrubs and century-old trees.

A little beyond the lawn stretched what the Calhouns liked to call their Friendship Garden. Here, among other trees and flowers, stood a fine hemlock given to Calhoun by his fellow statesman, Daniel Webster, as well as an arborvitae, also presented to him by another

On either side of the handsome English spinet piano are brass floor candelabra, each holding nineteen candles, from Dumbarton Oaks, the Calhouns' Washington home. Portraits of the Clemson children, Floride and John, were painted during the family's stay in Belgium.

Above: In the outside kitchen are many heavy iron cooking vessels representative of the mid-nineteenth century. The sturdy pine table at left holds baking utensils from the Calhoun family. Below: Sunlight filters across the native rock floor, highlighting a once-indispensable spinning wheel.

fellow statesman, Henry Clay. One more gift was a varnish tree from Madagascar, sent by Commodore Stephen Decatur. Still standing today on the grounds of Fort Hill are such outbuildings as Calhoun's office or library, a kitchen and a springhouse.

There are fourteen rooms in the house, nearly all of them furnished with original Calhoun and Clemson family heirlooms. Among objects of interest in the ornate entrance hall are Calhoun's desk, pier table, mirror and banjo clock. In the parlor are two pieces of furniture that once belonged to George Washington—a Windsor-type chair and a Duncan Phyfe-style sofa, which is an especially fine example of colonial furniture. It is upholstered in black horsehair and the black mahogany frame is elaborately carved. Curving, twisting dolphins form the legs; the straight back is broken at each end by a deep oval which frames the head and wings of a serpentine eagle.

These pieces came into the Clemson family through the marriage of Thomas Clemson's sister to Samuel Washington, grandnephew of the first President. The parlor also contains a small English spinet, with a music book on it, used by Mrs. Calhoun when she was a young girl. A chair and tiny footstool, upholstered in crimson velvet, were presented to the Clemsons by King Leopold I of Belgium.

In the State Dining Room, where the Calhouns entertained so many distinguished guests, attention centers on the Duncan Phyfe African mahogany banquet table and its twelve matching chairs. Here, too, is a sideboard presented to John Calhoun and made from mahogany paneling that originally came from the officers' quarters of the famous frigate *Constitution*, known as "Old Ironsides." On the top of the sideboard is Mrs. Calhoun's elegant silver coffee urn engraved with her initials. The oil paintings in the dining room are of John Calhoun and his wife, Floride. A side table contains a chest of Calhoun silver. The "Berry Patch" wallpaper blends well with the gold velvet drapes framing the long, narrow windows and the original green and gold cornices over the windows.

In addition to a large oil painting of Calhoun, the master bedroom of the house displays a combination wardrobe-bureau designed by Mrs. Calhoun and modeled after the one used by Dolley Madison. But of particular interest here is the four-poster canopied Calhoun bed, said to have been the one used by the Marquis de Lafayette when he was an overnight guest of the Calhouns in Washington during his triumphal return visit to the United States in 1825.

John C. Calhoun died a man haunted by the future. He saw "dark forebodings." "I would die happy if the Union could be preserved," he said, although he knew otherwise. It is well that his beloved Fort Hill survived along with the Union, for its quiet distinction serves well to recall the life and times of one of the nation's finest statesmen.

Above: The mahogany bed in the master bedroom was
reportedly used by Lafayette in 1825 when he visited the
Calhouns in Washington. The attractive chintz spread was
made by Calhoun's daughter, Cornelia. Left: An epergne
of silver and cut glass provides a graceful centerpiece
for the Duncan Phyfe table in the State Dining Room.

JOSEPH MANIGAULT HOUSE
Charleston, South Carolina
AN ARCHITECT'S MASTERPIECE

Entrance to the Manigault House is gained through the charming circular gate lodge, an unusual substitute for the wrought-iron gate typical of early Charleston.

Opposite: In its upward sweep toward the second-floor level, the circular staircase dramatically frames the antique crystal chandelier in the entrance hall below.

Among the numerous architects who, in the eighteenth and nineteenth centuries, designed many of the fine old mansions still standing in Charleston, South Carolina, one of the best known was Gabriel Manigault. Today, one of his most admired works is the masterpiece he designed for his brother, Joseph Manigault. This house, standing on its original site at 350 Meeting Street, has been restored and refurnished by the Charleston Museum and is now open to the public as an early nineteenth-century period museum.

Although Gabriel Manigault was influenced by the architect brothers, Robert and James Adam, he managed to create a style that was highly individual, that showed his own flair for architectural design and ornamentation. This capacity is revealed in other Charleston buildings he created and which were to affect a later generation of city architects, such as South Carolina Hall, built in 1804; the First Bank of the United States, built in 1801, later to become City Hall. The Joseph Manigault House is dated 1803.

The Manigaults, among the earliest of the French Huguenots to settle in South Carolina, had long been one of the state's most distinguished families. The founder of the family in America was Pierre Manigault, who had embraced the Protestant faith in France and so laid himself open to religious persecution. Manigault was among the many Huguenots who fled to America where they settled in various colonies, including South Carolina. In the years following, the Manigault family apparently prospered. One of Pierre's sons, Gabriel, who was to become the grandfather of the architect, is recorded as having been among the wealthiest men in South Carolina during colonial times. The family was a leading one in pre-Revolutionary days when Charleston was the social, political, cultural and economic center of the South, a city containing many handsome town houses of the wealthy and aristocratic planters of South Carolina.

Gabriel Manigault, the architect, did not begin his career as an architect. A few years before the outbreak of the American Revolution in 1775, he was sent abroad to study law at Geneva and in London. He later returned to Charleston and was present in his home

Above: Every portion of the house offers the same aesthetically pleasing detail as the hand-carved door and frame to the ballroom. Below: The chest-on-chest, which can be separated into three traveling trunks, is an outstanding example of the craftsmanship of Charleston cabinetmaker Thomas Elfe.

city when, during the War of Independence, the British, under Sir Henry Clinton, captured and occupied Charleston from 1780 to 1782.

During this period, too, he showed increasing talent in the field of architecture, a talent that eventually became genius. With the close of the American Revolution, Gabriel Manigault apparently renounced his allegiance to the Crown and became active in the formation of the new State of South Carolina. His principal contribution was in the creation of private homes and public buildings.

In designing and supervising the construction of his brother's house in 1803, Gabriel Manigault built better than he knew. For the house has survived quite a few calamities that have struck Charleston during its long and colorful history. In addition to several large fires, the South Carolina city was bombarded twice—once during the American Revolution when the British captured it, and once during the Civil War when Northern cannon raked it. In addition to manmade disasters, there have been hurricanes, tornadoes and earthquakes.

During the long years of the nineteenth century, the Joseph Manigault House passed through the hands of a number of successive owners and gradually deteriorated. When the decision was made to demolish the house, it was bought for taxes by Princess Pignatelli, who presented it to the Charleston Museum. Since then, the house has been restored and refurnished in the early Federal period.

It is generally believed that this house represents Gabriel Manigault at his best in the field of domestic architecture. Usually described as late Georgian, the house has unique Gabriel Manigault touches and refinements that greatly enhance its appeal. As with so many early Charleston houses, this one is fronted by a low brick wall. Instead of a wrought-iron gate, however, the entrance here is a circular gate lodge of classic design, an outbuilding much admired by visitors.

The house itself, situated on a wide green lawn, is three stories high, of brick construction, with a hip roof and with another characteristic feature of Charleston architecture—a two-story piazza on its front elevation. It was on these piazzas that Charlestonians found relief and comfort during the torrid summer months. The Manigault residence also has an open semi-circular bay on the north enclosing the stairway. This stairway ascends from the first to the second floor in a sweeping curve bringing the spacious hall to a grand climax directly opposite the entrance from the piazza. Hanging near the staircase is a magnificent crystal chandelier, a gift from Princess Pignatelli.

The interior rooms of the Manigault mansion are tastefully furnished with pieces that harmonize with the delicacy and lightness of the mansion's mantels, doorways, ceilings and cornices. Some are the work of famous Charleston craftsmen such as Thomas Elfe.

Among the notable pieces which grace the home are a clothespress bearing the label of its maker, a Rice bed, a chest-on-chest in

Above: The classical lines of the English-made,
Grecian-style couch and chairs form a pleasing contrast to
the ornate Waterford crystal chandelier and hand-carved
cornice-work. Left: The rectangular balcony
of the Georgian-style home is partially supported by
a series of elaborate iron brackets.

the bedroom, and two Charleston-made sideboards in the dining room. Also of interest in this room are the mahogany Sheraton Grecian-style chairs, dating from around 1810. Each is inlaid with a silver plaque bearing the crest of the Mathews family, descendants of the man who was Governor of South Carolina during the American Revolution.

Perhaps the mansion's outstanding room is its elegant ballroom. The walls are French gray, which was the original color of the room according to paint scrapings. The design of the apricot and gold silk curtains is appropriate to the period. The fireplace is faced in pink marble and the double columns of the mantel are repeated on each side of the door. Over the mantel is a large, almost full-length, portrait of Mrs. Peter Manigault, painted by an eighteenth-century Charleston artist. The English-made Grecian-style couch and chairs, dating from around 1810-1815, were once the property of the United States Minister to Great Britain, General Thomas Pinckney, of Charleston. This room and the others in the Joseph Manigault House are eloquent reminders of the gracious way of living of early nineteenth-century Charleston.

Courtesy The Charleston Museum

Fine Charleston-made antiques grace the entrance foyer, but the focal point is the breathtaking sweep of the stair-case which swings up past the delicate chandelier.

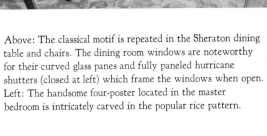

Above: The classical motif is repeated in the Sheraton dining table and chairs. The dining room windows are noteworthy for their curved glass panes and fully paneled hurricane shutters (closed at left) which frame the windows when open. Left: The handsome four-poster located in the master bedroom is intricately carved in the popular rice pattern.

Above: A most eminent example of the Adam style, the Nathaniel Russell House in Charleston has its characteristic delicacy and grace. Right: One of the home's three oval rooms, the library, contains a revolving Sheraton drum table. A portrait of Nathaniel Russell by John Wesley Jarvis hangs above the relief-decorated mantel.

NATHANIEL RUSSELL HOUSE
Charleston, South Carolina
IN THE BROTHERS ADAM STYLE

If any house in America might be selected as this country's most outstanding example of the brothers Adam style of architecture, that honor could well be claimed for the Nathaniel Russell House in Charleston, South Carolina. Both its exterior and its interior have all of the lightness, grace, delicacy and fine proportions of the popular eighteenth-century Adam style of architecture and interior design, a style originated in London by the Scots-born architects and brothers, Robert and James Adam. Built shortly before 1809, this residence is now not only a public museum but the headquarters of the Historic Charleston Foundation, which maintains many of the historic houses in the famed old Carolina city on the Atlantic Coast.

In his time, the builder of the mansion, Nathaniel Russell, was one of the most successful merchants of Charleston and of the South. But he was not a Southerner by birth, coming originally from Rhode Island, where his father was a chief justice of that state's Supreme Court. After settling in Charleston before the American Revolution, in 1769, Nathaniel Russell forged rapidly ahead as a merchant. He also became president of the Charleston New England Society, and, as such, was known to some of his friends as "The King of the Yankees."

It was rather late in his life when Nathaniel Russell decided to build the mansion on the then new and fashionable Meeting Street that would one day outrank many of the residences of his fellow-merchants. He must have completed his elegant house sometime before 1809 since he is on record as living in it by that year. It is said that he spent more than $80,000 on it—a large sum in those days—and he employed the best architects and craftsmen in Charleston, who were the most skillful in the South.

Although the name of the mansion's principal architect is not known, there is a belief in some quarters, according to Talbot Hamlin, the noted architectural historian, that it might have been the conception of Russell Warren, one of the great architects of early Rhode Island days who went down to the South and designed some of Charleston's most distinguished houses.

In 1809, an outstanding social event occurred in the new Russell house when Russell's eldest daughter was married to Arthur Middleton, of Stono, nephew and namesake of South Carolina's distinguished Revolutionary War leader and a signer of the Declaration of Independence. When, in 1811, a tornado unroofed his house, and broke windows and furniture, Nathaniel Russell promptly repaired the damage at a cost of $20,000.

Members of the Russell family continued to live in the Meeting Street mansion until 1857 when it was sold to Governor Robert F. W.

A free-flying staircase ascending from the first to the third floor has slender banister rails of Honduran mahogany which add to the feeling of lightness and the sweeping curves of the apparently unsupported stairs.

Above: The second-floor bedroom, with walls of Wedgwood blue and white, has a bed of New York workmanship, probably from Duncan Phyfe's shop. Below: A large mahogany Chippendale-style breakfront bookcase of the eighteenth century is found in the Russell library.

Allston of South Carolina. Besides being a public official, Governor Allston was one of the foremost planters of his time and won wide recognition for his scientific advances in the growing of rice.

Following Governor Allston's death in 1864, the Nathaniel Russell House served for some time as a school, and was then occupied by two successive private owners. Few alterations were made during these years and thus its Adam-style exterior and interior were preserved. It was in 1955 that this unique architectural landmark was purchased by the Historic Charleston Foundation, assisted by a grant from the Richardson Foundation and by public donations.

Since then, the house has been restored and its rooms furnished with period pieces, none dated later than 1820. Here may be found furniture from England, Ireland, France and Italy, as well as many pieces from early cities on the Atlantic seaboard and from early days in Charleston. All of this elegant furniture is of the kind that a wealthy merchant such as Nathaniel Russell would have owned.

From the street, one observes, behind a low brick wall topped by an ornate wrought-iron fence, a three-story brick residence with a four-sided bay projecting from one wall of the house into a garden. The facade, in its entirety, is a pleasing Adamesque composition, employing two kinds of brick as well as marble, wood and wrought iron. An unusual decorative feature here are the high attenuated arches spanning the second-floor windows, which open on a wrought-iron balcony. An ornamental parapet on the roof of the house provides an elegant finishing touch for its front elevation.

Inside, one is immediately astonished by a remarkable sight in the entrance hall—a free-flying staircase that, apparently unsupported, swings upward in sweeping curves to the third floor. It is a sight that no other Charleston house can offer. Also of interest in the entrance hall are an oil painting said to be of a governor's son, often attributed to the English artist, William Hogarth (1697-1764), an antique New England clock, a stenciled Sheraton-style settee dating from 1810 and a pair of black-lacquered armchairs.

In laying out the floor plan of his house, Nathaniel Russell followed the Adamesque formula of a square room, an oval room and a rectangular room. The reception room in his house is rectangular in design. Among its outstanding features are the Karabagh rug, of about 1800, and a pair of Chinese Chippendale chairs, upholstered and with elaborately carved legs.

There are three oval rooms in the residence, made possible by the three-story bay projecting outward into the garden. The oval room on the first floor is the library. Striking, with walls of Pompeian red and buff woodwork, it contains interesting pieces such as a Sheraton revolving drum table and a globe, dated 1799, with a compass in its base. The library mantel contains a relief of the god Bacchus and his chariot against a Wedgwood-blue background. Over the mantel is a portrait, by the American artist John Wesley Jarvis (1781-1839), of the builder of the house at the age of eighty-one.

In the oval Gray Room on the second floor may be seen numerous pieces of approximately the Russell period. The Empire settee here is American, but the harp on one side of the room is French, the work of Erard Frères. Also French is the *vernis-Martin* armchair, one of a collection of such chairs brought back from France to Charleston in 1797 by General Charles C. Pinckney, member of the famous Pinckney family of diplomats and statesmen. He had been sent to France on a government mission by President Adams. An

eighteenth-century French painting over the fireplace mantel may have been an original Russell family possession. It belonged to Alicia Middleton, of Bristol, Rhode Island, a great-granddaughter of Nathaniel Russell.

Among objects of particular interest in the handsome dining room are numerous examples of Charleston-made furniture. The solid mahogany dining table came from a noted South Carolina plantation house, Spring Grove, and is set with part of a collection of China Trade porcelain in orange and gold that was popular during the early days in South Carolina. The Hepplewhite-style chairs around the table are, however, from New York. A sideboard in the dining room, of crotch mahogany veneered on pine, is from another noted early South Carolina house, Ophir Plantation.

On the second floor a bedroom with walls of Wedgwood blue and white was restored and furnished in memory of Josephine Pinckney, founding trustee of the Historic Charleston Foundation and a noted author. The canopied, four-poster bed here is of New York workmanship, believed by some to be from the shop of Duncan Phyfe, the celebrated American furniture maker. The side chairs and sewing table in the room may also have come from the same shop.

Across the front of the house on the second floor is the distinguished green drawing room. The carving and stuccowork of the window and door frames and of the ceiling cornice constitute some of the finest Adam ornamentation to be found anywhere. The slender recessed double columns on each side of the doorway match those of the window frames, while its architrave displays iris and honeysuckle in relief. The mantelpiece has single columns and an inner facing of white marble.

As a consequence of the care and superb workmanship which Nathaniel Russell expended on his house, it displays in almost every room the perfections of delicacy, gracefulness and balance which are the hallmarks of the Adam style.

One of two elaborately furnished drawing rooms on the second floor, the oval Gray Room has an American Empire settee, and a French harp by Erard Frères.
The eighteenth-century French painting may be part of the home's original furnishings.

ROBERT MACKAY HOUSE
ANDREW KILPATRICK HOUSE
Augusta, Georgia
Two Houses from Colonial Georgia

Among the many handsome colonial and antebellum mansions in eastern Georgia, few are older and more historic than the Robert Mackay and Andrew Kilpatrick houses in the Savannah River city of Augusta, Georgia's second oldest community. Both survive from the days when Georgia was one of the thirteen colonies, and both are associated with outstanding episodes in the state's long history.

One of the most tragic and atrocious events in the South during the American Revolution occurred in the Mackay dwelling, which, both before and during the war, was widely known as Mackay's Trading House. It was here that, in 1780, Colonel Thomas Brown, an Augusta Tory fighting on the side of the British, executed thirteen wounded American soldiers by hanging them over the stairwell on a porch—each victim representing one of the thirteen colonies. Slightly wounded himself, Colonel Brown observed the gruesome spectacle from a nearby bedroom, feeling that at last he was exacting vengeance for having been tarred and feathered a few years earlier by the American patriots of Augusta.

The hanged soldiers were his prisoners, captured from the troops who had attempted to dislodge him and his own men from his headquarters at the Trading House. When the Americans were driven off by the arrival of British reinforcements, they had to abandon twenty-nine of their wounded. After the thirteen were hanged, the remaining sixteen were turned over to Indian allies of the British, who put them to death by slow torture. At the end of the war, Colonel Brown fled the country to settle on a grant of land in the British West Indies island of St. Vincent, where he died in 1825.

The actual building date of the Robert Mackay House is not firmly established. The story of the house begins with its Savannah River site, part of a five-hundred-acre tract of land granted to Thomas Red, a Virginia planter, in 1757. Red retained the property until 1761 when he sold it to John Francis Williams, a trader among the Cherokee Indians of colonial Georgia. The consensus is that it was either Thomas Red or John Williams who built the Robert Mackay House sometime in the four-year period between 1757 and 1761. As was often done at the time, the house was built large enough to serve both as a home and a place of business.

Above: Thirteen wounded American soldiers were hanged over the porch stairs of the Mackay House in 1780 by Tory Colonel Thomas Brown.

Opposite top: Horseshoe stairs flanked by graceful iron railings lead to Augusta's handsome Andrew Kilpatrick House. Opposite bottom: The Robert Mackay House was widely known as a trading center by both colonists and Indians in the 1770's.

Above: Eighteenth-century English brass andirons and fender grace the finely molded fireplace in the Mackay drawing room. The Sheraton-style pianoforte case is believed to be by Duncan Phyfe. Right: A Chinese Chippendale bed and Southern pine chest-on-chest are the focal points of a first-floor bedroom.

Not until after Robert Mackay became a business partner of John Williams in about 1768 did the house become widely known among colonists and Cherokee Indians alike as Mackay's Trading House. As with many Scots of that day, Robert Mackay had a marked talent for making friends with the Indians. When he became sole owner and occupant of the Augusta trading house in 1770, Mackay set up subsidiary trading stations among the Cherokees, placing clerks in charge. But the Augusta establishment remained the focus of his extensive trading operations.

At some date prior to 1775, Robert Mackay acquired a new business partner, Andrew McLean, and the trading firm became known as Mackay and McLean. However,Robert Mackay died soon afterwards, during the year of the outbreak of the American Revolution. Andrew McLean then gained full control of the company, and when Mackay's former partner, John Francis Williams, died in that same year, Andrew McLean married his widow, Catherine Williams. At the time of the Colonel Brown atrocity in the Mackay Trading House in 1780, there were no members of the Mackay family living in the Savannah River mansion.

In the years after the War of Independence, the Mackay dwelling came to be known locally as the White House. It had been assumed that, because one Mr. McCall, writing in 1811, asserted the dwelling "was designated the White House," it had been a white-painted house from the beginning. When the building was restored in 1956, however, the Georgia Historical Commission, discovering that the white paint had not been applied until late in the nineteenth century, returned the house to its original color—grayish blue.

After the house was designated as "an important example of fast-disappearing early American architecture" in 1934 by the Historic American Buildings Survey of the United States Department of Interior, it was transferred to the Richmond County Historical Society. In 1956, the society conveyed it to its present owners, the Georgia Historical Commission.

When the commission retained the services of the late Thomas G. Little, noted historical architect, to restore the house, he stated that it was "the finest example of colonial frame residential architecture south of the Potomac." The building is two and a half stories high, with a gambrel roof, chimneys at each end, clapboarded exterior and a cornice featuring dentil decoration. Of commanding interest is its two-story porch, which occupies the entire front and is supported by square columns.

At the suggestion of Mr. Little, the Georgia Historical Commission furnished the interior of the Robert Mackay House in such a way that antique pieces and household articles of the eighteenth century are displayed on the first floor, relics and other material pertaining to the Southern theater of operations during the American Revolution are exhibited on the second floor, and memorabilia associated with the early traders among the Cherokees is on the third floor.

The entrance hall contains an exquisite small Queen Anne-style maple tea table, circa 1750. In the dining room a mahogany banquet table in the style of Duncan Phyfe, dates from about 1790. This is complemented by mahogany eighteenth-century American Chippendale side chairs.

Perhaps the outstanding room in the house is the drawing room with its finely molded, yet simple, blue-painted wood mantelpiece surmounted by a pair of single-arm ("mantel-arm") brass lamps, a

This silver tea service, circa 1790, at Mackay House is engraved with the initials "ACT" for Ann Clay and her husband, Thomas Cummings, first Intendent (Mayor) of Augusta.

The Kilpatrick mansion is often referred to by local people as "the house of a thousand chandeliers," as their crystal prisms are reflected in the home's many mirrors.

Above: A nineteenth-century Empire sofa, upholstered in green velvet, is a luxurious complement to the Carrara marble mantel and pier mirror in the Kilpatrick House living room. Below: The home's dining room is warm and gracious, featuring an eighteenth-century harvest table, and ladder-back chairs from Virginia.

large antique Oriental Kashmir rug and three smaller Oriental rugs; a silver tea service, circa 1790, engraved "ACT" for Ann Clay and her husband, Thomas Cumming, the first Intendent (Mayor) of Augusta; and an early nineteenth-century piano with a Sheraton case believed to have been made by Duncan Phyfe. Most of the rooms have Venetian blinds which accurately reproduce the blinds that were so popular in eighteenth-century England and America.

Another Augusta landmark is the colonial eighteenth-century Andrew Kilpatrick House. Built in the classic Georgian style in 1761, it is another example of a dwelling built both as a home and a place of business. In colonial times it served as a wayside inn and relay station for the changing of horses on the old stagecoach road from Charleston, South Carolina, through Augusta, to Athens, Georgia.

When the great French statesman and general, Marquis de Lafayette, paid a return visit to the United States in 1824-1825 and traveled through the South, it was from the handsome Doric portico of what is now the Andrew Kilpatrick House that the celebrated Frenchman addressed the people of Augusta. An outstanding wedding and social event took place in this house later when Joseph Emerson Brown, the Civil War Governor of Georgia, married Miss Cora McCord, daughter of Zachariah and Harriet McCord.

Then, in 1896, Mrs. McCord took in as a boarder a young medical student from the Medical College of Georgia. His name was Andrew Jones Kilpatrick. Although he graduated from the medical college that same year, Dr. Kilpatrick chose to remain a boarder in Mrs. McCord's home. And so it came about that in 1900 Dr. Kilpatrick married his landlady's daughter, Miss Jennie Lou McCord. The Kilpatricks continued to live in the old house at Seventh and Greene streets, and in the years following it became widely known as the Kilpatrick House.

As time passed, however, and the streets of central Augusta grew increasingly crowded and nosier, Dr. Kilpatrick became restless and finally announced to his wife that he would like to move to a new location on The Hill, a residential section where life was quiet and peaceful. When his wife objected, saying she did not want to leave the old house, Dr. Kilpatrick immediately made plans to move the entire house to a new location at 1314 Comfort Road on The Hill. This was done in 1929 at a cost of $40,000. Included in the project was the planting of nearly mature magnolia trees on the new site.

Today, the revered old Andrew Kilpatrick House is one of the handsomest—both inside and out—of the many fine old homes in Augusta and the Savannah River countryside. It was recently purchased and restored as a private residence by Dr. and Mrs. A. J. Bollet, both professors at the medical college.

Walking up the graceful horseshoe stairs with their iron railings at the front of the house, the visitor passes through a Doric portico and a fanlighted doorway into a mansion of surpassing elegance. Here are spacious rooms with Carrara marble fireplaces, crystal chandeliers and attractive antique furniture.

Local people often call the old Kilpatrick mansion "the house of a thousand chandeliers" because of an optical illusion created by its crystal chandeliers and its numerous mirrors. At each end of the mansion's double parlor are French gold-framed pier mirrors, and over the mantel is hung another gold-framed pier mirror, and all of these, when the crystal chandeliers are lighted, create the spectacu-

lar illusion of an endless vista of glittering prismatic chandeliers—a unique effect that few old mansions of the South can offer. This double room is further enhanced by fine plaster work on the cornices and over the archway.

Other distinctive features here include the fireplace, which is embellished with one of the several unusual wrought-iron fire screens in the house, and some eighteenth-century English brass fireplace tools. The swag curtains are based on a pattern designed by Thomas Jefferson and were made in Charlottesville, Virginia, for Kilpatrick House. Here, too, is a John Rogers (1829-1904) chalkware group, "Going to the Parson."

The horseshoe staircase at the back of the house, duplicating the one in front, overlooks a charming garden and a pool, a fitting culmination to the oldest house in historic Augusta still serving as a residence.

The spacious and airy hallway of Kilpatrick House, with its "keystone" arches, holds an eighteenth-century grandfather's clock, antique organ and a handmade reproduction of a pedestal desk. The room's wide floor planks are of virgin Georgia pine.

Above: Greek Revival in style, the Jones Plantation House near Millen, Georgia, seems an almost spectral symbol of the architecture and history of the Old South. Right: The porticoed, white-columned entrance porch of two stories at Birdsville was added to the home in 1847.

JONES PLANTATION HOUSE
(BIRDSVILLE)
Millen Vicinity, Georgia
SAVED FROM GENERAL SHERMAN'S TORCH

Had it not been for the courage and heroic resistance shown by the mistress of the Jones Plantation House in southeast Georgia during General Sherman's famous and devastating March to the Sea, the mansion would have gone up in flames and Georgia would have lost one of its oldest antebellum residences, dating back to just after the close of the American Revolution. A porticoed and white-columned residence, it is located on its original magnolia-shaded site some twelve miles from the town of Millen. The house, with its plantation, is also known as Birdsville.

When General Sherman and his Union troops were marching through Georgia during the Civil War, a detachment of his men surrounded the Jones Plantation House and took immediate charge of the property. Then, noticing what appeared to be two freshly dug graves in the family cemetery, the soldiers began to uncover them, thinking that the family silver might be buried at the two sites. What they found instead were the remains of twin infants who had died a short time after their birth, the children of Mrs. William Beaman Jones, mistress of the Birdsville plantation house.

Still confined to her second-floor bedroom, Mrs. Jones watched horrified while the Union soldiers violated the family cemetery. She then watched them light a torch to apply to her plantation home. When the troops demanded that she get out of bed and leave the house, Mrs. Jones refused, insisting that she would rather burn to death than leave her home. In the face of such feminine resolve, the Union troops withdrew from her bedroom, extinguished the blaze they had begun at the basement level, and continued on their way. On that day in 1864 which was so terrifying for the mistress of the mansion, her husband, Dr. William Beaman Jones, was away from home, serving in the Confederate Army. Mrs. Jones was the former Sidney Ann Elizabeth Sapp, member of an old family of the region.

Although a state historical tablet near the plantation manor asserts that its original portion was built by Philip Jones in 1767, this date is believed to be incorrect by the present mistress of the mansion, Mrs. Ben (Jones) Franklin, Sr., a great-great-granddaughter of Philip Jones. Long research on the subject leads her to the con-

Corinthian columns, always elements of stature and grandeur, are found as supports on the plantation porch, and used as embellishments on the corners of the home.

clusion that the Birdsville plantation house was completed between the years of 1784 and 1789, or just after the American Revolution.

Among family records is a document, dated 1784, showing that Philip Jones had been granted a bounty tract of 287 acres in southeast Georgia for his services in the American Revolution, the date of the grant being 1784. A later plot of the land shows the Birdsville plantation house standing on this tract. Since Philip Jones died in 1789, five years after he acquired the tract, Mrs. Franklin concludes that the original portion of the house must have been built at some time between 1784 and 1789.

After the manor house was completed at the close of the American Revolution, a small settlement grew up around it and this was called Birdsville, after the village's first postmaster, Samuel Bird. In addition to having a post office, Birdsville possessed a wayside inn for stagecoach travelers on the road from Savannah to the state's second capital at Louisville, a road that passed through the Jones plantation. At a later date, Dr. William Beaman Jones, son of Philip, established an apothecary shop, or small drug store, at Birdsville.

It was Dr. Jones who, in 1847, made the first major addition to his ancestral seat. This was the porticoed, white-columned entrance porch at the front of the house, designed in the Greek Revival style, which was then a popular architectural mode. The Jones porch is two stories high, supported by four handsome Corinthian columns. Then during the 1880's, the Victorian style came into vogue, and with it another addition to the house—two characteristically Victorian bay windows on the front of the mansion. But these additions did not destroy the symmetry of the edifice; in fact, they enhanced its visual appeal.

As the dwelling place of five generations of the same family—something of a record in Georgia—the Jones Plantation House has an interior rich with old family furniture, heirlooms, relics and memorabilia, all attractively arranged in its various rooms by Mrs. Ben Franklin, Sr. Among the noticeable features of the interior are the numerous big wardrobes that served a family living in a house with only one built-in closet on its first floor. A curious exhibit in the mansion is a sterling silver pitcher won by Dr. William Beaman Jones in 1851 at a fair in Macon, Georgia, for having the best jackass at the fair. A likeness of the animal is embossed in silver on the pitcher. Another valued article is an ancient family watch made in Savannah and bearing the date 1794.

Among other articles of interest in the plantation house are "grandmother's biscuit table," on which thousands of biscuits were made over the years; an eighteenth-century flintlock musket; numerous old deeds, documents and maps; samples of the family silverware covering a period of more than a hundred years; and jars of arrowheads and other Indian relics found on the plantation.

Of all of the exhibits, however, few have greater appeal than the small walnut bed—dwarfed by a big four-poster bed next to it—in which Mrs. William Beaman Jones was lying ill on that day in 1864 when she defied General Sherman's soldiers. The soldiers went on their way marching through Georgia, and Mrs. Jones saved for posterity one of the truly historic landmarks of the Old South.

The large piano in the parlor at Birdsville was brought from New York by mule and wagon in 1829. Atop it are various family portraits and a Portuguese scale, a gift to the parents of Mrs. Ben Franklin, Sr., in 1895.

Above: The interior of Jones Plantation House is rich with collections and memorabilia of the family. In the dining room, a massive rounded-end sideboard and glass-doored cabinet hold the silver and crystal of five generations. Left: A variety of nineteenth-century pieces fill the mansion's comfortably furnished dining room.

ISAIAH DAVENPORT HOUSE

Savannah, Georgia

HOME OF A MASTER BUILDER

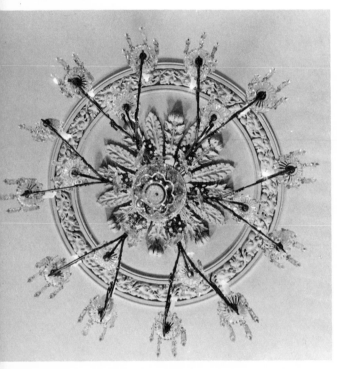

Davenport House in Savannah has some exceptionally fine ornamental plaster moldings, and among the best is the drawing room's ceiling medallion, which is patterned in an elaborate acanthus-leaf design.

Opposite: The austere lines of this three-story English brick residence are softened by the double semi-circular stairway and handsome wrought-iron balustrade.

A 150-year-old house built for himself by a master house builder survives today as one of the most elegant of the many distinguished old mansions in the time-hallowed city of Savannah, Georgia. Now a museum as well as headquarters of the Historic Savannah Foundation, Inc., it is widely acclaimed as the only colonial Georgian-style residence of its period left in Savannah.

The man who erected the mansion, completed in 1820, was Isaiah Davenport, a young master builder from New England and also a member of the noted Davenport family of that region. His great-grandfather was the Reverend John Davenport, a controversial clergyman of the Puritan faith and one of the two founders of New Haven, Connecticut. The builder's father was Jonathan Davenport, who distinguished himself in the Revolution. Another ancestor was John Davenport, a famous eighteenth-century English potter.

A native of Little Compton, Rhode Island, where he was born in 1784, Isaiah Davenport was only two years old when his father died, leaving his mother to bring up the family. At an early age, young Isaiah was apprenticed as a designer and builder of houses at New Bedford, Massachusetts. Then, at the turn of the nineteenth century, he went south to Savannah and there became a professional house builder. In 1809 he married Miss Sarah Rosamond Clark, a native of Beaufort, South Carolina.

Three years later he bought a parcel of land at State and Habersham streets, opposite Columbia Square in Savannah, and planned a comfortable home for the site. But he was not immediately able to realize his ambition because all of his time was taken in fulfilling the many commissions he was now receiving for the design and construction of homes. When, however, a national depression occurred in the second decade of the nineteenth century and all construction work came to a halt in Savannah and elsewhere, Isaiah Davenport finally had time to design the home he had long dreamed of for his choice tract of land.

Construction started in 1815, and the growing Davenport family was happy to move into the home from their small cottage. But their happiness was not to endure, for in 1827, just seven years after com-

Above: Handmade hanging lamps of brass illuminate the home's entrance hall, with its free-standing bone-white columns. Below: In the drawing room, muted colors on the shield-back chairs and settee and on Chippendale side chairs contrast with dark woods and flooring.

Photos: Courtesy Mrs. E. N. McKinnon

pleting his residence, Isaiah Davenport died at the age of forty-three. In addition to his widow, he left a family of six sons and one daughter. Since he died without a will, his estate had to be settled in the courts and by means of a public auction.

Eventually, Mrs. Davenport found herself in reduced circumstances and for a time was forced to take in boarders. Nonetheless, she managed to educate her children. A handsome woman, she was described as "sturdy" and "capable." The family lived in the Columbia Square home until 1840 when Mrs. Davenport, who lived fifty years after her husband's death, sold the house to William Baynard and moved to another location in Savannah. The house remained in the Baynard family until 1954.

Said to have brought up her children "to think for themselves," Mrs. Davenport allowed her sons to make their own choices in the Civil War. Two of them fought on the Union side and two with the Confederacy. Of these four, two were killed in action. As for the only Davenport daughter, Cornealia, she married General Henry Rootes Jackson of the Confederate Army, also a distinguished Georgia lawyer, judge and diplomat. In 1885 President Cleveland appointed him minister to Austria.

Although she had been forced many years earlier to relinquish her role as mistress of the mansion overlooking Columbia Square, Mrs. Davenport, in the years after the Civil War, became something of a legendary figure. A favorite story told of her during the war concerns the day in 1864 when some of General Sherman's Union troops, after their March to the Sea, surrounded Mrs. Davenport's carriage and insulted her.

Undaunted, she immediately ordered her coachman to drive to General Sherman's headquarters in Savannah. There, she reprimanded the general for the lax discipline of his troops and demanded protection. When she pointed out that two of her sons were fighting on the Union side, General Sherman promptly assigned an escort to see her safely home and also placed a military guard at her house for the remaining days of the Savannah occupation, the only house in Savannah to receive such protection.

In the years after 1840, when Mrs. Davenport sold her Columbia Square residence, the house passed through the hands of many successive Baynard family heirs and gradually deteriorated. Eventually, it became a tenement with eight families living under its roof. However, in 1954, when it was announced that the old landmark would be torn down to make way for a parking lot, seven women civic leaders promptly organized the Historic Savannah Foundation, Inc., for the purpose of saving and restoring one of the city's finest old mansions.

In designing his Savannah residence, Isaiah Davenport showed remarkable ability in the harmonious blending of various architectural styles both inside and out—styles as diverse as colonial Georgian, English Regency and Greek Revival. Although comparatively small in scale, the Davenport residence makes up in appealing design and attractive ornamental detail what it lacks in size and spaciousness.

The rich hue of the mahogany Sheraton dining table made about 1850 is complemented by place settings of rare Davenport china and silver. The candlesticks are also original Davenport pieces.

A Hepplewhite sideboard, circa 1790, in the dining room of Davenport House, is surmounted by a platter and tureen of English Davenport china. The portrait, after Gilbert Stuart, is of an unknown man.

At that time, many of Savannah's leading mansions were in the English Regency style, popularized by one of Savannah's most brilliant young architects, the Englishman William Jay. But Isaiah Davenport ran counter to this trend and designed his house—at least its exterior—in colonial Georgian, a style he grew up with in New England. His brick dwelling, revealing most of the familiar elements of the Georgian mode, has three stories over a full English basement, a gabled roof, dormers and twin end chimneys joined by parapet walls. The classic entrance portico is approached by a double semi-circular stairway with delicate wrought-iron handrails.

In contrast to its severely simple exterior, the interior of the house displays a skillful blending of the Georgian style with the newer Regency and Greek Revival styles. This is immediately apparent in the central entrance hall, which is painted in antique gold and embellished by a classic elliptical arch supported by two white, free-standing Ionic columns. Beyond the arch a circular stairway, with an attractive handrail, winds upward to the mansion's fourth story, or attic. A grandfather's clock, English tables, hanging brass lamps and Oriental rugs complete the hall's ornamentation.

To the right of the hall is the drawing room, acclaimed as one of the most beautiful rooms in Savannah. The elaborate plaster cornices, hand-carved woodwork and the acanthus-leaf ceiling medallion contribute much to the room's elegance. The door and window frames repeat the leaf motif in their corner medallions. From the ceiling hangs a French ormolu and crystal chandelier with eighteen candles. At each end, elliptical arches, supported by Ionic columns, add to the apartment's charm, as does an Italian marble mantel. Tastefully arranged about the room are Chippendale side chairs, a Queen Anne tea table, a settee and oil portraits on the walls.

Equally attractive in atmosphere and furnishings is the Davenport dining room. Occupying its center is an American Sheraton table, set with Davenport china, silverware and candlesticks. The room also contains a fine Hepplewhite sideboard, circa 1790, made in Baltimore. On it is a silver wine strainer, created in London about 1791 by Robert Hennell, as well as two old Sheffield candelabra. The oil portrait above, after Gilbert Stuart, is unidentified, but the one above the fireplace is that of General Charles Williams, a distinguished Georgian.

Upstairs a central hall with an archway and columns divides four large bedrooms and a dressing room. These rooms are the most recently restored and they hold most of the treasured mementos of the Davenport family, such as memory books and an 1827 inventory of the house. The two fourth-floor bedrooms with dormer windows have not been restored or furnished at the request of students of architecture who thus have more accessibility to the superior examples of materials and workmanship there from earlier periods.

Above: Off the drawing room is a small
sitting room containing several fine
Chippendale pieces. Left: An antique
cherry four-poster bed with a quilt
coverlet in a rich floral pattern graces
the room known as the "small" bedroom.

215

XIMENEZ-FATIO HOUSE

St. Augustine, Florida

A REMINDER OF THE SPANISH RÉGIME

One of the oldest houses in St. Augustine, oldest city in the United States, is the Ximenez-Fatio House. It is believed to have been built sometime between 1797 and 1802, which was during Florida's second Spanish régime. Now open to the public at 22 Avilés Street as an historic house museum, it is maintained by The National Society of the Colonial Dames of America in the State of Florida.

Showing evidences of Spanish, English and American colonial architecture, the Ximenez House was built by Andrés Ximenez, an early merchant of St. Augustine. Old Spanish records reveal that he purchased the lot on which his house stands in 1797. When, in 1802, Ximenez made a will, he stated, among other things, that he owned the lot and the house on it in which he lived. From this evidence, it seems that Andrés Ximenez, whose father-in-law was a master carpenter, built his dwelling between 1797 and 1802. A general store he operated was located in his house or in an adjoining outbuilding.

Here, then, Andrés Ximenez lived and conducted his business in the historic town near which, in 1513, Ponce de Leon discovered Florida and claimed it for Spain, the town that was founded in 1565 by Pedro Meméndez de Avilés and became the first permanent settlement in Florida. Although Spain ceded Florida to England in 1763, the English relinquished it to Spain twenty years later as part of a trade which returned the Bahamas to England .

When Andrés Ximenez built his St. Augustine house, Florida was still in the hands of the Spaniards. It was not until 1821 that Spain ceded the territory to the United States. Florida remained a territory until 1845 when it became the twenty-seventh state.

As it happened, either just before or just after Ximenez completed work on his house, his wife became ill and died, leaving the St. Augustine merchant with the task of bringing up two small sons and a daughter. They were later placed in the care of their mother's sister, Mrs. Gregorio Suarez. When Ximenez made out a second will in 1806, just seven days before his own death, the document revealed that he had been a man of considerable means. Among items

Opposite Top: Ximenez-Fatio House, dating from the late eighteenth century, is built of coquina stone and stucco. The picturesque buff-cream town house shows the influence of Spanish, English and American colonial architecture. Opposite bottom: The main room contains intricately carved, Spanish-style walnut pieces of late seventeenth-century vintage.

Above: The kitchen building displays hickory ladder-back chairs, a pierced tin lantern and various brass and iron cooking vessels. Below: Paintings of the Washingtons, a needlepoint fire shield and a rare Geib piano complete the English colonial atmosphere of the music room.

Photos: Courtesy National Society of the Colonial Dames of America in Florida.

listed in the inventory of his estate, besides merchandise, were his furniture, china and crystal ware, and his belongings in gold, silver and other precious metals.

After their father's passing, the three Ximenez heirs rented the two-story family home to a number of successive tenants. At one period the first floor of the dwelling was leased to Don Ventura Boix, who, at a sale of Ximenez's effects, purchased most of the storekeeper's merchandise and household furnishings. At that same period the second floor of the house was occupied by William Cook, who also had bought some of the Ximenez effects.

By 1830, however, the three Ximenez heirs had sold their interests in the house to Mrs. Margaret Cook, described as "the widow of Samuel Cook." What relation, if any, her husband was to the previous tenant, William Cook, is uncertain. She sold the house in 1838, and seventeen years later it was purchased by Miss Louisa Fatio, daughter of Don Francisco Felipe Fatio, for $3,000. It is said that after Miss Fatio acquired the house, it became "quite famous as a winter residence" where she welcomed many distinguished visitors. Miss Fatio lived here for twenty years and, because of this long occupancy, the dwelling is now usually referred to as the Ximenez-Fatio House. After she died in 1875, her heirs sold the property to David L. Dunham, a Fatio descendant. The last private owner of the place was Dunham's son, David R. Dunham, who, in 1939, sold the house to The National Society of the Colonial Dames of America in the State of Florida.

In several ways, the Ximenez-Fatio House bears a close resemblance to St. Augustine's oldest dwelling, the Hernández House. Both are two stories high, rectangular in shape, built flush with the sidewalk and covered with hipped roofs. The Ximenez House, however, features a second-story, cantilevered gallery or balcony and dormer windows in its roof—additions that might have been made by later English and American owners of the building. Painted a light buff-cream color, the exterior walls of the house are made of coquina stone and stucco, the former brought from the coquina rock quarries on nearby Anastasia Island.

At the back of the house there is a recessed, centrally located loggia and an extensive ell addition. Here, too, is a rectangular gabled kitchen building with two rooms, one the kitchen itself with a chimney and wall oven and the other a pantry.

Since acquiring the house in 1939, members of The National Society of the Colonial Dames of America in the State of Florida have carefully and tastefully refurnished it with late eighteenth-and early nineteenth-century pieces of the Ximenez and Fatio periods. In the main room on the ground floor a Spanish star lighting fixture hangs from the ceiling which retains its original cedar beams. Two intricately carved early eighteenth-century walnut chairs beside the fireplace and a handsome, carved storage chest strongly suggest the Spanish influence. The room also contains a seventeenth-century Moorish-style, carved stretcher table. In the beamed-ceiling library are two Savonarola chairs, a small Spanish stretcher table and a fine collection of books on Florida history.

The music room is furnished in the period of St. Augustine's occupancy by the English. George and Martha Washington are depicted in reverse paintings on glass which hang above the fireplace. An antique Yezd rug from Turkey covers the floor. The kitchen building contains a pierced tin lantern from around 1790, ladderback chairs of hickory and numerous copper, brass and iron utensils.

In addition to the picturesque street which it faces, the Ximenez-Fatio House is enhanced on the north side by an attractive garden, informally laid out in a series of flower beds, concrete walks and various types of bushes and palm trees. The cumulative effect is one completely appropriate to a landmark dating from the days of old Spanish Florida.

The library contains Savonarola chairs, a Spanish stretcher table and a fine collection of books on Florida history. As in the other rooms, the original ceiling beams are exposed, revealing the dwelling's sound construction.

FORT CONDÉ-CHARLOTTE MUSEUM HOUSE

OAKLEIGH

Mobile, Alabama

ON THE FAMED AZALEA TRAIL

Among the many distinguished antebellum homes in Mobile, Alabama, two are of particular interest because of the fidelity with which they represent the period of 1825-1860 when Mobile, due to its position as the principal city for exporting cotton from Alabama's rich agricultural Black Belt, was one of the South's most gracious cultural and social centers. These two are the Fort Condé-Charlotte Museum House (also known as the Kirkbride House), most historic dwelling in this "City of Five Flags," and Oakleigh, official mansion of the Historic Mobile Preservation Society. Both houses are open throughout the year as period museums, with many splendid examples of furnishings, from the French, Spanish, English, Confederate and American eras in Mobile history.

The Fort Condé-Charlotte House derives its name from the fact that it stands within the perimeter of Fort Condé de la Mobile, built of brick by French colonists under Jean le Moyne Bienville in 1717. It replaced an earlier and larger wooden structure, Fort Louis de la Mobile, also built by Bienville and the French, and named after the Maubila tribe of Indians in the region. It was from another tribe, the Alibamus, that the state received its name. Since the building of a fort was always Bienville's first move in founding a colony, Fort Louis de la Mobile marked the birthplace of the present huge seaport city of Mobile.

Antique silk draperies with pressed brass cornices and tiebacks in an acorn design harmonize with the elaborate antique rug in the Confederate Room. A three-piece rosewood set fashioned in the French rococo style is included among the furnishings in this typical Southern parlor of the 1850's.

Thigpen Photography

Photos: Thigpen Photograph

Above: On the second-floor level, slender
Corinthian columns connected by a crowfoot
banister enhance the delicate appearance
of Fort Condé-Charlotte House. Right: The
wrought-iron railing in the back Confederate
parlor encloses part of the brick flooring
(circa 1822) from the old jail.

222

One of the earliest French colonists in Mobile was Fifise Langlois, who, according to old records, planted the first azalea bush in Mobile in 1711, bringing the flower from his native Toulouse in France. Today, the azaleas blooming with handsome white, red and pink flowers in February and March, bring as much fame to the city as do its white antebellum houses.

When the Treaty of Paris was signed in 1763, ending the French and Indian War in America, the victorious English won not only Canada but all of the territory east of the Mississippi River, including the future State of Alabama. Although the French garrison at Fort Condé de la Mobile withdrew from the stronghold, most of the French colonists remained in the town. The name of the fort, however, was again changed, this time by the English, to Fort Charlotte in honor of the young English queen who reigned at that time.

During the American Revolution, the Spaniards captured Mobile in 1779 and held the city for the next thirty-four years. In 1813 the United States took possession of it, claiming it part of the Louisiana Purchase. When Mobile was incorporated as a town in 1814, a portion of the old fort property was converted into the town's first courthouse and jail. The historic fort remained standing until 1820 when it was demolished, although some of its foundation stones were left intact.

From what local historians can gather, it was in about 1822 that Peter H. Hobart built the original portion of the two-story residence now standing on part of the old French fort site. At a later period, during the 1840's, the house was acquired by Jonathan Kirkbride, who came to Mobile from Mount Holly, New Jersey. He is believed to have converted the old jail into his family residence. Part of the old jail floor and doors are still evident.

During the Civil War, when the Confederate flag flew over Mobile, the Fort Condé-Charlotte House did not suffer any damage in the Battle of Mobile Bay won by Admiral David Farragut in 1864, nor was it damaged during General R. S. Canby's capture of the city in 1865 and his restoration of the American flag to the community. In the years following, a number of successive owners have been in possession of the Fort Condé-Charlotte House. Finally, in 1940, it was purchased for a headquarters building by the Historic Mobile Preservation Society.

During World War II the house served as an officer's club for the United States Navy. With the aid of public donations, the society restored and refurnished the residence in 1944-1945. Then, in 1957, the society relinquished control of the property, and the National Society of the Colonial Dames of America in the State of Alabama purchased it from the City of Mobile and has maintained it as a museum house since that date. The Historic Mobile Preservation Society took control of Oakleigh and established its official headquarters there.

Built of brick and covered with smooth stucco, the Fort Condé-Charlotte House is architecturally interesting for its two-level gallery or veranda. In contrast to the four rather thick Tuscan columns on the first-floor level of the gallery are the four slender Corinthian columns at the second-floor level. The upper veranda also has a wooden banister of crowfoot design, which provides an additional ornamental touch.

Above: An elegant silver coffee service rests in a wood-lined silver tray below a portrait attributed to John Wesley Jarvis.

223

In keeping with the rich historical background of both the house and its site, each room in the residence has been refurnished with pieces reflecting different periods in Mobile's long and colorful existence. These include an English Room with pieces dating from 1763 to 1780, a French Room with Empire-style furnishings and a Confederate Room done in the manner of a Southern parlor between 1850 and 1860. One of the most popular rooms is the dining room, representing America's early Federal period and furnished with an attractive collection of pieces from the years 1812 to 1825. Especially interesting are a banjo clock by Simon Willard and an 1812 oil painting of Captain Thomas Swift attributed to John Wesley Jarvis (1781-1839). Displayed on a serpentine cherry and mahogany chest are a silver coffee pot, sugar bowl and creamer made in 1812 by the famed silversmith, Simon Chaudron.

In its setting of venerable oaks on what was known in early years as Simon Favre's Old Spanish Land Grant, the residence called Oakleigh survives today as one of the finest examples of Greek Revival architecture in Alabama—dignified, symmetrical, well proportioned. Shaded by ancient oaks and surrounded by a well-planned arrangement of azalea bushes, it is an appropriate home for the Historic Mobile Preservation Society.

The four brick pillars on the ground floor are rectangular; the wooden pillars on the gallery of the second level, which is the principal floor of Oakleigh, are square, tapering slightly at the top. The graceful, curving outside staircase which leads from the middle of the first-floor gallery to the main entrance door on the right side of the second-floor gallery is a striking feature without counterpart.

In view of the purity of its architecture, Oakleigh, surprisingly enough, was not designed by an architect but by a wealthy Mobile merchant, James W. Roper, who served as his own architect and contractor. It was in 1833 that Roper first began building his house, supervising slaves who, among other things, made bricks for the first floor from clay dug and baked on the Roper property. They also prepared the hand-hewn lumber used on the house's second floor.

As his own architect and contractor, James Roper, however, seems to have taken considerable time to complete his residence. It is said that the dwelling was "practically completed" by 1838 when the builder brought his new bride to the home he had designed. Another account has it that as late as 1852 some of the interior "was still unfinished." Whatever delays occurred, James Roper, it is generally agreed, achieved a Greek Revival masterpiece in his Mobile mansion. After the house passed out of the Roper family, it was acquired by various successive owners. For more than sixty-four years Oakleigh was occupied by members of the Irwin family.

Now restored and refurnished this unique landmark is literally an enchanting museum of early Victorian, Empire and Regency furniture, mementos and heirlooms. Especially notable is the second-floor Walton-LeVert Drawing Room, part of a double parlor, containing some of the possessions of the South's most famous belle, Madame Octavia Walton LeVert. Much has been written about her that is not verifiable, but she was a lady of great charm and ability who traveled widely and spoke several languages. She was a famous

Madame LeVert's portrait by Thomas Sully hangs above the rosewood piano in the Walton-LeVert parlor. According to Washington Irving, the charming belle was "a woman as appears once in the course of an empire."

Opposite: The front ground-level section of Oakleigh, originally divided from the rest of the house by a brick wall, had a hard-packed clay floor and was used as a cellar. The second story is actually the main floor of the mansion.

The east parlor, as viewed from the Walton-LeVert parlor, reveals the nearly floor-length Victorian pier mirror strikingly complemented by deep red draperies threaded with gold. Over the white marble mantel is a similar gold-leaf rococo mirror.

Opposite: Representative of the mid-nineteenth century are the portrait over the mantel, a world globe from Scotland, and the six-arm rococo chandelier in the library. The mahogany secretary-bookcase is a Victorian piece showing the influence of the Empire style.

hostess and, during the 1850's when Oakleigh was one of Mobile's most important centers of social activity, Mrs. LeVert maintained at her home elsewhere in the area (now demolished) what some have claimed was the only true salon of the period in this country. Among the close friends with whom she corresponded were Edwin Booth, Henry Wadsworth Longfellow, G. T. Beauregard, Millard Fillmore, Washington Irving and Henry Clay. She was apparently the first American woman presented to Queen Victoria.

The draperies in the LeVert drawing room and the other room of the double parlor were woven in France of deep red silk and strands of spun gold for a Louisiana home in the late 1850's. The swags were specially dyed and woven by Franco Scalamandré of New York City to be used with the draperies. Empire and early Victorian furniture, upholstered in silk and striped brocade, varies in color. The heavily carved rosewood piano dates from 1850. Two large oil portraits in the room are of Madame LeVert, painted by the celebrated American portrait artist, Thomas Sully (1783-1872), and of her husband, Dr. Henry S. LeVert, by the early Mobile artist, Thomas S. Officer.

This elegant room and other rooms in Oakleigh, Fort Condé-Charlotte House and other antebellum mansions in Mobile recapture well a colorful time and a way of life that is indelibly part of this region's living past.

ELGIN PLANTATION
CHEROKEE
HOLLY HEDGES
THE BRIARS

Natchez, Mississippi

LANDMARKS OF EARLY NATCHEZ

All the features of an elegant Victorian parlor are present in that of Elgin from rose-carved horsehair chairs and stools to an ornate what-not and gilt mirror.

The historic old town of Natchez, Mississippi, high on a Mississippi River bluff contains the largest collection of antebellum plantation houses of any city in America—rich in history, legend, architecture and authentic period furnishings. The most grandiose of these homes date from the period between 1815 and the Civil War when the combination of cotton and the steamboat made Natchez one of the wealthiest towns in the country. However, four of its most distinguished houses date from a slightly earlier period—Elgin, Cherokee, Holly Hedges and The Briars.

As a result of the French and Indian War and the Treaty of Paris, in 1763, the area came under British domination. During the American Revolution, however, the Natchez region was relatively neutral and the Spanish, taking advantage of the situation, moved in around 1779. They remained until the American flag was raised at Natchez in 1798, and it was during this Spanish period that Elgin, Cherokee and Holly Hedges were built.

Elgin mansion, in its park-like setting of moss-draped live oaks and magnolia trees, may be considered the earliest of the houses from the Spanish period because the oldest part of the structure was occupied in 1780. The rooms in this section of the house, such as the dining room, have low ceilings, typical of Spanish colonial dwellings. When the plantation house was purchased in 1840 by Dr. John Carmichael Jenkins, a physician as well as a noted horticulturist, he built an almost new residence around the early 1780 section. This enlargement, in which all rooms have high ceilings, now comprises the front, or main, part of Elgin.

It was just one year earlier that Dr. Jenkins had married Annis Dunbar, granddaughter of William Dunbar, a Scotsman who settled in Natchez during the Spanish régime and became a planter and large landowner. The belief is that Dr. Jenkins purchased Elgin Plantation because it was originally part of a land grant given to William Dunbar by the Spanish authorities. The place was named

Courtesy the Pilgrimage Garden Club

Elgin by Dr. Jenkins after a Dunbar family property in Scotland.

Upon settling down at Elgin Plantation, Dr. Jenkins began the planting, cultivation and study of fruit trees. His orchard became widely known for its luscious fruits and berries. He also experimented in the grafting of trees, a field in which he paved the way for the latter-day plant wizard, Luther Burbank. In all of this work, Dr. Jenkins kept a strict written record, and many of his notes, diaries, observations and letters are in the Library of Congress.

After Dr. Jenkins and his wife died of yellow fever during the epidemic that struck Natchez in 1855, Elgin was owned and occupied by the doctor's eldest son, Captain John F. Jenkins, who continued his father's interest in horticulture. Descendants of this family sold the property in 1914 to Thornton Green, a Northerner who formerly lived in Michigan. At the present time Elgin Plantation is owned and occupied by Mrs. W. S. R. Beane and family.

The Elgin house has all the inviting charm expected of an early Southern plantation residence. It is a white, two-story, frame dwelling with a gable roof that sweeps out over spacious double galleries supported by eight slender Doric columns. All windows opening on the upper and lower front galleries have "Gibbs doors"—that is, doors under the windows which can be opened for further ventilation during hot humid weather.

All rooms in the house have been refurnished with pieces of the Jenkins era. Here, too, are many items from The Oaks at New Albany, Mississippi, ancestral home of the present owner Mrs. Beane. Of special interest are Elgin's double parlors, which are on the left as one enters the house from the ninety-foot front gallery. The furniture is upholstered in the original horsehair. In each parlor are matching pier mirrors, eleven and a half feet tall with marble-top consoles. Between the parlors is a great black marble fireplace, flanked on either side by high double folding doors that reach from floor to ceiling.

The oldest portion of historic Elgin was probably built during the Spanish period, around 1780. After its purchase in 1840 by a well-known physician and horticulturist, Dr. John Jenkins, the home was greatly expanded, and named after a family property in Scotland.

229

The beautiful grandfather's clock in the hall, made in Liverpool by Hadwin in 1720, is a family heirloom from the Warwicks of Virginia and England. The hall leads into the low-ceilinged dining room, which dates from the Spanish period. Its unusual floor of "blue" poplar (tulip poplar) displays, along with darker wood tones, wide blonde streaks frequently found in this wood. A punkah, a hand-hewn oaken fan, is suspended above the mahogany table. In antebellum days it was the duty of a Negro child to pull the punkah's cord to keep the flies away.

The graceful stairway with tapering spindles and mahogany hand-rail leads to the second floor and several large bedrooms. One of these contains a four-poster bed which Jefferson Davis once slept in, as well as a rarity for the period—a closet.

One of the most conspicuous of antebellum Natchez houses is Cherokee, named after an early tribe of Indians in the region. Built in 1794, this house is also among the oldest in the city. Its conspic-uousness arises from its location on top of a small hill at Wall and High streets. A series of stone steps lead up to Cherokee's impres-sive, recessed Greek Revival entrance.

In its long history, this house has had numerous owners who were prominent in early Natchez. Old Spanish records reveal that the original portion of Cherokee was built in 1794 by Jessie Greenfield, member of a well-known Natchez family who had been given a grant of land on the hill by the Spanish authorities. Constructed of brick, the original dwelling now forms the mansion's rear section. In 1810, it was sold to David Mitchie, well-known plantation owner, banker and restaurateur. Following his death, about 1820, the house on the hill was inherited by his son, David Mitchie, Jr., but the younger Mitchie lost it through debts during the depression of 1839. In 1846, Cherokee was purchased by Frederick Stanton, at that time a rapidly rising Natchez merchant. It was probably Stanton who enlarged the house and added the facade of Greek Revival design, an archi-tectural style then at the height of popularity. The Stanton family

Cherokee's parlor, particularly well proportioned, is the setting for rosewood chairs and sofa with deep rose carving. A portrait of the home's present mistress, Mrs. Charles J. Byrne, hangs above the sofa, which is flanked by an English mahogany tripod table on the left and a rosewood table on the right. Both are surmounted by Bristol vases made into lamps.

Above: A bronze and crystal French chandelier illuminates the drawing room replete with antique pieces and *objets d'art*. At left is an early Natchez wing chair.
Left: Cherokee, which antedates most of the larger Natchez homes, is an interesting combination of Spanish and Greek Revival architecture. Its recessed gallery is also unusual to houses in this historic city.

Courtesy the Pilgrimage Garden Club

Above: The original section of the house now known
as Holly Hedges was completed in 1796 on land
deeded to John Scott, an early Natchez settler.
Right: The attractive cypress-built cottage presents
a pleasing symmetrical facade with central doorway.

remained here until 1857 when it moved into Stanton Hall, one of the most lavish and ornamental antebellum houses in Natchez.

The following year, Frederick Stanton sold Cherokee to Duncan K. Metcalfe, member of the celebrated Metcalfe family of pioneer days. He sold Cherokee for $8,000 in 1861.

The present owners, Mr. and Mrs. Charles J. Byrne, both members of old Natchez families, have restored the house on the hill and re-furnished it with handsome early American, French and English antiques. Of particular interest here is the drawing room with its high ceiling, attractively paneled doors and uncommonly wide windows which provide fine views of the garden. The chandelier in this room is a masterpiece of crystal and bronze. Above a black and gold marble mantel hangs a very decorative French gold-leaf mirror. Other rooms in the house display such pieces as a Sheraton sofa, an early Natchez wing chair, a Chippendale reading table, and, in the bedrooms, four-poster beds.

Also dating from the Spanish era is Holly Hedges, located not far from the business district of Natchez. Holly Hedges, although of modest appearance, is a veritable treasure house of rare period pieces, antiques, historical items, bric-a-brac and heirlooms—all collected and tastefully arranged by the house's present owners, Mr. and Mrs. Earl Hart Miller, who are interior decorators as well as antiquarians.

When John Scott, an early Natchez settler, petitioned the Spanish authorities to build a town house, he was granted the land on condition that he be remarried in the Catholic Church, that he would not leave Natchez, and that he would not stage any bull fights in his side yard. He evidently agreed to these provisions and in 1796 completed the original section of the house that is now Holly Hedges. The original deed, written in archaic Spanish, refers to him as "Don Juan Scott."

In was in 1818, a year after Mississippi was admitted to statehood, that John Scott's heirs sold the house to Judge Edward Turner. Here the judge lived with his family until 1832 when he presented the house as a wedding gift to his daughter, Mary, who had married a brilliant young attorney, John T. McMurran. In the years following, John McMurran became one of the wealthiest men in Natchez. In 1845 he built Melrose, one of the showplaces of Natchez. Among subsequent owners was Henry Carson, whose long ownership of Holly Hedges caused it to be called the Carson Cottage.

After Mr. and Mrs. Earl Hart Miller purchased this landmark in 1948, they not only restored and refurnished it but changed its name to Holly Hedges, now one of the best known names in Natchez. They learned, among other things, that it was the McMurrans who, after 1832, enhanced this cypress-built cottage of two and one-half stories with attractive details of a style of architecture then becoming popular, the Greek Revival. This ornamentation is exemplified in the handsome entrance door, with its sidelights and elliptical fanlight.

As with numerous Southern colonial homes of the earliest period, Holly Hedges has a central entrance hall which, at its rear, can be converted into a formal dining room. This portion of the hall has been dramatically covered with mural wallpaper of 1832 Zuber design which depicts early American scenes. At the front of the hall may be seen Empire wallpaper printed in Paris.

The lovely drawing room at Holly Hedges is distinguished by an eighteenth-century Broadwood piano. A portrait of Sir Archibald and Lady Grant, 1735, is credited to Hogarth and his students.

Courtesy the Pilgrimage Garden Club

Set high on a bluff overlooking the Mississippi River and the Louisiana lowlands, The Briars is a typical plantation home of the early nineteenth century. It was here that Jefferson Davis, later the Confederate President, married Varina Howell, the "Rose of Mississippi."

Opposite: Regal blues enhance the Louis-Philippe double parlor set, Florentine tea table and handmade Battenburg lace curtains. Presumably, Jefferson Davis wed Varina Howell before the Adam-style mantel in 1845.

All rooms of the house have been furnished with fascinating eighteenth- and nineteenth-century period pieces, not only from America but from England, France and the Orient. Among these are Queen Anne, Chippendale, Regency, Hepplewhite and Sheraton pieces. Here, too, are precious collections of china, silverware, pewterware and glassware, as well as such rare items as Lowestoft porcelains, Staffordshire figurines and Brittany statuettes.

One of the most interesting rooms in the house is the library, with its walls paneled in Ponderosa white pine. On one side of the room is a gracefully carved Adam mantel that originally came from La Grange Plantation House. The opposite wall from the fireplace is covered with a large antique map of Paris, done in black on lime green. It is from the original *Plan de Paris* by Torgot, dated 1739, which depicts the old Paris before Napoleon had many buildings torn down to make way for the grand new boulevard system devised by the city planner, Baron Haussmann.

Perhaps the most revered of these four early Natchez houses is The Briars. Situated a little distance from the city and reached by a winding road canopied with magnolia trees, vines and briars and which crosses several dry bayous, The Briars, located on a hill overlooking the broad Mississippi River, was the scene, in 1845, of the marriage of Jefferson Davis to Varina Howell, the "Rose of Mississippi." It is almost certain that Varina Howell could not have realized then that the man she was marrying would become President of the Southern Confederacy during the Civil War.

Above: The striking portrait above the mantel in the dining room of The Briars is of an ancestor of the current owner. A rare Hepplewhite sugar chest rests against the far wall. Below: Nineteenth-century Hepplewhite and Chippendale furnishings are found in the spacious living room, with its floor-to-ceiling windows.

The future Mrs. Jefferson Davis was born and brought up at The Briars, the daughter of William Burr Howell who had acquired the plantation house in 1820. He was a Yankee, the son of Governor Richard Howell of New Jersey and a cousin of the famed statesman, Aaron Burr. After serving honorably with the United States Navy in the War of 1812, William Burr Howell moved to Natchez and in time became owner of The Briars.

The question of when this plantation house was built, and who built it, are matters so far undetermined by local historians. One building date often given is 1812, which would be during territorial days in Mississippi. Since it is of record that William Burr Howell bought the house in 1820 and that his daughter, Varina, was born there in 1826, it is obvious that The Briars was built early in the nineteenth century.

In the year 1850 this historic plantation house was purchased by Walter Irvine, who lived there with his family during the Civil War. Neither the Irvine family nor the house were molested when Union troops occupied Natchez in 1863. Descendants of Walter Irvine lived in The Briars for more than half a century. In 1927, it was purchased by Mr. and Mrs. William Winans Wall, who set about restoring the now-aging mansion and the grounds around it. At the present time the house is owned and occupied by Mr. and Mrs. Charles Kelley.

The Briars is properly described as a typical prosperous Southern planter's house from the early nineteenth century rather than a mansion of the later, more extravagant era. It is a handsome, well-proportioned building, with many attractive architectural details. Here is a white frame building, two stories high, with a gable roof featuring lovely dormer windows. A wide gallery, supported by ten slender columns, occupies the entire front of the house. An ornamental main doorway and two side doorways, enhanced with sidelights and fanlights, open on the gallery.

The lower floor contains six rooms. On the right of the central entrance hall is the parlor, centering on an Adam-style mantel of sunburst design before which, it is assumed, Jefferson Davis married Varina Howell. The wedding was a hurried, rather informal, affair, postponed several times due to an illness of Miss Howell's. When Davis appeared unexpectedly for a visit in February of 1845 and found her recovered, the ceremony was held on short notice. The room has wide-plank floors, a large fireplace and contains a Louis-Philippe double-parlor set and a rosewood etagére, or what-not. The dining room contains an American Hepplewhite three-piece dining table, a Baltimore Sheraton sideboard, a cherry sugar-desk with false drawers concealing a bin used to hold unrefined sugar and a Moravian chest of drawers, also of cherry, with tulipwood inlay in the shape of tulips. The Southern china cabinet displays apple-green Sèvres.

A wide variety of furniture, heirlooms and other household articles of the late eighteenth-century period are exhibited in the remaining rooms of The Briars. The upper floor contains four large rooms, particularly the two center ones which are connected by folding doors that allow it to be converted into a ballroom where it is believed the wedding breakfast for Jefferson Davis and his bride was served.

The Pink Bedroom contains a cradle once owned by the Davis family; mosquito netting or a toy could be hung from the ring attached to the swan neck. A colorful silk quilt fashioned in the log-cabin pattern brightens the pale pinks on the four-poster bed made from Southern cherry.

LOCHINVAR
Pontotoc, Mississippi
SHOWPLACE ON PONTOTOC RIDGE

Of great interest in the central entrance hall at Lochinvar, Robert Gordon's dream mansion on Pontotoc Ridge, is the dizzying cantilevered stairway which winds upward to the third floor of the home.

When Robert Gordon, an early Indian trader and land speculator of Mississippi, acquired sufficient means and a handsome wife, he vowed that he would build for her one of the most palatial mansions in all Mississippi. He lived up to his promise. Work on his mansion was started in 1834 and when the house was completed, Robert Gordon, a Scotsman by birth, named it Lochinvar. He had in mind Sir Walter Scott's ballad hero "Young Lochinvar" in the author's *Marmion*. Sir Walter had died only four years before Robert Gordon began work on his house in America.

Today, that dwelling survives on its hill-top site near the northern Mississippi town of Pontotoc as one of the truly magnificent mansions in a state of many imposing mansions. Although now privately owned, the Gordon house is identified by an historical marker just south of Pontotoc.

Previous to building his plantation house, Gordon had, among other things, founded the present city and cotton center of Aberdeen on the Tombigbee River in northeast Mississippi, naming it after his favorite city in Scotland. He also built there a roomy hotel, the Gordon House, to accommodate the ever-increasing number of settlers who were flocking into the Chickasaw Indian country of northeast Mississippi. During the height of his career as a land speculator, Robert Gordon owned acreage stretching from Aberdeen to Pontotoc, a distance of sixty miles.

When Gordon first arrived in Mississippi in the early 1800's he engaged in barter with the Chickasaw Indians and quickly won their friendship. Then, in 1832, the Chickasaw signed the Treaty of Pontotoc, whereby the Indians ceded their lands to the government. Gordon was present at the treaty-signing held at the home of Topulkah, the Chickasaw chief, and was one of the signers.

The government then set up a land office at Pontotoc so Robert Gordon left Aberdeen and established his headquarters in the town. In the years immediately following, he engaged in land speculation on an ever-increasing scale, became a banker, and soon was one of the wealthiest men in northeast Mississippi. It was during this period that Gordon met and married Mary Elizabeth Walton, handsome daughter of a well-to-do planter and one of the society belles of that part of Mississippi.

Robert Gordon spared no expense in building his home. Four massive Doric columns made from solid timber were taken from his ancestral home in Scotland while every timber in the 133-year-old mansion was hewn by hand from the heart of huge old forest pines.

Above: The sparsely furnished foyer is dominated by a ten-foot-tall clock and the spare beauty of the ascending spiral staircase. Below: The second-floor landing foyer is a repository for many books, some of them owned by the original Gordon family.

Determined to give his wife a proper and elegant setting for her charms and social graces, Robert Gordon immediately began the task of building for her the most stately mansion in Mississippi. And thus it was that Lochinvar came into being on the ridge two miles south of Pontotoc. Work on it was completed in 1836. In constructing Lochinvar, Gordon employed the services of architects, master builders, craftsmen and artisans specially brought over from Scotland.

In the years following, Lochinvar became the leading social center of the region, a popular gathering place for the beaux and belles of the countryside. As he grew older, James Gordon, only son of the master and mistress of the house, played a larger and larger role in the entertaining of guests at Lochinvar. When James reached maturity, he became a well-known sportsman, writer and poet, and at Lochinvar he welcomed many distinguished visitors from the sports and literary worlds. He traveled extensively in Europe and recorded his impressions of life at Lochinvar in a published volume of verse, *The Old Plantation.*

With the outbreak of the Civil War in 1861, however, life at Lochinvar altered abruptly, becoming more serious than before. A patriotic Southerner, James Gordon promptly organized the "Chickasaw Rangers," a company of cavalry which he armed and equipped at his own expense. It was assigned to the Confederate defenses at Richmond, and James Gordon rose to the rank of colonel. While he was in the field, Lochinvar was converted into a hospital for Confederate wounded.

When the war ended in 1865, Colonel Gordon returned to his ancestral home on Pontotoc Ridge. Although the colonel inherited Lochinvar after his father died in 1867, he soon ran into difficulties in maintaining the big place. His fortune had already been depleted by the cost of outfitting and commanding the cavalry company. Eventually, Lochinvar was mortgaged, and the plantation house was finally lost by the Gordon family.

In 1900 a prominent Pontotoc attorney, J. D. Fontaine, bought the historic property. Fontaine never lived at Lochinvar but in 1926 his son, J. B. Fontaine, and his wife moved into the house and did much to restore it to its original state of magnificence. Among numerous guests welcomed by the Fontaines to Lochinvar was Governor Theo G. Bilbo of Mississippi, who visited there in 1930. In 1966 the Fontaines sold the mansion to Dr. Forrest T. Tutor of Jackson, Mississippi.

Located atop the highest hill in the county and surrounded by large oaks, English boxwoods and cedars, Lochinvar has a setting to match its imposing architecture. In outward appearance, the house presents an impressive facade in the Greek Revival style. It is three stories high, rectangular in shape, gable-roofed and with paired chimneys at each end of the roof. Originally, an octagonal observatory or cupola was centrally located on the roof, but this was later removed when it fell into decay.

According to one of the numerous traditions associated with Lochinvar, the four stately columns which support its classic portico, as well as the ornamental entrance door of the house, were brought over from the Gordon ancestral home in Scotland. Unlike the columns on most mansions, those at Lochinvar are not hollow but made of solid wood, rising to a height of two stories. They were shipped to Mobile, Alabama, and hauled overland to Pontotoc in log wagons drawn by oxen, a distance of two hundred miles.

There are twenty-two rooms in Lochinvar. Eight of them are twenty-two feet square. The lumber used in building the mansion was made of hand-hewn, solid, heart pine, much of it cut from Pontotoc Ridge. The floors of the rooms are made of two-inch thick pine planks, each plank running the full length of the apartment. Instead of using nails, the builders of the house used small wooden pegs to join together the inside paneling. Also of interest is the fact that much of the interior woodwork, such as doors and banisters, was carved in Scotland in old English lace designs.

Of chief interest in the central entrance hall is a winding, cantilevered stairway which, apparently unsupported, continues upward to the third floor, arousing the curiosity of most visitors to the house.

On the walls of the entrance hall hang portraits of previous occupants of the house—Robert Gordon and his son, Colonel James Gordon, and J. B. Fontaine. The foyer also contains a fine, old grandfather's clock, ten feet in height.

To the left of the central hall is the double parlor. Each room is twenty-two feet square and the wall between is made up of folding doors which can be opened to create one large room. It was here that the many dances and other social events that made Lochinvar famous during the mid-nineteenth century were held. Each room of the double parlor contains an antique piano, and one has a Chippendale and a William and Mary chair, both mahogany. Most of the remainder of the furniture in these two rooms is Empire.

To the right of the foyer is the master bedroom with a huge tester bed, marble-top dresser and wardrobe cabinet, all of walnut. In the dining room is a sideboard which originally belonged to Robert Gordon and an elegant curved glass china cabinet.

In addition to the large spiral staircase there is a small servants' staircase leading from the dining room to the upper floors. It is sometimes called the "secret staircase," and many servants in the past claimed that it was haunted because air currents often blew out their candles as they climbed.

The attic is of interest with its hand-hewn beams pinned together with wooden pegs. From the attic a staircase leads out to the roof where there was once a small observatory which the present owner, Dr. Tutor, plans to rebuild, following plans and pictures of the original. The view of the lovely surrounding countryside from the top of the house is spectacular.

Above: A half-tester bed, about one hundred years old, is part of a set at Lochinvar which includes a marble-top dresser and wardrobe.

RINGROSE AND MAGNOLIA RIDGE PLANTATION HOUSES

Opelousas Vicinity, Louisiana

IN THE HEART OF THE BAYOU COUNTRY

In the midst of the famed Bayou Teche region of central Louisiana, an area as renowned for its white antebellum mansions and ancient live oak trees draped with Spanish moss as for its production of sugar cane, pecans, cotton and rice, stand two plantation houses of unusual distinction, both architecturally and historically. These are the Ringrose Plantation House at Opelousas and Magnolia Ridge at Washington. Although now in private hands, both mansions have been restored and furnished with remarkable collections of period pieces from early years in the county where they are located, St. Landry Parish, known in Louisiana annals as the "Imperial Parish."

Oldest of the two historic dwellings is Ringrose Plantation House, a leading attraction of the old city of Opelousas, which derived its name from an early Indian tribe in the region. Ringrose was built about 1770 by Michel Prud'homme, a member of the famous French family that settled at Natchitoches, Louisiana. When Michel Prud'homme built the house, Louisiana was still owned by Spain which had acquired it from France in 1762. After France had reacquired the territory by secret treaty with Spain in 1800 and then, in 1803, sold it to the United States in the famous Louisiana Purchase, the builder of Ringrose Plantation House found himself a citizen of the new American republic.

Now believed to be the oldest dwelling in St. Landry Parish, the Prud'homme house is a typical early French-Spanish colonial dwelling. In its garden setting on Prud'homme Lane, the house presents an attractive and symmetrical appearance. It is two stories high, with an upper and lower gallery across its front, and with a high-pitched hip roof from which dormers project on four sides. The first floor of the house is of brick and the second floor of *briqueté entre poteaux* covered with cypress siding. Round red brick columns are featured on the first-floor gallery and slender cypress posts on the second-floor gallery.

Two unusual outbuildings, typical of the Louisiana bayou country, once flanked the front grounds of Ringrose Plantation House. Of these two ancient frame *pigeonniers,* or dove-cotes, one is still in use. Also on the grounds of the plantation house is a famed tree known as the Opelousas Pink. It is believed by horticulturists to be one of the largest camellia trees in America—more than twenty feet high and twenty feet wide. The tree blooms spectacularly in February and March.

The motif of the bedroom downstairs is centered around an early Victorian, Belter-carved rosewood bedroom set.

Opposite: Historic Ringrose, one of the earliest homes of raised cottage style in the area, features unusual rounded-brick columns along the first-floor gallery. The bricks were handmade from a mold by slaves right on the plantation.

Two clustered-column, clover leaf beds lend dignity to an upstairs bedroom. The matching beds are family heirlooms, dating from 1820.

The plantation house is now owned and occupied by Mrs. Ruth Robertson Fontenot, an artist and writer and a leader in various historical associations in the state. She is also a discriminating antique collector, as the various rooms of Ringrose Plantation House eloquently testify.

The interior plan of the house is typical of French colonial dwellings in the South. Across the front of both floors are three rooms which open into each other. Behind each side room is a *cabinet,* or small back room. The stairway and hall are at the back of the house. Originally the living room and dining room were separated by a wall which had a fireplace on each side opposite one another. This was torn down several years ago and one freestanding fireplace, with simple cypress-wood mantel and ornamental molding, remains, facing the living room side and closed on the other. The floor of this combined room is solid polished terra-cotta, without carpet or rugs.

In the dining room is a mahogany banquet table in the Duncan Phyfe manner with square center pedestal and small legs on the sides, which was made to order in Augusta, Georgia, for the present owner's grandmother. Also in the dining room is an interesting English mahogany silver chest.

Of particular interest to Mrs. Fontenot are the bookshelves lining one wall of the living room, where she has collected many rare books, documents, maps and records of pioneer times in Louisiana. The hand-hewn and hand-sawed cypress bookshelves were made of lumber from the ancient Ringrose barn.

The first-floor bedroom contains an early Victorian Belter rosewood set. In the upstairs bedrooms are a pair of clover-leaf beds, dating from about 1820, which belonged to Mrs. Fontenot's great-grandmother and a cherry and pecan field bed with tobacco-leaf and acanthus carving, circa 1800.

Left: The richly varied collection of antiques at Magnolia Ridge includes a ruby glass kerosene lamp on a Louis XIV center table made about 1700, an early Georgian fall-front secretary and several Victorian pieces in the parlor. Below: Simplicity is the keynote in the exterior design of this graceful Southern plantation home.

A pine desk used by General Banks graces one corner of the house he occupied. Above it are a banjo clock and a painting of Magnolia Ridge Plantation House.

Six miles north of Opelousas lies the old town of Washington, once an active shipping point and social center on Bayou Courtableau. Maintaining much of the quiet dignity and charm of the antebellum South is Magnolia Ridge, a plantation house built on a knoll overlooking Bayou Courtableau. It has been restored and refurnished with attractive antebellum pieces by descendants of the builders and the present owners, the Valery Mayer family.

Magnolia Ridge was built by slaves and completed in 1830 under the direction of Judge John Moore. It was constructed of bricks made from clay on the plantation, and today a beautiful lake is located where this clay was dug. The year the house was completed Judge Moore married the widow of David Weeks, the builder of The Shadows, the beautiful plantation at New Iberia.

The judge's daughters later married Prescotts and the dwelling became known as the Old Prescott Home. Later, when the plantation had grown to thirty thousand acres, it was called Oakland Plantation. When purchased in 1938 by George M. Wallace of Baton Rouge, Magnolia Ridge was given its present name because of the many lovely magnolia trees growing on the place.

For a period during the Civil War, the Union commander, General Nathaniel P. Banks, established his headquarters at Magnolia Ridge. From here, General Banks, who was a former governor and congressman of Massachusetts, directed his unsuccessful Red River expedition in Louisiana. After the war, he was again elected a Massachusetts congressman. At the time of the conflict, the owner of Magnolia Ridge was Captain Lewis D. Prescott, a Confederate officer who was on duty in the field.

Magnolia Ridge is a typical Southern Classical-style plantation house. It is two and a half stories high, with a gable roof, and fronted by a magnificent two-story gallery supported by six Doric columns.

The entire interior of the house is natural white plaster with nine-foot ceilings and random-width plank floors of heart pine, which are original. The lower floor of the house contains a large living room with an open fireplace, a dining room, a breakfast room, butler's pantry and a modernized kitchen. The second floor has four large bedrooms and three baths, and the third has two bedrooms and a bath. At each of the levels, a central hallway goes through the house.

Furnishings from the Louis XIV to the Belter period are numerous throughout the house. Three of the bedrooms are furnished with four-poster, clover-leaf beds and dressers made by Prudent Mallard, the noted, early nineteenth-century cabinetmaker from New Orleans. A French daily calendar clock, dated 1710 and operated by weights, is an outstanding piece in the first-floor hallway.

Among other rare period pieces and antiques in Magnolia Ridge are a three-hundred-year-old *secretaire*, a Wells Fargo desk, an English Chippendale breakfront, Oriental porcelain vases, Chippendale mirrors, French candlesticks, marble-top tables and a desk said to have been used by General Banks when he occupied Magnolia Ridge during the Civil War. The house also contains a number of paintings—madonnas, landscapes and still-lifes—by eighteenth- and early nineteenth-century European masters.

THE SHADES

Jackson Vicinity, Louisiana

OLDEST HOUSE IN EAST FELICIANA

Venerated throughout the surrounding countryside, rich in history and an architectural landmark, the plantation residence known as The Shades near Jackson, Louisiana, survives today as the oldest house in East Feliciana Parish. It was the seat of the famed Scott family of Louisiana for more than 170 years. The red brick house is now owned and occupied by George Berger, formerly of Victorville, California, a cousin of Miss Eva Scott, last of the Scott family to reside in The Shades. She died in 1961 at the age of eighty-four after living her entire life in the East Feliciana dwelling. Both Mr. and Mrs. Berger have done much to restore the house and refurnish it with nineteenth-century period pieces, including many Scott family heirlooms.

Had it not been for the kindness and compassion of a son of the builder of this house, Major E. A. Scott of the Confederate Army, in releasing a captured Union soldier, The Shades might have been put to the torch during the Civil War. When a contingent of Yankee troops invaded the house, they learned that it was the family home of the same Major Scott who had released one of their own number earlier, a soldier on leave who was captured while returning North to attend a funeral. Because of this, the Union troops spared The Shades and went on their way burning numerous other houses.

The builder of this East Feliciana landmark was Alexander Scott, a native of Scotland who had emigrated to America and become one of Louisiana's earliest planters and landowners. At first he settled in Black Mingo, South Carolina, but as more and more reports came to him of the fertile lands in what was then the "Florida Parishes" of Louisiana, he decided to resettle in that region. Thus Alexander Scott, who was as much a sportsman and hunter as an adventurer and landseeker, made his way along the trails and through the forests of South Carolina and Mississippi, riding his horse and carrying his favorite long rifle, which he nicknamed "Old Black Mingo," after his former South Carolina home.

He finally arrived in the East Feliciana region of the future state of Louisiana and decided to stake his claim there. He had found

One of the most beautiful Scott family heirlooms which has been preserved at The Shades is this white Wedgwood pitcher with corn-husk-and-leaf design.

what he wanted, "seven springs and seven pastures," as he was to write later. Eventually, he came into possession of a seven-thousand-acre tract, which was an old Spanish land grant. He is believed to have settled in this region in the late eighteenth century.

Almost immediately, Alexander Scott began making plans for the building of a comfortable, two-story plantation house of brick material, selecting a site for it in the shade of a group of old live oaks laced with gray Spanish moss, a setting that caused Scott to name his place The Shades. As a first step, however, he had to set up several kilns to make bricks from clay on his property. He also obtained timber from his land for the interior finishing of the house.

While the house was under construction, Alexander Scott lived in a nearby log cabin from which, with his Black Mingo rifle, he went out on hunting trips through the woodlands of the area. His brick house was finally completed in 1808. Four years later he married Miss Eleanor Norwood and she became mistress of the mansion in East Feliciana Parish. When she died at a later date, leaving him with two small daughters, Scott brought a new wife to the mansion, the former Miss Sarah Allen.

Already a planter, landowner, sportsman and host, Alexander Scott eventually took on a new role—that of philanthropist. In addition to rearing six children of his own, he brought up a number of foster children under his roof. It was his son, Major E. A. Scott, of the First Louisiana Cavalry, who by an act of generosity in freeing the captured Union soldier, saved The Shades from destruction.

Major Scott had inherited the family mansion when his father died in the 1840's. With the death of the major himself in 1903, the plantation house became the property of the major's own son, Alexander Scott II. It was Alexander II's daughter, "Miss Eva" Scott, who became the next owner of The Shades.

Described as "a jolly, well-loved little lady," Miss Eva did the most to preserve the many Scott family pieces and heirlooms which now make a veritable treasure trove out of The Shades. And this rich heritage is being carefully nurtured by the house's present owners, Mr. and Mrs. George Berger. In addition, the Bergers maintained a dairy farm on the plantation, which over the years has been reduced to 1,600 acres.

As seems evident, Alexander Scott, a practical man who liked worldly comfort more than worldly display, built a solid brick house intended to be a commodious home rather than a gaudy showplace. It appears he had no desire to out-rival other planters' mansions. And so he chose a simple, early Federal type of design for his house—rectangular in shape, two stories high, with central entrance door, gabled roof and end chimneys. Stretching across the entire front of the house is a one-story gallery or veranda supported by six round plastered columns.

Above: Early American decorating tastes are reflected in almost every room of the comfortable two-story home.

Opposite top: The Shades was built by Alexander Scott from bricks baked on his property. The house was completed in 1808. Opposite bottom: The attractive oval dining table where Scott and his family dined is a prized possession.

This extra-long deacon's bench in front of a spacious fireplace was provided for the comfort of guests.

The ground floor contains four rooms divided by front and back hallways which cross at the center of the house. The stairway rises from this point to the second floor and its two large bedrooms. The woodwork of walnut, oak and pine lacks ornateness; most of the rooms have wide-plank flooring.

On one side of the central entrance hall is located the living room, which contains numerous Scott family pieces and heirlooms. Above the fireplace in this room hangs a large oil portrait of Alexander Scott painted by the celebrated American portrait artist, Thomas Sully (1783-1872). It shows a smooth-shaven man with a thin face, black hair, piercing eyes, a firm jawline and patrician features. On one side of this elegant room hangs a ten-foot-high, beveled English mirror in a gilded frame, an adornment that reflects, on the other side of the room, a huge Mallard breakfront bookcase. Most cherished piece in the living room, however, is Alexander Scott's double-barreled flintlock rifle, Old Black Mingo.

Equalling the living room in interest is the large dining room, which measures fifteen by twenty feet. Here may be seen exposed ceiling beams made of hand-carved walnut. In front of the handsome, spacious fireplace is an extra-long deacon's bench for the comfort of family guests. Most prized possession in this room is an attractive oval dining table, the same table where Alexander Scott and his large family enjoyed feasts after his numerous hunting trips. Among other Scott family heirlooms here is a white Wedgwood pitcher in corn-husk-and-leaf design and a white syllabub set, its small lidded cups on a tiered china stand.

Attached to the rear of the house is the old kitchen with its great black hearth and original iron cooking pots hanging from hand-forged cranes. Alexander Scott's plantation smithy forged the andirons for the huge fireplace and his slaves carved the now smoke-darkened walnut rafters in the ceiling.

This historic East Feliciana landmark also contains the late Miss Eva Scott's amazing bell collection. Amounting to more than a thousand bells, it caused some of her neighbors to give another name to The Shades—the "House of a Thousand Bells." It was in 1898 that Miss Eva began her collection, when her brother, Ned Scott, fighting in the Spanish-American War, sent her a souvenir bell from Cuba. Before the bell arrived, however, she received a message that her brother had died of yellow fever.

Although she used her brother's gift as a dinner bell in the dining room, her many friends objected to its raucous sound and began sending her more soothing bells to replace it. She appreciated their replacements, but Ned's bell stayed on the table. In the years following, more bells came to her, such as ones once owned by Robert E. Lee and Jefferson Davis, and her fame as a collector grew.

The plantation surrounding The Shades is much reduced in size now, but the approach to the house along a winding driveway to the hilltop and the trees and abundant flower gardens still provide a suitable setting for this unpretentious but distinguished dwelling.

Above: The large oil portrait revealing Scott's patrician features is a Thomas Sully original. Left: A magnificent breakfront bookcase by Prudent Mallard completes the living room décor.

Above: The rustic Christian Waldschmidt House offers
an authentic portrayal of pioneer life in Ohio. Right:
The back porch was probably a favorite place to chat
after the day's work was finished.

CHRISTIAN WALDSCHMIDT HOUSE

Camp Dennison, Ohio

OHIO HOME OF AN EARLY GERMAN PIONEER

One of the oldest, most noteworthy and appealing memorials to the early German pioneers who colonized southern Pennsylvania and southern Ohio is the Christian Waldschmidt House near the Cincinnati suburban village of Milford on the Little Miami River. Built in 1804 by a man who migrated westward from Pennsylvania to settle in the Ohio country, this solid stone house is also of interest as an architectural landmark, a fine example of what has been called Pennsylvania "Dutch" design (because the Germans referred to themselves as *Deutsche*). In 1941 the Waldschmidt residence was presented to the Ohio Society, Daughters of the American Revolution, whose members restored it and opened the house as a public museum.

The builder of the sturdy stone house in Ohio, Christian Waldschmidt, was born and reared in the vicinity of Reading and Lancaster, Pennsylvania, focal points for the state's colonial German families. His father was a Pietist minister (Lutheran) who had emigrated from Germany. Christian Waldschmidt was married, the father of two daughters and six sons, and a veteran of the American Revolution, when, in the year 1794, he resolved to move westward to the exciting, undeveloped new Ohio country. That was just after General "Mad Anthony" Wayne, at the Battle of Fallen Timbers, defeated the Indians and made the region safe for settlement.

Under the leadership of Waldschmidt, a group of about ten or twelve men undertook a preliminary reconnaisance trip to the Territory of Ohio, traveling over the mountains on horseback and on the Ohio River in flatboats. On arrival near the future site of Cincinnati, they sought out John Cleaves Symmes, who had served in the Continental Congress, had been a colonel in the Revolutionary War and who was now the Ohio Territory's largest land speculator. Symmes was then in the possession of some 300,000 acres, land that included the site of Cincinnati.

The Waldschmidt group bought some land for their new settlement from Symmes, selecting an area on the Little Miami River some twelve miles north of the Ohio River village of Columbia. Then most of the men in the party, including Waldschmidt, returned to

An oil of Sarah, youngest of Waldschmidt's daughters, hangs on the west wall of the parlor.

The massive china cabinet built from cherry-wood cut near the house is surprisingly devoid of ornamentation.

Pennsylvania to gather up their families. Those who were left behind immediately began building log cabins. Waldschmidt, who was among the largest purchasers, acquired 1,140 acres at a reported cost of "one Spanish dollar" per acre.

It was in the spring of 1796 that Waldschmidt and his family, and five other families, left the Reading and Lancaster areas of Pennsylvania for their new homes. By 1798, there were twenty families living in the settlement. A strong and enterprising man, one who had the makings of an industrialist, Christian Waldschmidt took the lead in developing the little colony sixteen miles northeast of Cincinnati. By 1800 the village now known as New Germany had a church, a general store, a school and a number of mills and shops, including saw and grist mills, a paper mill and a distillery. The paper mill is believed to have been the first in the Northwest Territory.

As his wealth increased, Christian Waldschmidt began making plans for the construction of a comfortable stone house in the Pennsylvania "Dutch" style he had admired as a young man in Pennsylvania. The house, completed in 1804, was built of native field stone held together with white mortar and heavy oak timbers. The contractor was Joseph Boone, who came from the Reading area of Pennsylvania and who was a cousin of Daniel Boone, famed frontiersman and Indian fighter.

Among the many residents of New Germany often entertained by the Waldschmidts in their spacious residence overlooking the Little Miami River was their daughter, Catherine, and her young husband, Matthias Kugler. Coming to the village in 1797 and hiring out as a Waldschmidt mill hand, Matthias Kugler had early shown unusual abilities as an administrator, which Waldschmidt was quick to notice. A year after his arrival he married the Waldschmidt daughter and was later to play an important role in the history of the community.

By the time Christian Waldschmidt had completed his stone house, he was already well known as a leading exporter of the region, loading his flatboats at Columbia on the Ohio River with lard, flour, linen and whiskey for shipment to the New Orleans market. When a banking and exporting firm was founded in Cincinnati to facilitate river shipping, he was elected a member of its board of directors. In 1810 his wife Catherine died and a year later he married a widow, Magdalena Kern Custard. All told, Waldschmidt had eight children by his first and second wives.

In the fateful year of 1814, both Christian Waldschmidt and his son, John, died suddenly of influenza. Although he left a fortune of $25,000 in addition to large tracts of land, warehouses, mills and stock in the Miami Exporting Company, Waldschmidt had not made a will. After his estate was probated, most of his holdings, both by inheritance and purchase from other heirs, passed to his daughter, Catherine, and her husband, Matthias Kugler. In the years following, the Kuglers, later assisted by their son, John, developed the community into a leading paper-manufacturing center. But the Waldschmidt settlement gradually declined as Cincinnati advanced to the position of principal city west of the Alleghenies in the years before the Civil War.

During the Civil War, the old stone residence made history by serving as the headquarters of General Joshua Bates, who was in command of Camp Dennison, a recruiting and training center for

Above: The solidly built cherry-wood table was made for Sarah
after her marriage. Around the table are brightly painted
and decorated yellow kitchen chairs from Pennsylvania.
Left: In the parlor is the only original wood mantel still
intact. The rocker at left, known as the "tobacco chair,"
has been in the Waldschmidt family for years.

some thirty thousand Union troops billeted in the immediate vicinity of the residence. Since that time, the site has been known as Dennison, so-named after an Ohio governor. After the war, the Waldschmidt house was occupied by tenant farmers, and later was used as a grain and corn storage barn.

Although apparently neglected, the old stone house near Milford remained in sound condition. And such was its situation when, in 1941, Mr. and Mrs. Chester Kroger, of Cincinnati, bought the landmark and presented it to the Ohio Society, Daughters of the American Revolution. The old Waldschmidt place was restored and furnished with period pieces to reflect German home life in Pennsylvania and Ohio during the early nineteenth century.

Although classified as Pennsylvania Dutch, the house has all the outward characteristics of what is now known as the Federal style. Here are such typical Federal aspects as a basic rectangular shape, four windows and a central doorway at its first-floor level, five windows on the second floor, a gable roof, and end chimneys.

In furnishing the house authentically, members of the Ohio Society, Daughters of the American Revolution combed the Pennsylvania and Ohio countrysides for furniture and other household articles that would be contemporaneous with the life and times of Christian Waldschmidt and other German-born or German-descended settlers of early America. As a result, the house has become an outstanding period museum.

The parlor contains several family portraits including an oil of Sarah, the youngest daughter of the first owner, and another of Matthias Kugler's son, John. The interesting "tobacco chair" in this room is a family heirloom and the small rocker was made for Ambrose Waldschmidt, grandson of Christian, for a birthday gift. Another outstanding piece in the parlor is the inlaid, butternut wood, dropleaf table of Hepplewhite design. The fine mantel here is the only original one in the house.

The attractive cherry hutch in the dining room was cut from wood on the property while the house was being built. It now holds china originally owned by the Waldschmidts. Also in this room are an inlaid cherry Hepplewhite chest of drawers, a cherry corner cupboard, a cherry banquet table which was a wedding gift to Sarah, and yellow-painted chairs with painted decoration which came from Lancaster, Pennsylvania.

The low-ceilinged kitchen, which contains a flour and meal bin that belonged to Matthias Kugler, is believed to pre-date the rest of the house. It may have been the building where the family lived while the rest of the house was being built.

Perhaps the most superb piece in the entire house is the German *kas*, made in 1714, which is in the north bedroom on the second floor. It is inlaid lemon wood and has the bride's initials carved into it. Many rooms of the Waldschmidt House have been enhanced with items from the Gaston Collection of Lighting Devices, one of the most valuable such collections in the country. The adjustable candlestand in the parlor is particularly rare.

This durable stone house, one of the oldest dwellings along the historic Ohio River, serves well to recapture something of the lives of those who were among the first to settle and prosper west of the Alleghenies.

The trundle bed, common in the seventeenth and eighteenth centuries, was used at night and hidden underneath the large walnut bed during the day. On the bed is a lovely quilt handmade around 1830-1840.

Opposite: Two blue and white coverlets brighten the round-post, four-poster bed. The handwoven plaid belonged to the Waldschmidts. The unusual cradle in front, which has a platform under the rockers so that it will not creep as it is rocked, and the small prayer bench at the foot of the bed were probably much-used items.

257

JEREMIAH SULLIVAN HOUSE

Madison, Indiana

AN ARCHITECTURAL MASTERPIECE

Among numerous landmarks in the historic Ohio River town of Madison, Indiana, none has been photographed, sketched, painted and described more than the handsome Jeremiah Sullivan House. Built more than 150 years ago, the Sullivan residence is considered by architectural historians to possess all the best features of the Federal style. This style was initiated primarily by Thomas Jefferson's efforts to develop a fashion for America which would be indigenous to this country and which would replace the English Georgian style which had been popular throughout the colonies.

The house was built by Judge Jeremiah Sullivan, who arrived in the state only one year after it was admitted into the Union in 1816 and quickly became a leader in its public affairs. It was Judge Sullivan who bestowed the name "Indianapolis" on Indiana's capital city. A son and grandson were elected Mayor of Indianapolis.

A native of Virginia, where he was born in 1794, Jeremiah Sullivan studied law at William and Mary College, and, during the War of 1812, served as a captain in the army. It was in 1817 that young Sullivan, riding on horseback, journeyed westward to the then booming Ohio River town of Madison, Indiana, because he had heard that the new town was in need of lawyers.

Madison was located at a point where it was relatively easy to cross the river and which had long been used by the Indians in their travels over the Michigan Trail. Settlers coming down the river on flatboats, rafts and canoes found it convenient to leave the river here and strike north over the trail into the wilderness. Thus Madison became a major entry point into the Northwest Territory.

Sullivan's abilities as a competent attorney soon became apparent, and not long after his arrival he was appointed prosecuting attorney of Jefferson County by Indiana's first governor, Jonathan Jennings. About the same time, too, Sullivan married Charlotte R. Cutler. It was in 1818 that he completed his Madison house, apparently unaware that it would survive him as an architectural masterpiece. He lived here for the remainder of his long life, rearing his children, entertaining his many friends, holding conferences and meetings on public issues of the day.

The handsome wrought-iron railing is one of the few ornamental touches on the Sullivan House exterior.

Opposite: According to architectural historians, Jeremiah Sullivan's home incorporates all the best features of the Federal style of architecture.

Above: A modern addition to any Midwestern settler's home was the tin bathtub. Bath water was kept hot on the Franklin stove which came up river from Pittsburgh in 1800. Below: The law office of Jeremiah Sullivan now contains his portrait, his Empire-style secretary-bookcase and other personal possessions which reflect his busy career.

Two years after he moved into his new residence, Jeremiah Sullivan was elected to the Indiana State Legislature. While serving there, he gave Indianapolis its name. At a later period, in 1836, he was elected a justice of the Supreme Court of Indiana, an office he held for the next ten years. When a criminal court was created in Jefferson County in 1869, Jeremiah Sullivan was appointed its first judge. As it happened, however, he held this post for only one year, for he died in 1870 at the age of seventy-six. In addition to his son Thomas, who became Mayor of Indianapolis in 1889, Judge Sullivan and his wife were parents of five other children.

In 1962 the Jeremiah Sullivan House at Second and Poplar streets was acquired by Historic Madison, Inc. Since then, the residence has been restored and refurnished with early nineteenth-century period pieces. Among the latter are many Sullivan family heirlooms, a few of them brought to the house from Virginia when Judge Sullivan invited his parents to live with him. These had been given to the Indiana State Museum by the wife of George Hammond Sullivan, a grandson of the judge, and when the house was restored, they were returned to the house.

Built flush with the sidewalk, the Sullivan house is of brick construction, white-painted, two stories high, with a gable roof. Its handsome doorway, approached by steps with ornamental wrought-iron railings, is in the Palladian style. It is characterized by delicate moldings, Corinthian-capped fluted pilasters, side panels of glass and an elliptical fanlight above the door. A Southern-style gallery, two stories high, is at one side of the house, overlooking a low brick wall that encloses lawns and a garden.

In his authoritative volume, *Indiana Houses of the Nineteenth Century,* Wilbur D. Peat notes in particular the paired chimneys at one end of the Federal-style house designed for Judge Sullivan, observing that they "impart an air of stateliness" to the dwelling. He adds, "Other elements help, of course, in giving it charm, such as pleasing proportions, intimate scale, and an exceptionally beautiful door."

In restoring the house, officials of Historic Madison, Inc., found that all of the plaster walls in the rooms were whitewashed. No evidence has been uncovered of early paint or wallpaper; whitewashing was then considered the easiest way to clean a house each spring. In the entrance hall a staircase, with a simple turned cherry handrail and square spindles, leads to the second floor. This is almost identical with the staircase displayed in the Winterthur Museum as an excellent example of Federal interior design.

The wood used throughout the house is poplar, except for the floors, which are ash. The green of the woodwork in the entrance hall and the unusual mustard color of the stair risers authentically reproduce the original colors used in this way.

In the back parlor or law office is a three-section bookcase with wrought-iron handles which belonged to Judge Sullivan. It held his law books, and he could put one or more sections into his wagon and take them with him on his circuit-riding missions. Also in this room is the judge's Empire-style secretary-bookcase with writing board that could be lifted at an angle.

The dining room contains two English, cut-crystal, Georgian compotes which the judge brought from Virginia with him in 1817 and an Empire-style mantel mirror made in Philadelphia, which was originally purchased by Thomas Sullivan, the judge's father.

The serving kitchen at the rear of the main floor connects with the basement kitchen and the bedrooms on the second floor by narrow stairs. Food was brought from the basement in pots and pans and transferred in the serving kitchen to the china. The pottery and porcelain, such as the flow-blue, mulberry and pink Staffordshire, now displayed in the serving kitchen cupboards belonged to Judge Sullivan at the time he lived in this house.

The front bedroom on the second floor has been furnished as an early nineteenth-century bedroom typical of a prosperous family in Virginia to reflect the Sullivans' background. The four-poster canopied bed, which may have been carved by the notable Samuel McIntire of Massachusetts, is accompanied by a Sheraton chest and some Hepplewhite pieces. The other bedroom, with its New Orleans half-canopy bed, demonstrates the new look of the Federal period. Wealthy families living on the river often followed French fashions and had items brought up-river to them from New Orleans.

The English cut-crystal Georgian compotes gracing the dining room table came with the Sullivans from Virginia in 1817.

Above: The Ménard home, a fine example of French colonial architecture, overlooks the Mississippi River where once the village of Kaskaskia stood. Right: The quaint kitchen, lighted by a simple candle chandelier, contains the original fireplace and bake oven mantel lined with pewter plates and other cooking necessities.

262

PIERRE MÉNARD HOUSE

Fort Kaskaskia State Park, Illinois

A Social Center of Territorial Days

When the Territory of Illinois was organized in 1809 and its capital established in the old Mississippi River town of Kaskaskia, the official seat of government was temporarily set up in three rented rooms in the home of one George Fisher, a dwelling located conveniently in the center of town. But a more commodious capitol building could have been found in the residence of a leading citizen, Pierre Ménard, except that it was too remote from town, standing on a bluff above the Mississippi River. That house was built seven years before Illinois Territory was formed and it was a social center during territorial days and the early years of Illinois statehood.

Still standing today, the Pierre Ménard House is the most appealing landmark of Fort Kaskaskia State Park. It has been restored and refurnished with Ménard family pieces by the State of Illinois and is now open to the public as a period museum and memorial to Ménard, the first Lieutenant Governor of Illinois. The dwelling has great value as a reminder of one of the pioneer founders of Illinois and as a rare surviving example of the French colonial architecture that prevailed during early territorial times in the upper Mississippi River region.

It was in 1802 that Pierre Ménard, a Quebec-born fur trader who became a prosperous merchant, built his home above the Mississippi. He was living here when, in 1809, the Territory of Illinois was established and he was appointed by Territorial Governor Ninian Edwards to be the presiding officer of the Illinois Territorial Legislature. Here he also saw Illinois become a state in 1818, and he was elected the state's first lieutenant governor under Governor Shadrach Bond, another Kaskaskian.

At that time, Illinois was principally a region of prairies and had a population of about fifty thousand, with most living in such early French towns on the Mississippi as Kaskaskia and Cahokia (both named after Indian tribes). What is now Chicago was a settlement of about fifteen fur traders' log cabins clustered about a military reservation known as Fort Dearborn.

Although Kaskaskia served as Illinois's first capital, it held that title for only two years. After the capital was moved in 1820 to the more centrally located Vandalia (it was later moved to Springfield),

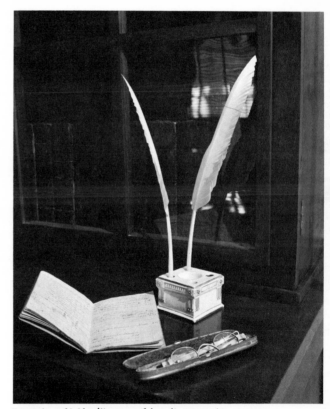

Reminders of Ménard's successful trading operation include his china inkwell with quill pens, spectacles and well-worn record of accounts book.

Kaskaskia gradually declined and its main section finally was swallowed up by a Mississippi River flood in 1881. But Pierre Ménard's residence, high on its bluff, was not touched by the flood waters.

Despite the decline of Kaskaskia in the early nineteenth century, Ménard continued to live in his comfortable house overlooking the town. At the end of his term as lieutenant governor, he retired to his Kaskaskia home, intending to spend the rest of his days here with his family. But he was called back to public duty in 1828 when President John Quincy Adams appointed him to an Indian commission headed by Governor Lewis Cass of Michigan Territory. President Andrew Jackson reappointed him to what would be his last public post. He died in his Kaskaskia home on June 13, 1844, at the age of seventy-eight.

The Ménard house was occupied for many years by various descendants of its builder and later by others, who kept it in good repair. It was in 1927 that the State of Illinois purchased the house, and, after refurnishing it with many original Ménard family pieces, opened it as a public museum.

Although Ménard was a French-Canadian, born and reared in Quebec, his house is of the French colonial type that originated in early Louisiana. Constructed primarily of oak, it was evidently built by carpenters who came up-river from that state. The house, resting on a solid stone foundation, is long and low, just one story high, with a hip roof featuring dormers. The roof sweeps out over a columned gallery occupying the entire front of the house.

The colors are very close to those originally used. The floor of the gallery is painted buttermilk red. Inside, most of the woodwork is painted a desert gold and the doors are Pompeian red. Most rooms have wallpaper which reproduces early patterns. There are light green Venetian blinds throughout the house and Aubusson rugs in the parlor, dining room and master bedroom.

In the walnut-trimmed central entrance hall of the dwelling are displayed numerous personal belongings of Pierre Ménard's, including his compass, Bible, spectacles, watch, flute and flageolet. The handsome French fireplace in the drawing room has a mantel of carved poplar and pine with geometric designs and triple colonnettes. Over it hangs a large oil painting of the builder of the house. Here, too, is Ménard's favorite walnut secretary with bookshelves.

Additional personal possessions of Ménard in the house include his books (some in French), an embroidered velvet vest and wardrobe. Another curious item is a barber chair from early Kaskaskia. Separated from the main house is the kitchen, containing a huge fireplace and a capacious Dutch oven.

Not least interesting about the Pierre Ménard House is that its windows retained, until recent times, their original hand-pressed panes, imported from France. On the outside of one of these panes was an inscription, evidently scratched in with a diamond ring, that spoke tantalizingly of a possible romance in the Ménard family. It contained two names, "L. C. Menard" and "Augustin Louis Cyprian," a place name, "Ste. Genevieve," and a date, "August 14, 1842."

Among original Ménard pieces in the master bedroom are the mahogany chest of drawers and the baby bed. The cherry-wood bed, similar to Ménard's high poster, is intricately carved with pineapple and tobacco-leaf designs. The wedding gown was worn by Ménard's daughter.

Above: The central section of Roi-Porlier-Tank Cottage, circa 1776, is one of the few examples left of the "wattle-and-daub" type of construction. Right: A clay idol doll from Tank's missionary venture in South America sits atop the handmade pine bureau in his daughter Mary's bedroom.

ROI-PORLIER-TANK COTTAGE

Green Bay, Wisconsin

OLDEST HOUSE IN WISCONSIN

The small, white frame dwelling in Green Bay's Tank Park, widely known as Tank Cottage, survives today as Wisconsin's oldest house. Named for Nils Otto Tank, a Norwegian religious leader who once owned and occupied it, the house is now a period museum maintained by the Green Bay Historical Society. In official records of the society, the house is identified as the Roi-Porlier-Tank Cottage, after the three most prominent families to own and occupy it successively during the nearly two hundred years of its existence.

Tank Cottage, located just west of the Fox River, is well preserved and has a richness of history and colorful background that few other old houses in the Great Lakes region can equal. In addition to its historical appeal, this cottage is of especial interest to architectural chroniclers as being one of the few surviving examples of what is known as the "wattle-and-daub" type of construction used during early French days in the Mississippi Valley.

It was in 1776, when what is now Wisconsin was part of British territory, that a French-Canadian fur trader, Joseph Le Roi, settled at Green Bay and built the wattle-and-daub house that forms the original, or central, part of today's Tank Cottage. At the end of the Revolutionary War and the formation by the United States of the Northwest Territory, which included future Wisconsin, Joseph Le Roi was still living in his wattle-and-daub dwelling at Green Bay, but now he was a resident of the new nation.

In building his house, Roi constructed a rectangular framework of rough uprights that had been shaped by a portable whipsaw. He then stuffed into the spaces between these uprights such material as branches, twigs and leaves (the wattle) and plastered them together with mud and clay (the daub). It was a form of construction popular with the early French settlers of Cahokia, Kaskaskia, Ste. Genevieve and other Upper Mississippi River towns.

The second phase of the history of Tank Cottage began in 1805 when the house was purchased by Jacques Porlier, who also was a fur trader but who, in addition, was an educated French-Canadian. Because of his academic background and agreeable personality, Porlier soon became a leading figure iin the Green Bay settlement. At this time, although the future state was now part of the new American republic, the British were still dominant in the Wisconsin fur trading villages.

One of the many Delft ware pieces in the home is this gaily decorated jar below a portrait of Nils Otto Tank.

Above: This rare marquetry cabinet, an unusual example of seventeenth-century Dutch artistry, had been in the Tank family for nearly two hundred years. Below: Part of the Delft ware collection hangs above the finely crafted butler's sideboard.

Thus it came about that the British at Green Bay took the liberty of appointing Jacques Porlier a justice of the peace, and he thereafter held court in the former Roi house. Here, too, he taught the children of the settlement and so became Wisconsin's first schoolmaster. During the War of 1812 local British officers established a temporary headquarters in the Porlier cottage and appointed its owner a captain in the British militia.

At the war's end, when the British were completely driven out of the Northwest Territory, Jacques Porlier became an American citizen and was reappointed a justice of the peace by Governor Lewis Cass of Michigan Territory, which then included Wisconsin. Judge Porlier also became an agent of John Jacob Astor's new American Fur Company. It was in his Green Bay cottage that Jacques Porlier died in 1839 at the age of seventy-four.

The third phase of the cottage's history began in 1850, two years after Wisconsin was admitted to statehood. In that year Nils Otto Tank, a Norwegian-born missionary of the Moravian Church, arrived at Green Bay with his new wife, an aristocratic and well-to-do Dutch woman, the former Caroline Van der Meulen. The couple purchased the Porlier house and enlarged it, clapboarded the exterior, plastered its interior walls, and added wings on either side of it. The wing on the right was designed as a meeting place and prayer room for the local Moravian Church.

As it happened Nils Otto Tank's dream of setting up a Moravian religious community around his cottage failed to materialize, but he and his wife continued to live there until his death in 1864. His widow, who lived until 1891, remained in the house near the Fox River, becoming widely known as Madame Tank.

During the half-century that she lived there, Madame Tank, a cultivated woman of independent means, one who appreciated the arts and the refinements of living, either collected or inherited from her aristocratic Dutch forebears a large number of antiques and family heirlooms. Many of these were shipped to her from Holland. Eventually, the time came when she did not have room enough in her cottage for these articles, and, after her death, unopened crates of rare china, silver and glassware were found in an attic storeroom.

When a public auction of her possessions was held most of the antique furniture and family heirlooms were purchased by the people of Green Bay and vicinity—a fortunate circumstance. So it was possible for the Tank Cottage Committee to recover many of the Tank family pieces when, in 1917, George H. Rice deeded the Tank Cottage to the South Side Improvement Association. Today the building is owned by the City of Green Bay.

A white, clapboarded, one-story house with a gable roof and with wings at either end and a simple porch across its front, the Tank Cottage has little in its outward appearance to suggest the interior richness and variety of its period furnishings, whose cumulative effect renders the house an outstanding period museum of the Midwest. Especially notable here are the many fine examples of Dutch marquetry furniture, delicate inlay work in which the Dutch excelled in the seventeenth century. In the parlor and several other rooms hang oil portraits of Nils Otto Tank, Madame Tank and other family

members, on loan from The State Historical Society of Wisconsin.

Also in the parlor, with its beamed ceiling, is a fireplace made by the original builder of the cottage, Joseph Le Roi. On the mantel above the fireplace in the charming parlor is displayed a handsome Sèvres clock with matching candlesticks flanking it, and portraits of Madame Tank's grandparents, General and Baroness Van Boetzelaer, painted by William Hendrick Schmidt (1819-1849), a Dutch artist. The parlor also contains a fine Dutch marquetry cabinet, and on the hearth are many quaint utensils and pieces of old brass.

Several cupboards in the cottage contain rare pieces of china, most of them Tank family heirlooms. Here, too, is a sizable collection of Delft ware from Holland and numerous examples of Chinese Export ware. An early nineteenth-century canopied, four-poster bed is the principal exhibit in Madame Tank's elegantly furnished bedroom, along with an old Spanish marquetry dressing table given to her mother, who was a lady-in-waiting in the royal Dutch court before her marriage.

It is because of these authentic furnishings, as well as the age of this dwelling and the continuous span of history it represents, that Tank Cottage has a truly unique place among historic houses of the upper Midwest.

Over the piano in the library are pastel portraits of Mme. Tank's younger sisters. The larger portrait between the two is of Mme. Van der Meulen, their mother, who was a lady-in-waiting at the Holland court.

JEAN BAPTISTE VALLÉ HOUSE

Ste. Genevieve, Missouri

HOME OF THE LAST COMMANDANT

The spacious *galerie* of Jean Baptiste Vallé's picturesque home originally ran around the entire house.

During the many years when France and Spain successively laid claim to the vast region west of the Mississippi River, the early French settlements along the upper river were divided into districts and a civil and military commandant placed in charge of each district. One of the most famous and respected of such commandants was Francois Vallé, founder of a family of commandants at Ste. Genevieve, Missouri, that long made the Vallé name one of the most familiar in the Mississippi Valley. After this huge region became part of the United States in the Louisiana Purchase of 1803, the last of the Ste. Genevieve commandants, Jean Baptiste Vallé, was so highly regarded that he was promptly appointed governor of the Ste. Genevieve district by the new American administration. Although he remained at this post until his death in 1849, he was always called by the title of "Commandant."

Now one of the oldest and most historic towns in Missouri, Ste. Genevieve still has numerous French Creole houses dating from French and Spanish colonial days. Of them all, however, interest centers on the picturesque home of Jean Baptiste Vallé. It was built by Vallé nearly two centuries ago and has since been well preserved by his descendants and by the descendants of Leon Vion, who acquired the house in 1867. Vion's great-granddaughter, Vion Papin Schram, and her husband, Bernard K. Schram, now own and occupy the historic house.

It is believed by local historians that Jean Baptiste Vallé erected his house in 1785. In that year, the original town of Ste. Genevieve, founded about 1750, was moved to a new and higher site four miles northwest of the old town, which had been inundated by a Mississippi River flood in the spring of 1785. When Vallé completed his house, his older brother, Francois Vallé II, was serving as commandant of the district, a position he held until his death in 1803.

After Jean Baptiste Vallé was appointed commandant, his house became the social as well as governmental center of Ste. Genevieve. And it continued in this dual role during the many years he served as American governor of the district. Here, Governor Vallé entertained a host of distinguished visitors, among them John James Audubon, the great American ornithologist-artist.

It is believed that Commandant Vallé also entertained the young King Otto I of Greece when that monarch visited the interior of the United States in 1835. A story is told that King Otto overstayed his welcome in the Vallé household. For three months the young man spent most of his time playing cards and shooting pigeons—all of which placed great strain on his host. But Commandant Vallé remained patient and tactful to the end, aware that his guest was a reigning European monarch.

General Lafayette is also said to have stayed here, when the aging French statesman and Revolutionary War hero paid his triumphal return visit to the United States in 1825. A handsome, four-poster spindle bed in one of the house's first-floor bedrooms is said to have been the one General Lafayette slept in during his visit. It is known, of course, that Lafayette came up the Mississippi River from New Orleans and that he and his party were entertained at St. Louis. But no documentary evidence has been uncovered to show that the

Sometime during the 1850's, the French Creole-style residence was transformed by the addition of a dormer window and a kitchen and a maid's room which cut off the *galerie* on either end.

Victorian furnishings in the library include a spool-turned lamp stand and oval-back love seat. The upholstered back panel of the love seat has a conforming finger-molded frame with carved cresting in low relief.

French statesman actually landed at Ste. Genevieve, oldest French town west of the Mississippi River.

It was about the middle of the nineteenth century, after the death of Jean Baptiste Vallé, that his house was transformed from the French Creole style into something resembling a Victorian residence. Among the alterations were extending the stone basement under the porches, repartitioning the main-floor rooms, widening the hallway, building a kitchen and maid's room at one side of the house, replacing with a staircase the ladder-like steps that originally led to the second floor, and enlarging the French Creole hip roof to include bedrooms and dormer windows.

Left intact, however, are the original heavy oak beams that remain exposed in the ceilings of the first-floor rooms. They are forty-six feet long, running the entire length of the house. Although these were given a coat of painted graining and brown varnish during the Victorian remodeling of the house, they were later stripped of such finishes and the original adz marks of the pioneer carpenters who built the house in 1785 were exposed to view.

With all of these changes, however, the old Vallé house still retains much of its French Creole architectural appearance, both inside and out. Here, for example, is the familiar French Creole *galerie,* or porch, which spreads out on all four sides of the house. Here, too, is the typical Creole stone foundation enclosing a basement with a food storage room and wine cellar. Although tradition has it that the food storage room, because of its iron-barred windows, was a "dungeon," this is unlikely as the bars were probably used to keep out trespassers, human or animal.

One of the most attractive rooms in the house is its parlor. Tastefully furnished with Belter-carved rosewood pieces of the Victorian era, it has a fireplace in the mid-nineteenth-century style. The six fireplaces in the house, one for each downstairs room, were installed after the house was enlarged. Originally, the dwelling contained only two fireplaces.

In the dining room stands an eighteenth-century sideboard, believed to have been made in French Canada. The rest of the room is furnished with Victorian pieces. The only remaining original walnut door in the house connects the library with a downstairs bedroom. All other doors are of pine and of a later period.

The four-poster bed in which General Lafayette is supposed to have slept is unique in that it has interchangeable winter and summer posters. Tall posters were used to support the tester in winter and shorter ones in summer, mainly to bring the mosquito netting closer to the sleeper. A modern bathroom in the house features an antique piece in the form of a nineteenth-century shaving stand with an adjustable mirror.

As with the house in which he lived, Commandant Jean Baptiste Vallé was himself a unique link with the past, with the *ancien régime* of early Ste. Genevieve years. It is said that even after he was appointed first American governor of the Ste. Genevieve district, the beloved old commandant continued to wear the cocked hat, knee breeches and broad-cuffed coat that typified men's clothing during colonial days in his district.

Above: The focal point of this bedroom is the decorative spindle-post bed where Lafayette allegedly slept. The original heavy oak ceiling beams remain exposed in all first-floor rooms. Left: Wide double doors open onto the parlor which is attractively decorated in the Victorian style with Belter-carved rosewood pieces. To the left is a fine reproduction of an early American wood mantel.

VARNER-HOGG PLANTATION HOUSE

West Columbia Vicinity, Texas

HOME OF A NOTED GOVERNOR

In the center of the sixty-five-acre Varner-Hogg State Historic Park at West Columbia, Texas, stands one of the state's oldest, most imposing houses. It is a fitting memorial to the man who once lived in it, James Stephen Hogg, generally regarded as one of Texas' most distinguished governors. The house was presented to the State of Texas in 1958 and is now, together with the sixty-five-acre tract of woodlands and grasslands surrounding it, administered by the Texas Parks and Wildlife Department. Completely refurnished, the Hogg residence is open to the public as a period museum.

In addition to being a memorial to Governor Hogg, its last owner, it is also something of a memorial to the first owner of the site, Martin Varner. A true Texas pioneer, Martin Varner was a trader on the Red River when Moses Austin received permission from the Spanish provincial authorities to colonize three hundred Anglo-Americans in Texas. In 1821, after the death of Moses Austin, the work of colonizing fell to his son, Stephen F. Austin, and the trader on the Red River left his post, joining the Austin colony in southeast Texas.

In that same year, Mexico won its independence from Spain, rendering future Texas a Mexican province. Then, in 1824, Martin Varner, being among the original settlers of the Austin colony, received from the Mexican government a grant of some 4,500 acres of land in present Brazoria and Waller counties. His grant was the twelfth of the three hundred issued by the Mexican authorities in compliance with the terms of Moses Austin's original contract. These grants are known in Texas history as the "Old Three Hundred."

Selecting a site on his land near a creek, now known as Varner Creek, the pioneer Texan built a two-room log cabin, moved his wife, daughter and two servants into it, and became a farmer and stock raiser. As more and more settlers came to the region, however,

Varner-Hogg Mansion, named after its first and last owners, was once the center of a bustling sugar cane plantation. It now stands serenely in the sixty-five-acre park of the same name.

Ornate white-painted lawn furniture furthers this idyllic scene of plantation life at Varner-Hogg Mansion.

Martin Varner grew restless, and finally in 1834 sold his land. While making final arrangements for the disposition of his property in 1836, he joined the army of General Sam Houston and helped free Texas from Mexico. After the war, Martin Varner resettled in northeast Texas.

The man who bought his land in what is now Brazoria County was Columbus R. Patton, another pioneer Texan. It was in 1835 that Patton built, on the site of the early Varner cabin, a two-story brick house—the original portion of the present Varner-Hogg Plantation House. Intending to convert the land into a sugar cane plantation, Patton also constructed several outbuildings, including a kitchen, a large sugar processing house and slaves' quarters.

While Patton was building, there was established, just two miles south of his plantation in the early town of West Columbia, the first capital of the new Republic of Texas, with Sam Houston as its first President. The first Congress convened at West Columbia on October 3, 1836. A few months later, however, the capital was moved to the new town of Houston, and eventually to Austin.

By the time of Patton's death in 1856, his plantation, widely known as the Patton Place, had become a major sugar cane producer. The property remained in the Patton family until it was sold in 1869. It is said that at this sale the property also included a racetrack and a stable of thoroughbred horses. A number of successive owners operated the plantation during the remaining years of the nineteenth century.

It was in 1901 that James Stephen Hogg, the first native-born Governor of Texas and one of that state's ablest chief executives, became proprietor of the plantation house originally built by Columbus R. Patton in 1835. A native of the countryside near Rusk, Texas, where he was born in 1851, James Stephen Hogg early in life went through the experiences of plantation living. When, however, both of his parents died before he was thirteen and the family plantation had to be sold, young Jim Hogg had to go out into the world and earn his own living.

At first he served as an apprenticed typesetter on a newspaper in Rusk. He then became an editor, and also took up the study of law. Admitted to the bar in 1876, he was then elected a justice of the peace. Eventually, he began to attract state-wide attention when he started his fight against corporations, especially railroads, which he saw were gaining unreasonable advantages at the expense of the people of Texas. In 1886 he was elected Attorney General of Texas, an office he held until 1890.

Now a popular figure among the farmers and stockmen of the state, James Stephen Hogg won easily over his opponent when he ran for governor in 1890. Among his outstanding achievements were the creation of the Texas Railroad Commission and the enactment of a body of strict anti-trust laws. It was at a later period that the Federal government created a similar body of laws under the heading of the Sherman Anti-Trust Act. On his retirement from public life in 1895, and with the death that same year of his wife, Governor

Above: This unusual bed, one of a pair in the west bedroom, was made from the mahogany banisters of the old St. Louis Hotel in New Orleans. The fancy marble-topped washstand holds a Copeland Spode chamber set. Left: The pioneer atmosphere of the kitchen is enhanced by a spinning wheel, a hearth crane with hand-wrought iron hanging pots, and several pierced tin candle lanterns, all early American pieces.

Above: Also in the west bedroom are furnishings dating from before the Civil War, including a graceful swan-neck-style dresser mirror. Below: A comic figure of Uncle Sam stands jauntily on the windowsill beside an early American captain's desk.

Hogg devoted the rest of his career to a number of private business interests in Houston and Austin.

When not involved in business, he spent much time at the plantation house he had acquired in 1901. Here, he lived as a country gentleman, relaxed with his four now motherless children, entertained his many friends, and engaged in farming and stock raising. It is said that Governor Hogg suspected there was oil under his plantation acres and therefore stipulated in his will that his children could not sell the property for at least fifteen years after his death. As it happened, eleven years after his death in 1906, oil was discovered under the plantation grounds.

It was in 1920 that the governor's four children—William, Ima, Michael and Thomas—found it necessary to do some restoration on their old plantation house. What is now the mansion's most commanding feature, a spacious veranda supported by six, white, two-story columns, replaced a second-floor gallery that was originally attached to the facade. The edifice is a fine example of Southern-style architecture, two stories high, with a gable roof and a square decorative cupola centered on the roof. A permanent stucco was applied to the house's exterior.

All of the rooms in the plantation house have been furnished with period pieces of the years from 1835 to 1850, although there are some later pieces that belonged to the Hogg family. In the parlor are a red settee, chair and marble-topped table, the work of New York craftsman, John Henry Belter. In addition, there are furnishings of the Hogg family, covered with the popular black horsehair of the era. A color lithograph of Jefferson Davis and his cabinet presides over the room from above a melodian.

Upstairs, in the west or Pink Bedroom, the furnishings are from New Orleans, including a pair of beds made from the mahogany banisters of the old St. Louis Hotel in that city. The pictures on the walls, however, are part of Texas and French history, and illustrate the life of French refugees who, after the fall of Napoleon, settled in "Champ d'Asile," a French colony situated near what is now Liberty, Texas. Other furnishings in the house include antique pre-Civil War pieces, some in the French Empire style, and historic items relating to the Mexican War.

The kitchen building, which includes a formal dining room, smokehouse and kitchen, is now connected to the main house by a breezeway. Restoration work of 1920 also included the rebuilding and modernizing of the kitchen, dominated by a center work table with a pot rack holding hand-wrought copper pans. Both kitchen and smokehouse are furnished with early pioneer furniture, china and utensils.

In 1958 the governor's daughter, Miss Hogg, presented the plantation to the State of Texas as an historic park, along with an endowment fund. Since then, the state has made this sixty-five-acre area near West Columbia into one of its most attractive historic landmarks and state parks. In the midst of its magnolia trees and extensive pecan grove stands the white-pillared, historic Varner-Hogg Plantation House, a tribute to early Texas settlers and a much admired former governor.

A portrait of Governor James Stephen Hogg hangs above Belter-carved settee in the parlor. The rosewood chair, upholstered in black horsehair cloth, is from the Hogg family.

SAN FELIPE COTTAGE

Houston, Texas

OLDEST HOUSE IN HOUSTON

In the simple living room of San Felipe Cottage hang the
charming and primitive portraits of two young girls,
northern European in origin and dating from around 1820 .

The San Felipe Cottage in Houston, Texas, is the oldest surviving house in that huge and historic city of the Southwest. Aside from this, the dwelling has an interesting background story and is unique architecturally as a Southern-type cottage with some Greek Revival elements in its design. In 1962 it was moved to Sam Houston Park, where it is still within view of its original location on the old San Felipe Stage Route. The house, built alongside this storied road, could have been erected as early as 1837, a year after the independent Republic of Texas was founded. It was from this old road that the cottage took its name. At that time the San Felipe Stage Route connected Houston with the early town of San Felipe, where, in 1823, Stephen Austin established his colony headquarters and thus made it the birthplace of American settlement in Texas.

Another name for the cottage might well have been the Widow Smith House. It was built for the widowed Mrs. David Smith, who originally came from North Carolina and whose maiden name was Obedience Fort. She moved to Texas with her eight children, a group of slaves and her household goods. Since she received her land grant alongside the San Felipe stagecoach road in 1837, local historians have assumed that, in accordance with requirements, Mrs. Smith had the cottage built immediately to establish her claim to the land grant.

Her husband, David Smith, was also a native of North Carolina where he had served in the American Revolution. Both the Smith family and Fort family, however, had moved westward to "The Cumberland Settlement" in Tennessee, and it was there that, in 1791, David Smith married Obedience Fort. In the years following, the Smiths were to become the parents of eleven children, ten of whom survived to maturity.

Of a restless disposition, David Smith had traveled a number of times to the Mississippi Territory. On one of these trips he met and became well acquainted with Andrew Jackson, who was to become the seventh President of the United States. Eventually, David Smith sold his land holdings at The Cumberland Settlement, and, with his large family, moved southward to Hinds County, Mississippi, where he acquired new land holdings in the region just north of Jackson.

It was here, in a house he called Soldiers Rest, that David Smith died in 1835 at the age of eighty-three. By that time, most of his children were mature and some already successful. One of his daughters, Obedience II, had married Hiram G. Runnels, who later became Governor of Mississippi. Another son, Ben Fort Smith, was elected to the Mississippi legislature.

It was Ben Fort Smith who, in 1833, caught the "Houston fever," aroused when two New York land speculators, the brothers Augustus and John Allen, announced they were planning a new town in East Texas to be called Houston. Ben Fort Smith immediately purchased a plantation on the Brazos River and moved his family to it. He also, in 1836, built Houston's first hotel, the City Hotel, which stood on the site of the present Southern Pacific Building.

With her son paving the way, Mrs. Obedience Smith decided that she, too, would like to move westward to the new and booming Houston area. And so it was that she, and her younger children, sold the Hinds County property in Mississippi and by 1837 had taken up residence near the city limits of Houston. Mrs. Smith immediately built a house which may have been San Felipe Cottage.

Her son, Judge John W. N. A. Smith, brought his family to Houston about the same time. He and other members of the Smith family lived in homes quite close to Mrs. Smith, so the area was sometimes referred to as the Smith Compound. In 1839 she sold most of her acreage here to Judge Smith, but three years later he deeded it back to his mother. In 1844 Mrs. Smith sold her home and the twenty-five acres around it to her daughter, Piety, and her husband, T. B. J. Hadley. Not until after this sale are the records clear that the dwelling on this site was the San Felipe Cottage. Eventually, the cottage came into the possession of Justine Ruppersberg. It was Ruppersberg and his descendants who did more to restore San Felipe Cottage than any other previous owners in the years after the house no longer belonged to the Smiths.

The cottage, believed to have been built around 1837, originally stood along an historic stage route, and was moved in 1962 to a fitting site in Sam Houston Park.

A Chippendale slant-top cherry desk in the cottage study is a New England piece, circa 1770. Its unusual complement, a maple corner chair of the late eighteenth century, has its original rush seat. On the wall hangs a Regency what-not, circa 1825-1835, of English make.

The functional study desk, hand-fashioned in 1840, was designed for either wall or table top. A massive trunk, typical of the mid-1900's, is the familiar dome-cover type.

Of simple design compared with some of the other early Texas houses, San Felipe Cottage is of frame construction, one story high, with an attic and a gable roof. Three dormers project from the roof, the central one decorated with a small balcony. A Southern feature of the house is its gallery, occupying the entire front facade. This has a few Greek Revival ornamental details, including four supporting columns with Doric capitals.

While the cottage does contain a few articles that originally belonged to Mrs. Obedience Smith, it is mainly furnished with period pieces of the early nineteenth century. Among objects of interest in the central entrance hall are a pair of fancy Sheraton-style chairs, dated between 1820 and 1830, and a blown-glass hanging lamp, with bronze bandings and burner, circa 1840.

In the parlor just off the entrance hall may be found, among many other pieces, an American love seat that probably belonged to Mrs. Obedience Smith's daughter, Piety, and which probably came from New Orleans. A mirror over the fireplace is framed in a mahogany pillar and scroll setting, circa 1830. This room also contains a black-painted Sheraton rocking chair of New England origin, circa 1820. The drop-leaf table and six fancy chairs in the dining room are American versions of late Sheraton design, dated 1820-1830. A pie safe, partly veneered in yellow knotty pine, is of the late Empire period, probably made in the deep South.

Among the interesting pieces in the study are a slant-top Chippendale-style desk of cherry wood, made in Rhode Island or Connecticut about 1770, and a mahogany, Regency-style what-not shelf of English origin, dating from 1825-1835. Another especially appealing room is the weaving room, which contains a shuttle, spinning wheel, handloom and other related articles and utensils. In the east bedroom upstairs is displayed a Staffordshire washstand set, made around 1830-1850 and owned by Mrs. Obedience Smith.

A strange story associated with the San Felipe Cottage property concerns an old leather trunk owned by Mrs. Smith's daughter, Piety, who, with her husband, T. B. J. Hadley, had acquired the land and cottage in 1844. In later years when their grandson, Richard W. Franklin, a prominent Houston attorney, filed suit to establish the exact boundaries of the original Smith tract of land in view of what he believed to be encroachments on it, he could not find any documentary evidence to eject the supposed trespassers.

Then came the day when his sister, Mable, quite casually accompanied a friend of hers to a famed Houston clairvoyant, Madame Watts. While Miss Franklin sat quietly to one side as the madame analyzed her friend's fate, the clairvoyant supposedly interrupted her seance, turned to Miss Franklin, and exclaimed, "You have never been here before, but there is a very elderly gentleman, tall, slender and distinguished in appearance, who insists on talking with you. He is waving some papers that look like deeds or documents, and exclaiming, 'Don't let them take my land!' You will find all the papers in your grandmother's old leather trunk."

On returning to her home that day, Miss Franklin thought of her grandfather, Judge T. B. J. Hadley, and told her brother about the curious incident. They quickly rummaged through their grandmother's old leather trunk, discovering the necessary documentary evidence to support Richard Franklin's suit, a suit which resulted in his regaining the property in question.

Pink lustre Staffordshire china and a Bristol blue glass with wooden top enhance the late Sheraton drop-leaf table. The fancy-painted, rush-bottom chairs in the same style were made in Connecticut in 1824. Pottery displayed on the pie safe is in the Bennington tradition.

Walter Barnes Studio

The French Legation was originally the home of France's chargé d'affaires in the new nation of Texas. Especially noteworthy for its sturdy construction, it was built of durable Bastrop pine. Window glass for the home was brought from France, hardware from England and de Saligny bought elegant furnishings in New Orleans.

FRENCH LEGATION

Austin, Texas

A RELIC OF THE REPUBLIC

One of the most unusual old houses in the State of Texas, a house perhaps more remindful than any other of the years it was an independent nation, is the dwelling in the state capital of Austin known today as the French Legation. It was built nearly 130 years ago and is now as much admired for its architecture as for its history. In 1945 the house was purchased by the State of Texas and placed in the custody of The Daughters of the Republic of Texas, a patriotic organization that refurnished the historic landmark and opened it to the public.

It was early in 1839, three years after the Republic of Texas was founded and Sam Houston elected its first President, that France sent a secretary, Count Alphonse Dubois de Saligny, from its Washington embassy to the new republic in the Southwest. His mission was to look into the possibilities of opening diplomatic relations with the new nation. De Saligny, seeing an opportunity to advance his own political career in the young capital, reported favorably on the proposal. The republic was officially recognized by France in the fall of that same year and de Saligny, as he had hoped, was sent back to Texas as the French chargé d'affaires. Arriving in Austin exactly a year after his first visit, the count presented his credentials to the chief executive, President Mirabeau B. Lamar.

Some months later, Count de Saligny bought a lot for his legation, which would also serve as his home, on what afterwards became Robertson Hill in East Austin. He purchased it from Anson Jones who was to achieve subsequent fame as the last President of the Republic of Texas. In the meantime, while preparations for the legation were under way, de Saligny first lived in the rustic Bullock's Hotel and later rented a house next door to the hotel.

One of his first political maneuvers was an attempt to have the republic pass a bill which provided that, in return for a promise to bring in at least eight thousand French immigrants to build forts on the western Texas frontier to protect the new nation from marauding Indians, de Saligny would receive three million acres of land and all the rights pertaining to it. He would become a wealthy man if the bill passed and he did not hesitate to suggest that its enactment would probably aid a great deal in securing the $5 million

University of Texas Library

Count Alphonse Dubois de Saligny, the cultured representative of the government of France to the Republic of Texas, was the builder of his official Austin residence in 1840.

loan for Texas which was then pending before a Paris bank. Entertaining at his rented quarters and later at the legation house, de Saligny plied some of the leading figures of the Texas Republic with elaborate French dinners, fine imported wines and Principe cigars, but his efforts were unsuccessful and the bill failed.

During this period, the curious "hog episode," which had been rankling de Saligny for several months, came to a climax. Hogs belonging to hotelkeeper Richard Bullock occasionally had broken into the count's neighboring stable, destroying his fences and eating his horses' corn. Finally one day, a de Saligny servant killed one of the hogs. Bullock thrashed the servant and forbade the count ever again to enter his hotel. In retaliation against the Texas government for not passing his bill, the Frenchman seized upon this hog incident to cause a major political issue. Thus, the already hesitating French government ceased negotiations with the Texas representative in Paris who was seeking the $5 million loan for his young country.

Offended by the failure of the republic's Secretary of State to apologize for Bullock's conduct, the count departed for New Orleans, leaving behind the recently completed dwelling with its sign on the veranda reading "Legation de France." It was the only foreign legation in Austin, even though the republic also had been recognized by England, Holland and the United States.

Although the record is unclear, apparently de Saligny eventually returned to Austin to take up full-time residence in the legation house. The French Legation closed its doors on December 29, 1845, when Texas was admitted to the Union as the twenty-eighth state and the republic came to an end. Later owners of this solidly built house were Bishop John Marri Odin of the Diocese of Texas; Captain Moseley Baker, who commanded a detachment in Sam Houston's army; and a prominent Austin physician, Dr. Joseph W. Robertson. The acquisition of the house by the state in 1945 was brought about mainly through the efforts of the late Mrs. Walter Prescott Webb, wife of the distinguished Texas historian and at that time president of The Daughters of the Republic of Texas.

In appearance, the French Legation presents a pleasing, well-balanced architectural composition within its setting of lawns, gardens and trees. It is a one-story building of frame construction, with a hip roof and end chimneys. The material used in its construction was a fine-grained pine found in Bastrop County, Texas. Usually described as in the Louisiana bayou architectural style, the house has a veranda extending across its entire front which is supported by pairs of square pillars with Doric capitals. Three dormers projecting from the roof provided light for the upstairs servants' quarters.

All rooms in the house have been furnished with early and mid-nineteenth-century pieces, some of them original Saligny belongings. An unusually wide entrance hall, in the center of the house, also served as a dining room, and, when the table was removed, as a ballroom. Among objects of interest in the entrance hall is a copy of a map of Texas made in 1840 by A. Brue, geographer for King Louis Philippe of France, and presented to Dr. Frederick Leclerc, once a guest at the French Legation in Austin.

The most frequented spot during the hot Texas summers was probably the legation's spacious porch.

Ellison Studios

Walter Barnes Studio

Perhaps the most opulent room in the house is its parlor, which has been tastefully refurnished with period pieces by the National Society of the Colonial Dames of America Resident in the State of Texas. The rosewood sofa in the parlor is an original Saligny piece. Among original Robertson family articles is the early eighteenth-century French clock on the mantel, which, according to tradition, Mrs. Robertson obtained by trading her pony for it. It is of European walnut inlaid with satinwood and has an ormolu mounting. The room also contains a handsome English piano dating from about 1760 and an oil painting of Louis Philippe, the French king at the time of Count Saligny's service in Austin.

Displayed with some early nineteenth-century books and other objects in the count's study is an old printing press that belonged to Saligny, and an oil portrait of the French explorer, La Salle. The legation's master bedroom is furnished with a French mahogany bedroom suite of the 1830-1850 period obtained by Dr. Robertson in New Orleans after he bought the French Legation. A wine cellar on the premises has been re-excavated and stocked with one hundred-year-old wine casks.

Of great interest to visitors here is an outbuilding, the French Legation kitchen. It is a reconstructed version of the original outbuilding and is said to be the only known authentic restoration of an early French kitchen in America. In this kitchen Count Saligny's *chef de cuisine* prepared the fine roasts and other meat dishes, seasoned with herbs from his garden, that made the legation dinners renowned in early Texas. The kitchen was reconstructed by Mr. and Mrs. J. W. Beretta of San Antonio and dedicated to the memory of Mrs. Beretta's great-great-grandparents, Mr. and Mrs. James Franklin Perry. Mrs. Perry was a sister of Stephen F. Austin, the "Father of Texas."

The authentic reconstruction of the legation kitchen, separate from the house itself, is the result of long research. Count de Saligny's kitchen was carefully supervised by a French chef and the home's excellent cuisine was famous throughout the district.

ÁVILA ADOBE
Los Angeles, California
OLDEST HOUSE IN LOS ANGELES

Ávila Adobe, once an eighteen-room mansion, belonged to Don Francisco Ávila, mayor of the Los Angeles Pueblo.

In the midst of what is now officially designated as El Pueblo de Los Angeles State Historical Monument—a forty-two-acre area surrounding the Old Plaza where Los Angeles was born in 1781—stands the oldest house in that great metropolis of southern California. This is Ávila Adobe on Olvera Street, built more than 150 years ago during the Spanish régime in Alta California. It is not only the oldest but the most historic private dwelling in the vast city. Together with the ancient Mission Plaza Church, Ávila Adobe is one of two principal monuments to the early Spanish pueblo that became the Los Angeles of today.

The most dramatic episode in the long history of Casa Ávila occurred in January 1847, when it became the headquarters of Commodore Robert F. Stockton of the American Navy, who was in command of the Pacific squadron during the Mexican War of 1846-1848. After capturing San Diego, Commodore Stockton sailed northward, and, following a short skirmish, captured the Pueblo of Los Angeles and there set up his headquarters. So it was that the American flag was raised for the first time above the plaza, having been preceded by the Spanish and Mexican flags.

In its early years, however, Ávila Adobe and the plaza witnessed a quiet, leisurely and uneventful way of life. The Pueblo of Los Angeles was founded in 1781 when the Spanish Governor of California province, Felipe de Neve, sent eleven families of Mexicans, Indians, Negroes and half-breeds to the site to lay out a village. Each family was granted a piece of land facing the plaza, as well as a few animals, some tools, provisions and a little money. The new community was named El Pueblo de Nuestra Señora la Reina de Los Angeles ("The Town of Our Lady Queen of the Angels"). This name was shortened to Los Angeles when Easterners began to settle in the area at a later period.

A few years after the pueblo was established, there arrived one Don Cornelio Ávila, who became the founder of the noted Ávila family of early Los Angeles history. It was his grandson, Don Francisco Ávila, who built Ávila Adobe in 1818, while California was still a province of Spain. Don Francisco Ávila had previously

Opposite: Ávila Adobe epitomizes the quiet leisurely pace of life in Los Angeles during its early years. The adobe is the oldest existing private dwelling in the city.

The sunny patio, dotted with earthen jugs and potted cacti, is delightfully reminiscent of early Spanish California life, still to be found in colorful restorations such as the Ávila Adobe.

married Señorita Encarnación Sepúlveda, daughter of Don Francisco Sepúlveda and Doña Ramona Serrano de Sepúlveda, early residents of the pueblo.

With the successful revolt of Mexico from Spain in 1822, the Mexican flag was raised over the Pueblo of Los Angeles. Soon afterwards, Don Francisco Ávila was elected *alcade,* or mayor, of the pueblo. In the course of time, however, he became involved in political intrigues, largely instigated by his brother, José María Ávila, involving the possibility of freeing California province from Mexico. At the height of this activity his adobe house became known as "La Casa de los Revolucionarios." But Don Francisco soon freed himself from that line of endeavor.

When Don Francisco Ávila died, the adobe house on Olvera Street passed to his widow, Doña Encarnación Ávila. She continued for many years afterwards the traditions of hospitality first established here by her husband. Ávila Adobe was the social center of the pueblo. Then came the electrifying news in 1846 that the United States had declared war on Mexico, had already taken Monterey, and had proclaimed California a part of the Union.

On hearing that the Americans were about to march on the Pueblo of Los Angeles, Doña Encarnación Ávila fled from her Olvera Street home to friends on the outskirts of the pueblo, leaving her house in the care of a Mexican boy. Finally, the Americans came, in charge of Commodore Robert Stockton and General Stephen Kearney, and headed up Olvera Street behind a military band playing "The Star Spangled Banner." With them was the famous Indian scout, Kit Carson, who had earlier saved General Kearney and his troops from annihilation at the Battle of San Pascual.

With the arrival of the American soldiers and the music of the band, the Mexican boy left in charge of Casa Ávila rushed out of the house to hear the music and witness the pageantry in the plaza, leaving the door unlocked. The American commanders, noting the suitability of the house for their purposes and finding no one at home, took charge of the adobe dwelling and set up their headquarters. It also became the focal point for General John C. Frémont's activities. However, the American forces moved out within a year and Doña Ávila returned to her home from the casa of a friend where she had taken refuge.

In the years after 1850, when California was admitted to statehood, Ávila Adobe continued to be owned and occupied by the descendants of Don and Doña Ávila. And so it survived into the twentieth century, into the coming of the railroad era to Los Angeles and the discovery of oil in the region. By the time, in 1927, when Los Angeles had a population of more than a million and a skyscraper City Hall soared upward just south of the ancient and original Pueblo of Los Angeles, Ávila Adobe was in a state of severe neglect and about to fall into ruins.

The old landmark had been condemned as unsafe and might have been demolished, had it not been for the timely intercession of Mrs. Christine Sterling, a well-known Los Angeles writer and historian.

John Howell

Don Francisco planned his home to be one of the Plaza's most luxurious. The adobe walls were constructed two feet in thickness, high-ceilinged rooms had beams hand hewn from local cottonwoods and the veranda along the front of the home led into living rooms approached by French doors brought around the horn by ship from Boston.

She launched a public project to save and restore the dwelling and other surviving adobe houses on Olvera Street and around the old Plaza de Los Angeles.

A group of public-spirited citizens was formed under the name of Plaza de Los Angeles, Inc., and this body raised funds to carry on the work of restoring the plaza, Ávila Adobe and other landmarks of the birthplace of Los Angeles. The group was greatly encouraged when, in 1934, architects of the Historic American Buildings Survey of the U. S. Department of the Interior made scale drawings, as well as detailed photographs, of La Casa Ávila, and placed this material in the permanent archives of the Library of Congress.

Since that time, and largely through the diligent efforts of the late Mrs. Sterling, who became known as the "Mother of Olvera Street," Ávila Adobe has been gradually refurnished with household articles, heirlooms and period pieces of the early Los Angeles pueblo era. One charming example is the small, early nineteenth-century piano built by Groesteen in Germany. As did much of the more sophisticated furniture in early Los Angeles, this piano came in a sailing vessel around Cape Horn and is believed to be the third piano to arrive in California.

Several of the rooms were refurnished by Señora Florencia Sepúlveda de Schoneman, a descendant of the Ávila family. When this work was started in 1929, the owners of Ávila Adobe, the Rimpau family, who also were descendants of its builder, opened their house to the public.

At the time Don Francisco Ávila first built his spacious adobe house in 1818, it had a flat roof, made water-tight with black brea (tar), mixed with sand and horsehair, from brea pits in the vicinity of the pueblo. At a later date, about 1825, the house was covered by the low-pitched gable roof it now bears and which extends outward to form the broad veranda at its front. The adobe walls of the dwelling are four feet thick, which helps to keep the house warm in winter and cool in summer.

In the many rooms of Casa Ávila are high ceilings supported by beams hewn from cottonwood trees that grew along the banks of what is now the Los Angeles River. From the long veranda at the front of the house numerous French doors lead into the living and other rooms of the Casa Ávila. The French doors are said to have been brought by ship around the Horn from Boston. Most of the original furnishings and hangings of the house were imported by Don Francisco Ávila from Europe. At the back of the adobe a long row of bedrooms looks out on a sunny patio or courtyard.

In 1953, the suggestion was made by silent-screen star Leo Carillo that the entire old plaza area of Los Angeles be made into a state park. At that time, Carillo, who was a descendant of one of the earliest settlers of the Pueblo de Los Angeles, was an influential member of the California State Park Commission. And thus the El Pueblo de Los Angeles State Historical Monument had its inception.

Photos: John Howell

Above and left: Ávila Adobe has gradually been refurnished with period pieces relating to the early Pueblo era. The early nineteenth-century piano, built in Germany, is one of the items originally brought to Los Angeles by ship and one of the first pianos to have arrived in California.

PETALUMA ADOBE

Petaluma Vicinity, California

A LANDMARK OF OLD ADOBE DAYS

Hand-hewn redwood beams and adobe (unburned) clay account for the solidity of Petaluma Adobe. This type of construction, common to the Southwest Indians, was inherited by Spanish and Mexican settlers.

Opposite: Vallejo's large labor force met in the huge courtyard every morning to call roll before dispersing for their various agricultural and industrial occupations around the prosperous hacienda.

One of the most historic of northern California houses is the Petaluma Adobe, located just north of San Francisco, three miles east of the city of Petaluma. It is a survivor of the Mexican era, a period when, among other things, the Mexican home government successfully prevented Russian settlers of extreme northern California from migrating southward and eventually taking over the whole region. The house is also a notable example of the unburned clay, or adobe, type of construction in American architectural history, a form of construction inherited by the early Spaniards and Mexicans from the Indians of the Southwest.

There is much history associated with Petaluma Adobe, which is the principal attraction of the city's Old Adobe Days Fiesta, an annual event, in the San Pablo Bay city. In 1834, the Mexican administrator and commandante-general of California province, Governor José Figuerosa, granted ten leagues of land "known by the name of Petaluma" in the region north of San Francisco Presidio to a capable and energetic young army officer, Mariano Guadalupe Vallejo. A few years later he was granted an additional five leagues of land, making a total of approximately 66,000 acres.

On this vast tract Vallejo established a hacienda that was one of the largest in Alta California. In 1836, he began building the main structure of his hacienda—the Petaluma Adobe that became his main ranch office, his workshop and storehouse. In erecting the house, he also had in mind its possible use as a fort in the event of Indian attack. As a result of the revolt of some Californians against Mexican authority in November 1836, Vallejo was appointed military and civil commander for the northern part of California province and elevated to the rank of general.

At the peak of its production, General Vallejo's hacienda, specializing in cattle raising and agriculture, had a work force of more than two thousand men, most of them Indians who lived in their own tule villages adjoining the huge hacienda. The great cattle round-ups were in the hands of skilled *vaqueros*, or Mexican cowboys. Other workmen labored as plowmen, harvesters, herders, domestic servants, weavers, tanners and artisans. The principal products of the ranch, hides, tallow and wheat, were sold to Yankee traders who called in sailing ships such as the one described in Dana's classic *Two Years Before the Mast*.

If General Vallejo became a prosperous *haciendado* he also turned out to be a successful military and civil commander of northern

Above: The nursery section of the master bedroom contains a quaintly decorated early cradle.

Opposite top and bottom: Guest rooms, although more crudely finished than the family apartments, were a welcome haven for weary travelers who could stay as long as necessary without charge. Each room was even furnished with a bowl containing a few coins so that the guest need not ask for charity.

California. When the tactful general formed an alliance with Chief Solano (Sem Yeto, "the Mighty Arm"), the number of Indian raids in the northern part of the province decreased substantially. He also succeeded in bringing to an end the southward migration of Russian settlers from Fort Ross.

Part of his success in this maneuver was his added ability as a colonizer. As time went on, he arranged to have more and more Mexican nationals become *rancheros* in his territory, and this resulted in discouraging the Russians. Finally, in 1841, they sold Rossiya (Fort Ross) to John Augustus Sutter, a Swiss-born army officer who became a Mexican citizen. A few years later gold was discovered in the river at Sutter's saw mill, a find that started the great California gold rush.

There were also many Americans who had settled in the Mexican province. They staged the successful Bear Flag Revolt against the Mexican Government in 1846, shortly after the United States had declared war on Mexico. When the Bear Flag Party looted his hacienda, Vallejo's fortunes and influence began to diminish, although he was appointed sub-Indian agent by the U. S. military government in 1847-1848.

However, this did not put an end to Vallejo's career as a public official. A resourceful, far-sighted man, he became an American citizen, and when California was admitted to statehood in 1850 he served as the first state senator for Sonoma County—the county of his vast early ranch. Incidentally, it was in 1965 that a nuclear submarine, launched at Sonoma County's Mare Island Navy Yard, was christened the *M. G. Vallejo* at the suggestion of President John F. Kennedy.

With his ranch now greatly reduced in size and no longer as productive as it was during the Mexican régime, General Vallejo sold it in 1857 to William Hill Whiteside. Two years later Whiteside transferred the property to William D. Bliss, a leading Petaluma attorney who had graduated from the Harvard Law School and settled in Petaluma in 1855. Bliss was a step-son of the great American historian and diplomat, George Bancroft. During the period, 1846-1849, when George Bancroft was ambassador to Great Britain, Bliss had served him as a private secretary in London.

In the years after General Vallejo sold Petaluma Adobe, he lived in a house he had built earlier in the nearby town of Sonoma. It was a Victorian-style residence he called "Lachryma Montis." Here, he and his wife continued the traditions of hospitality they had earlier established at Petaluma Adobe. Among guests entertained here by General Vallejo, the first citizen of northern California, was Admiral David Farragut.

William Bliss retained ownership of Petaluma Adobe until his death in 1886. Thereafter, it was rented by the Bliss heirs to a number of successive ranchers. When, in 1910, the historic building was deeded to Petaluma Parlor No. 27 of the Native Sons of the Golden West, it was showing worrisome signs of advanced age. Members of the organization, realizing the building's historic value, took immediate steps to begin restoring it. In 1951, title to Petaluma Adobe was transferred to the Department of Parks and Recreation of the State of California, which has since completed restoration and established it as the Petaluma Adobe State Historical Monument.

John Howell

297

Crudely wrought, but substantial table and chairs mark the Spanish colonial Mission style (1769-1834) in California. These pieces were probably made by Indians trained at one of the numerous missions in the area.

Petaluma Adobe was designed as a spacious, two-story building, rectangular in shape and with an open courtyard at its center. Surviving today, however, are only two sides of the original rectangular-shaped edifice. These are covered by a low-pitched gable roof that extends outward over two-story wooden verandas. All lumber used in the construction of Petaluma Adobe, most of it hand-hewn, came from the coast belt of redwood trees on the other side of Petaluma City. Thousands of adobe bricks, made by Indian labor, went into its three-feet-thick walls. All windows have been equipped with grills and shutters of the type used during the time when General Vallejo lived here.

The furnishings, which include both authentic pieces and careful reproductions, are in styles from one of two periods preceding the entry of California into the Union: The solid, plain, square-cut Mission style was prevalent from about 1769 to 1834. Its origins were in the crudely wrought but substantial pieces made by Indians trained at missions in Spanish colonial California. The Rancho style, which predominated between 1835 and 1846, was more finely crafted and somewhat more decorative.

In the courtyard of Petaluma Adobe, where roll calls of the ranch workmen were held each morning, may now be seen numerous exhibits representing the Vallejo era. One of these is a reproduction of a *caretta,* or Mexican ox cart. Other objects in the courtyard are an outside bake oven and blacksmith's forge. Inside can be found the granary, carpenter shop and a burro-powered grist mill.

On the northeast side of the adobe building there are rail racks hung with drying cow hides, the sort of hides that General Vallejo and *rancheros* sold to Yankee traders from the sailing ships. Offices, workrooms and storage areas were on the first floor of the hacienda, while the second floor contained the General's living quarters and family apartments, as well as numerous guest rooms.

The Petaluma Adobe thus authentically represents the many facets of life as it was lived on a California hacienda during the 1840's, a period of transition between the pioneer era and statehood.

DATE DUE

GAYLORD   PRINTED IN U.S.A.